Table of Contents

ESSENTIAL EARLY CHILDHOOD SKILLS

Everything for Early Learning is divided into five sections.

Basic Concepts

Activities in this section are designed to help your child:

- identify colors, basic shapes and sizes
- compare and describe the sizes and lengths of different objects
- classify objects according to common attributes
- understand the concept of opposites (in/out, up/down)
- understand positional concepts (behind, beside, between)
- develop and practice fine motor skills by coloring, cutting, gluing and manipulating objects

Mathematics Readiness

Activities in this section are designed to help your child:

- develop appropriate mathematical language
- match objects one-to-one
- develop concepts about quantity (more/fewer)
- develop general concepts about time (more time/less time)
- describe a simple sequence of events (before, after)
- describe events using ordinal numbers (first, second, third)

ESSENTIAL EARLY CHILDHOOD SKILLS

Reading Readiness

Activities in this section are designed to help your child:

- note similarities and differences among pictures, shapes, letters and words
- identify details that are missing from pictures
- identify parts of objects and the whole objects to which they belong
- identify rhymes in words and pictures
- follow directional paths from left to right and top to bottom
- form pre-writing strokes

Letters and Sounds

Activities in this section are designed to help your child:

- recognize and form the 26 upper- and lower-case letters of the alphabet
- identify the sound each letter makes at the beginning of a word

Numbers 0-10

Activities in this section are designed to help your child:

- recognize and write the numerals 0 to 10
- recognize and write number words from zero to ten
- count objects and sets of objects through ten

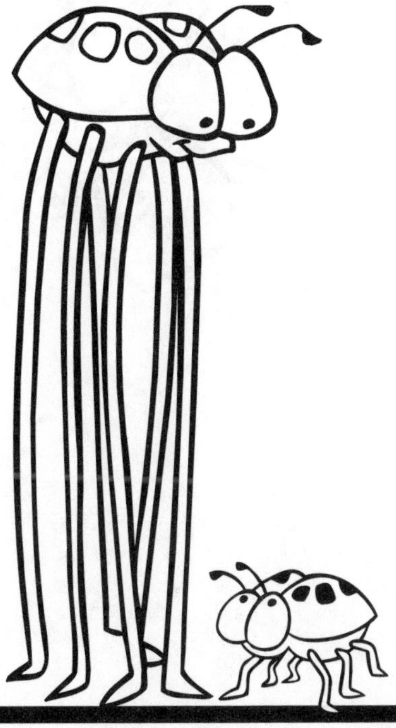

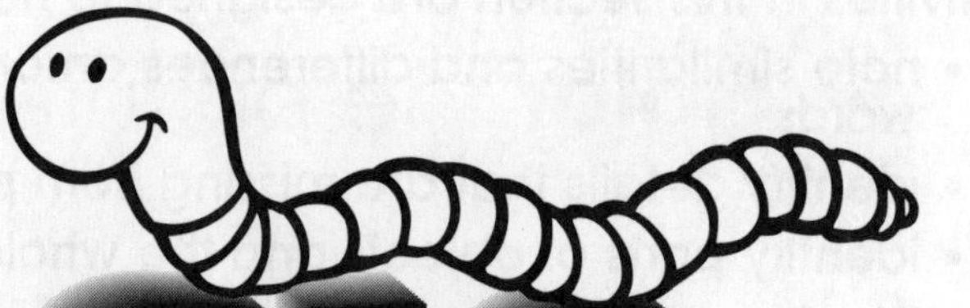

BASIC CONCEPTS

RED

Color the pictures **red**.

BLUE

Color the pictures **blue**.

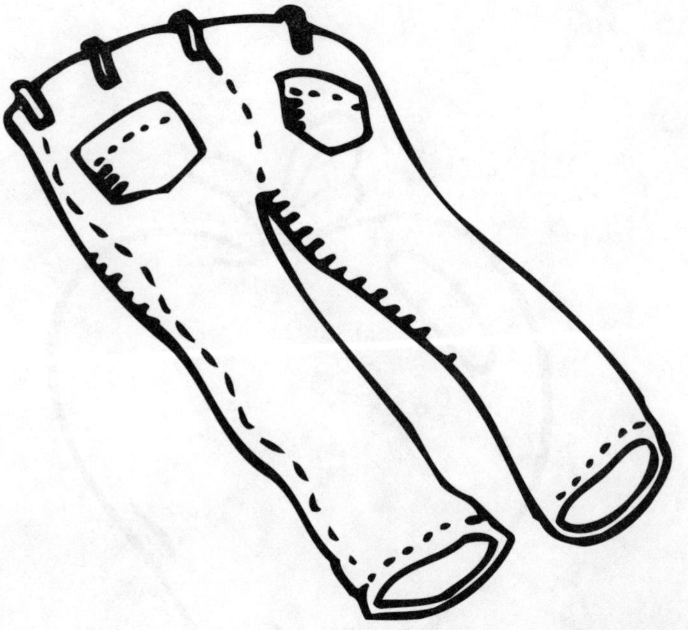

YELLOW

Color the pictures **yellow**.

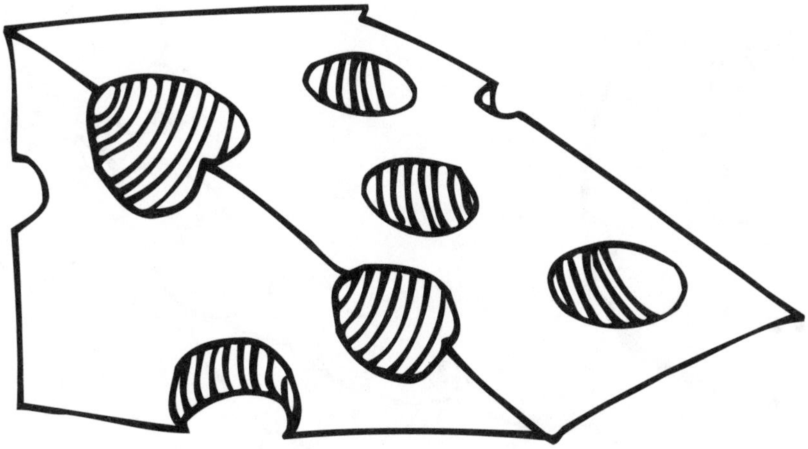

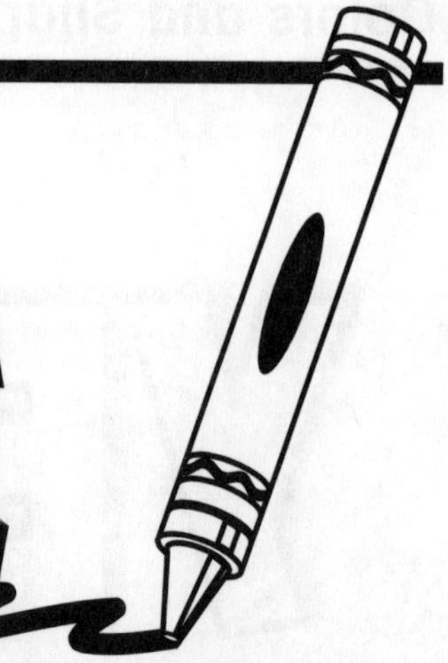

ORANGE

Color the pictures **orange**.

GREEN

Color the pictures **green**.

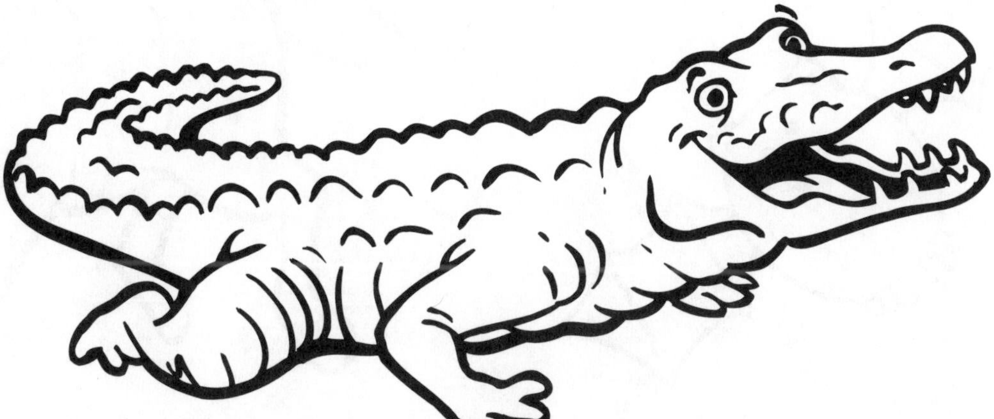

BLACK

Color the pictures **black**.

PURPLE

Color the pictures **purple**.

BROWN

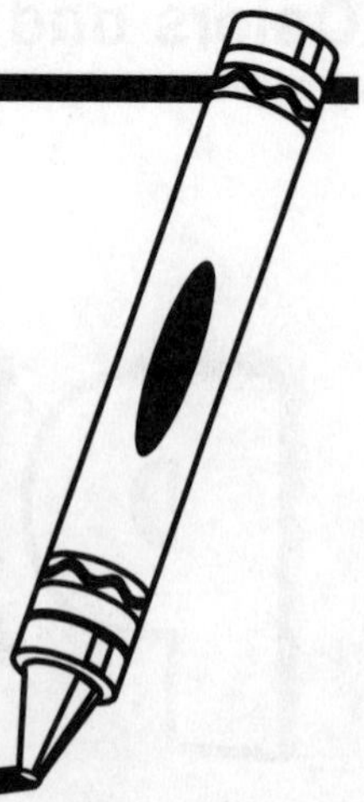

Color the pictures **brown**.

REVIEW COLORS

Color the picture.

REVIEW COLORS

Color the picture.

SORTING BY COLORS

Color and **cut out** the pictures at the bottom of the page. **Glue** the purple fruits in the purple basket. **Glue** the yellow fruits in the yellow basket. **Glue** the green fruits in the green basket.

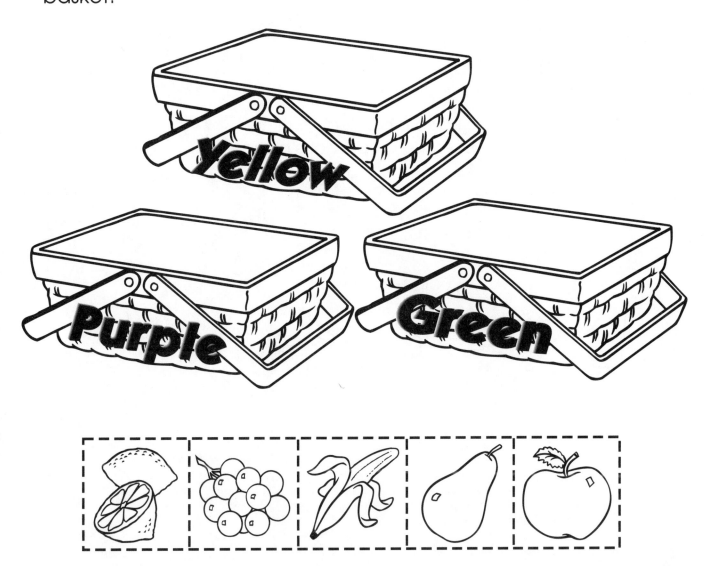

Page is blank for cutting
exercise on previous page.

COLOR PATTERNS

Look at the beads in each row. **Color** the next bead in the **pattern**.

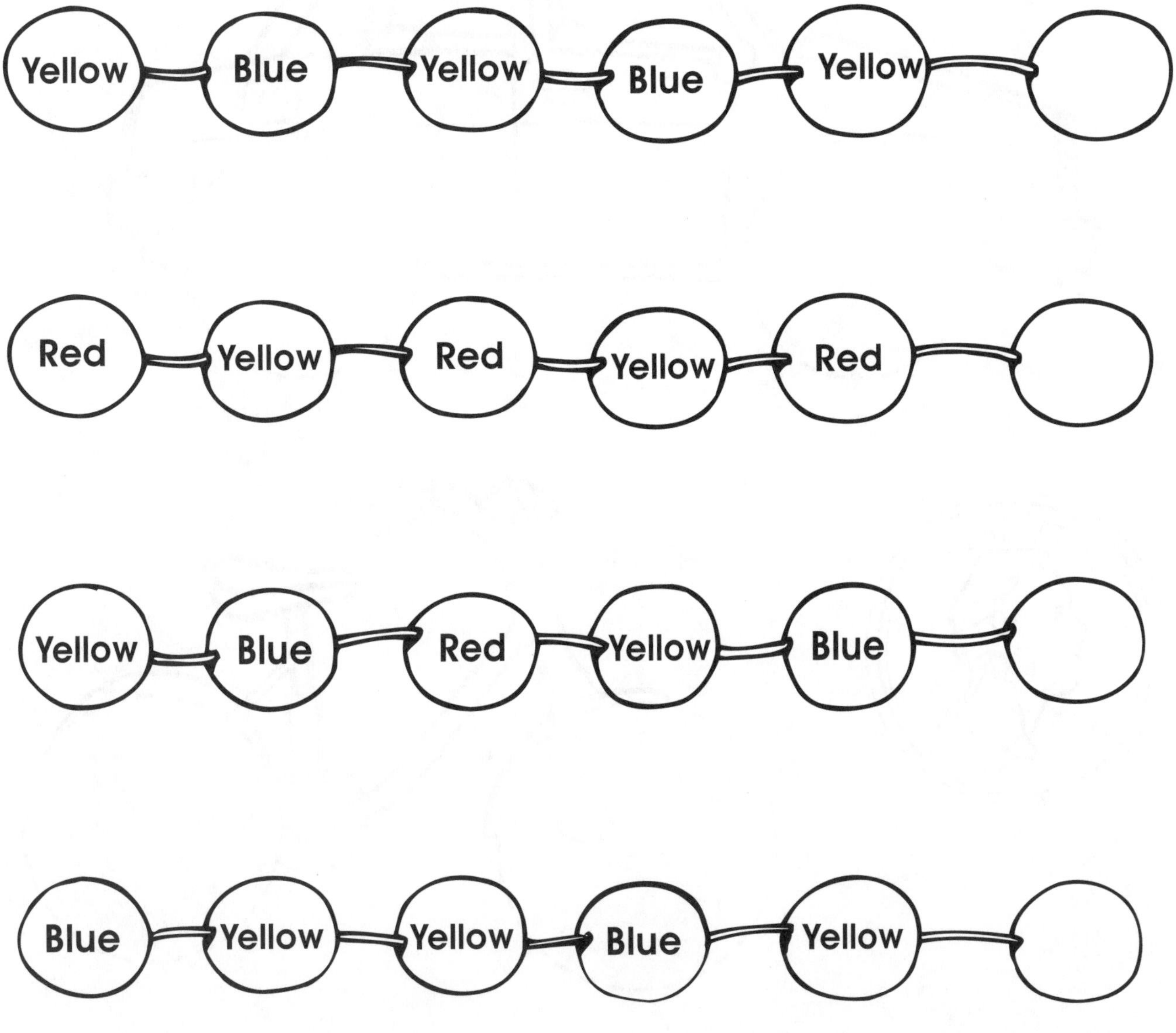

CIRCLES

We see many **circles** every day. **Trace** the circles. **Color** the pictures.

CIRCLES

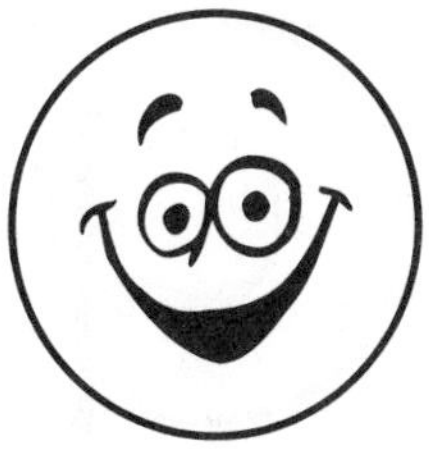

Circles can be different sizes. **Trace** the **circles**. **Color** the **circles**.

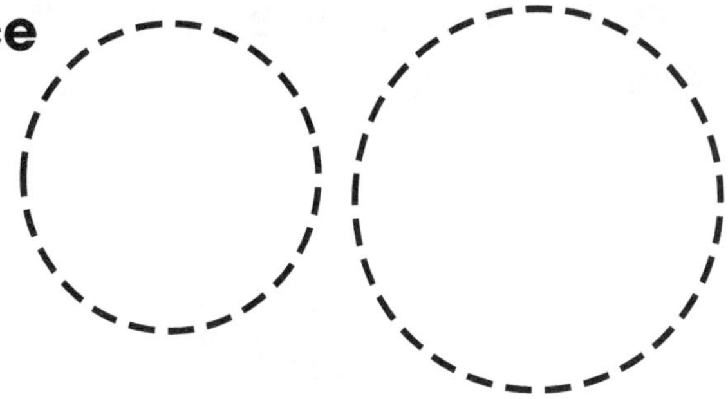

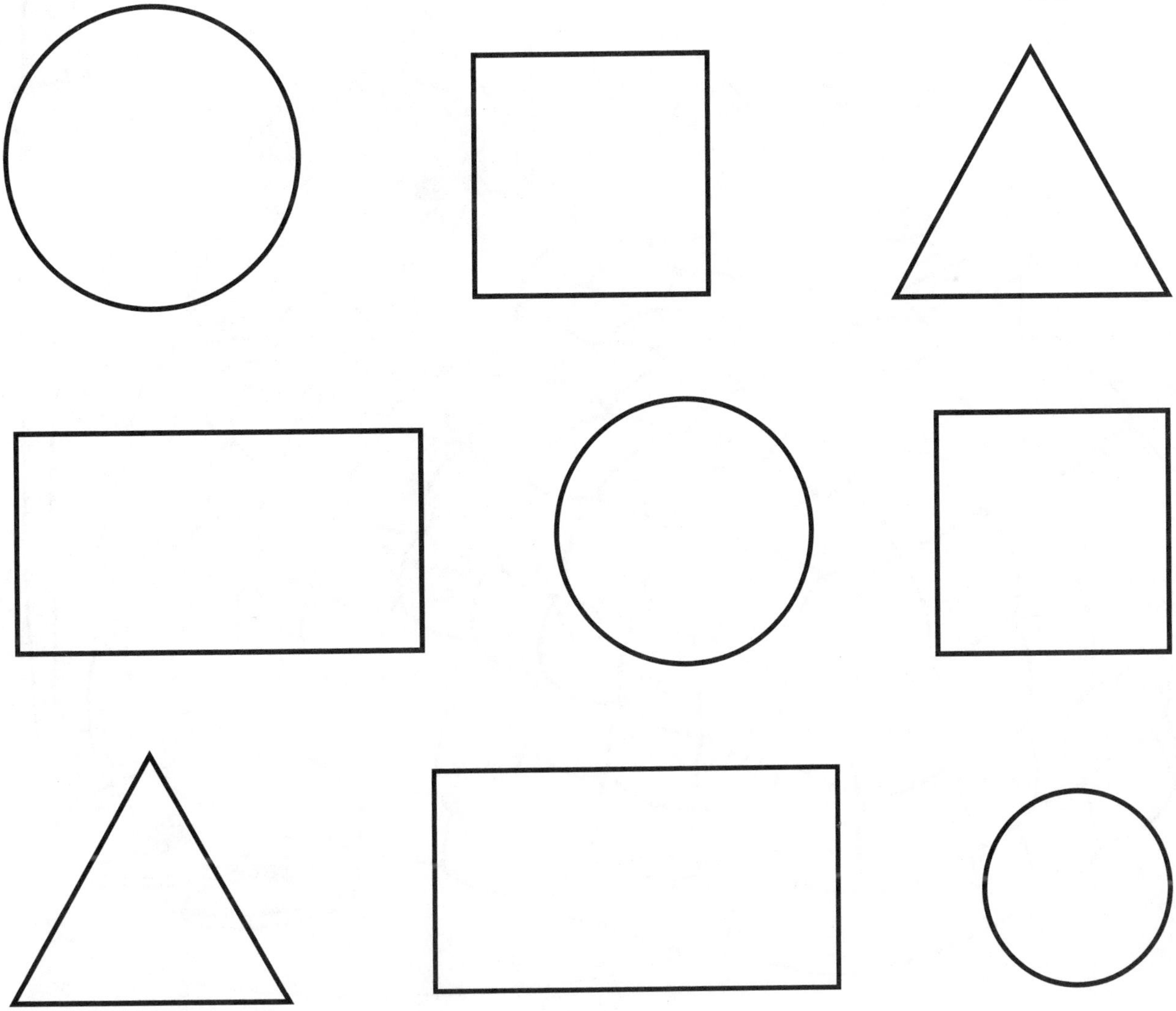

CIRCLES

Draw an **X** on the things that have the **shape** of a **circle**.
Color the picture.

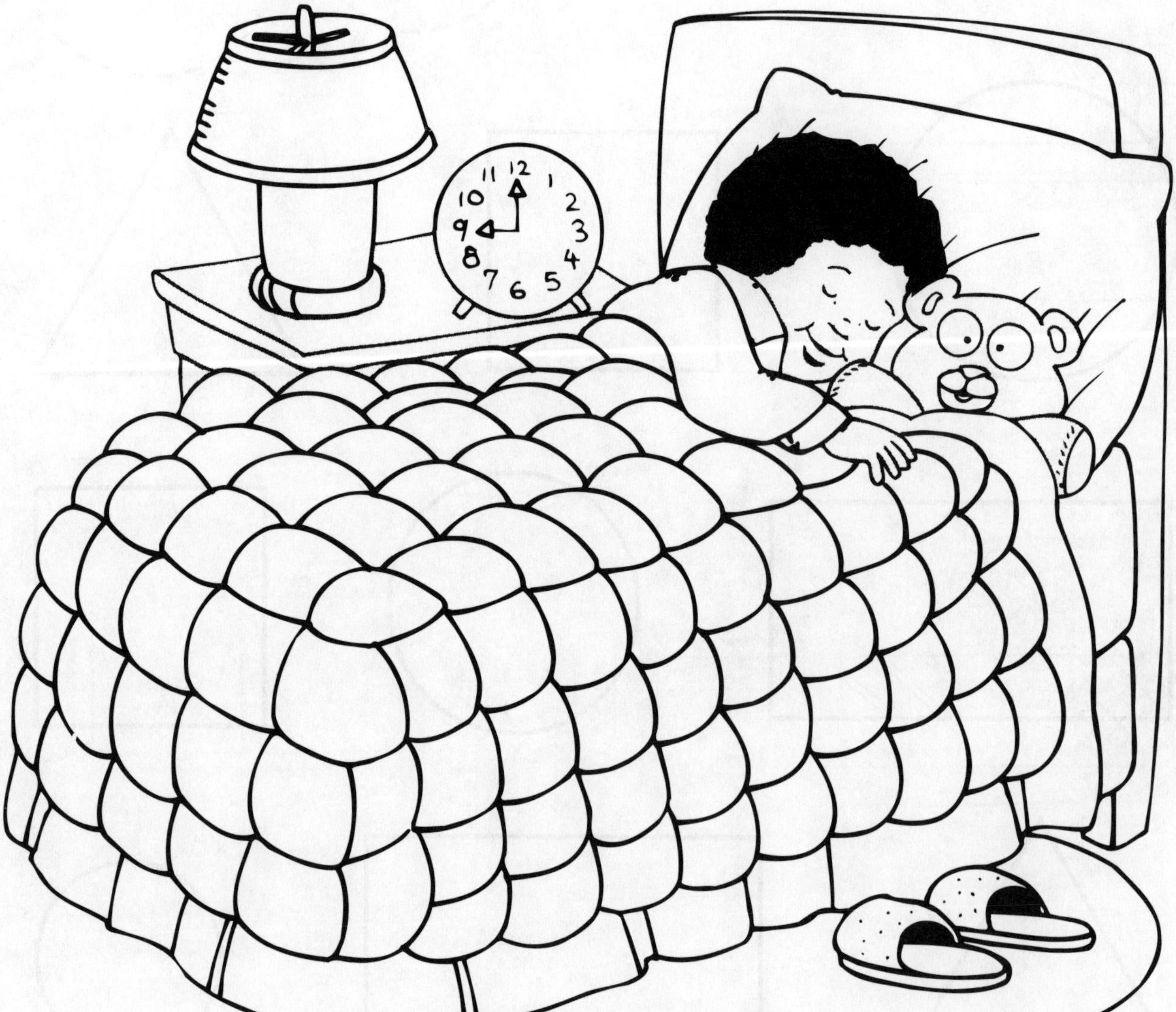

SQUARES

Draw an **X** on the things that have the **shape** of a **square**.
Color the picture.

RECTANGLES

We see many **rectangles** every day. **Rectangles** have 4 sides–2 long sides and 2 short sides. **Trace** the **rectangles**. **Color** the pictures.

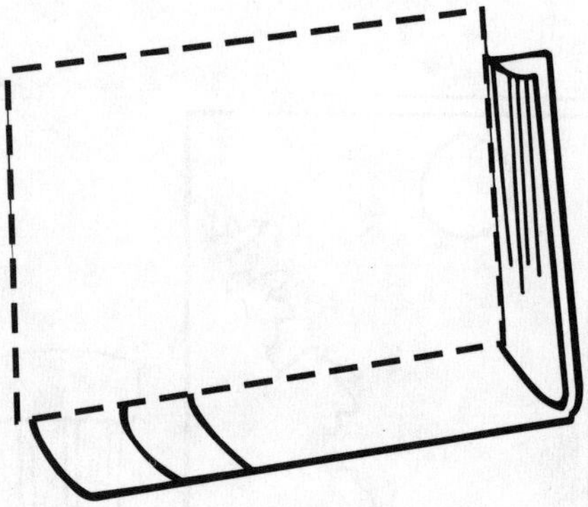

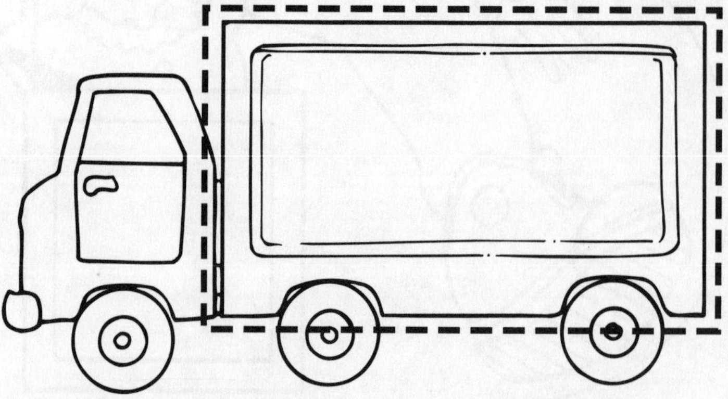

RECTANGLES

Rectangles can be different sizes. **Trace** the **rectangles**. **Color** the **rectangles**.

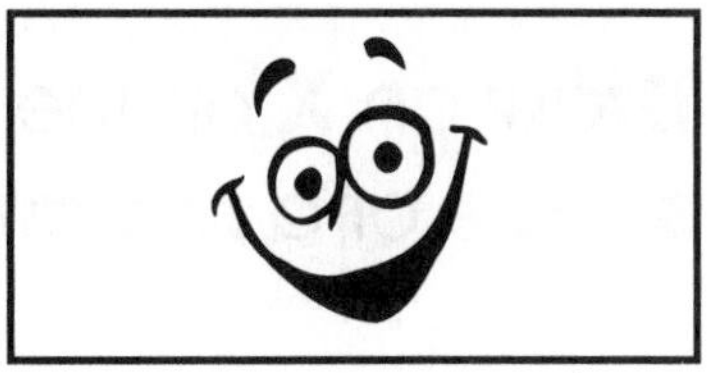

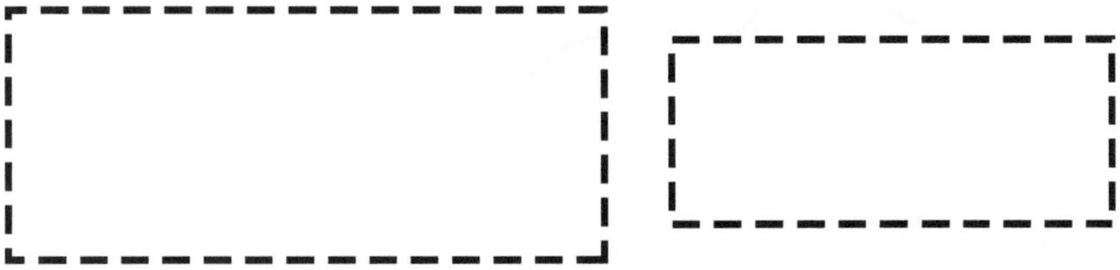

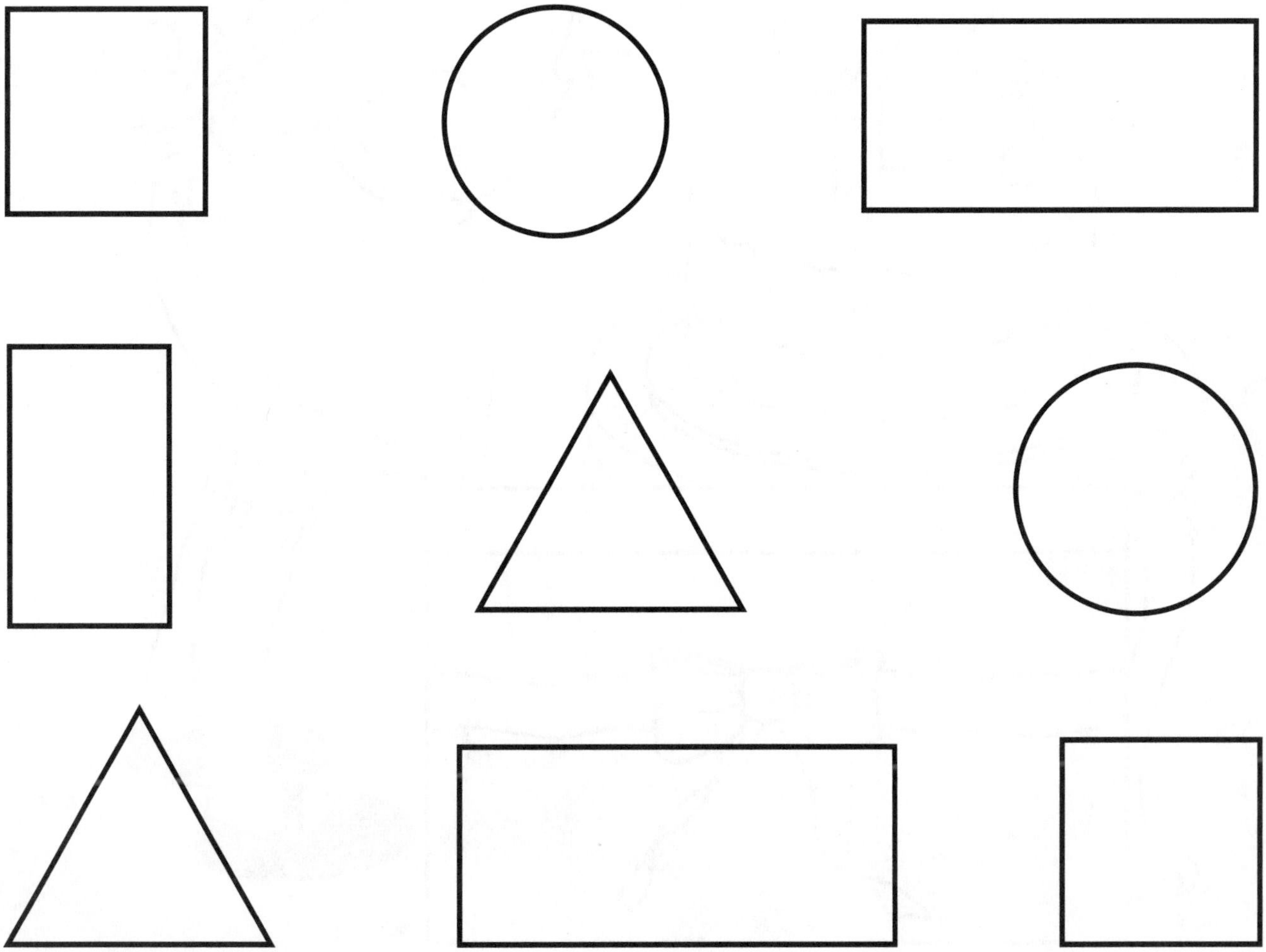

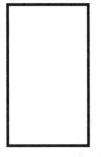

RECTANGLES

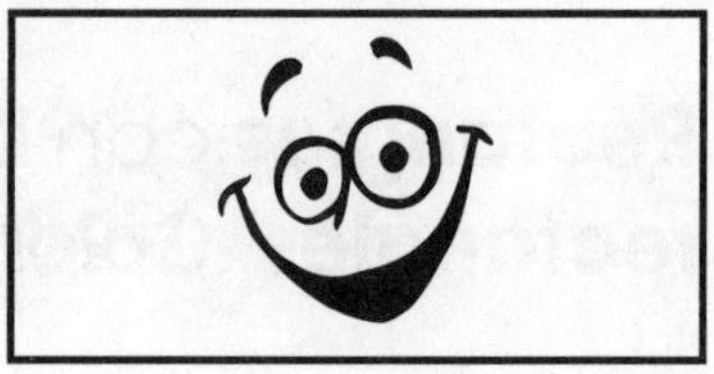

Draw an **X** on the things that have the **shape** of a **rectangle**. **Color** the pictures.

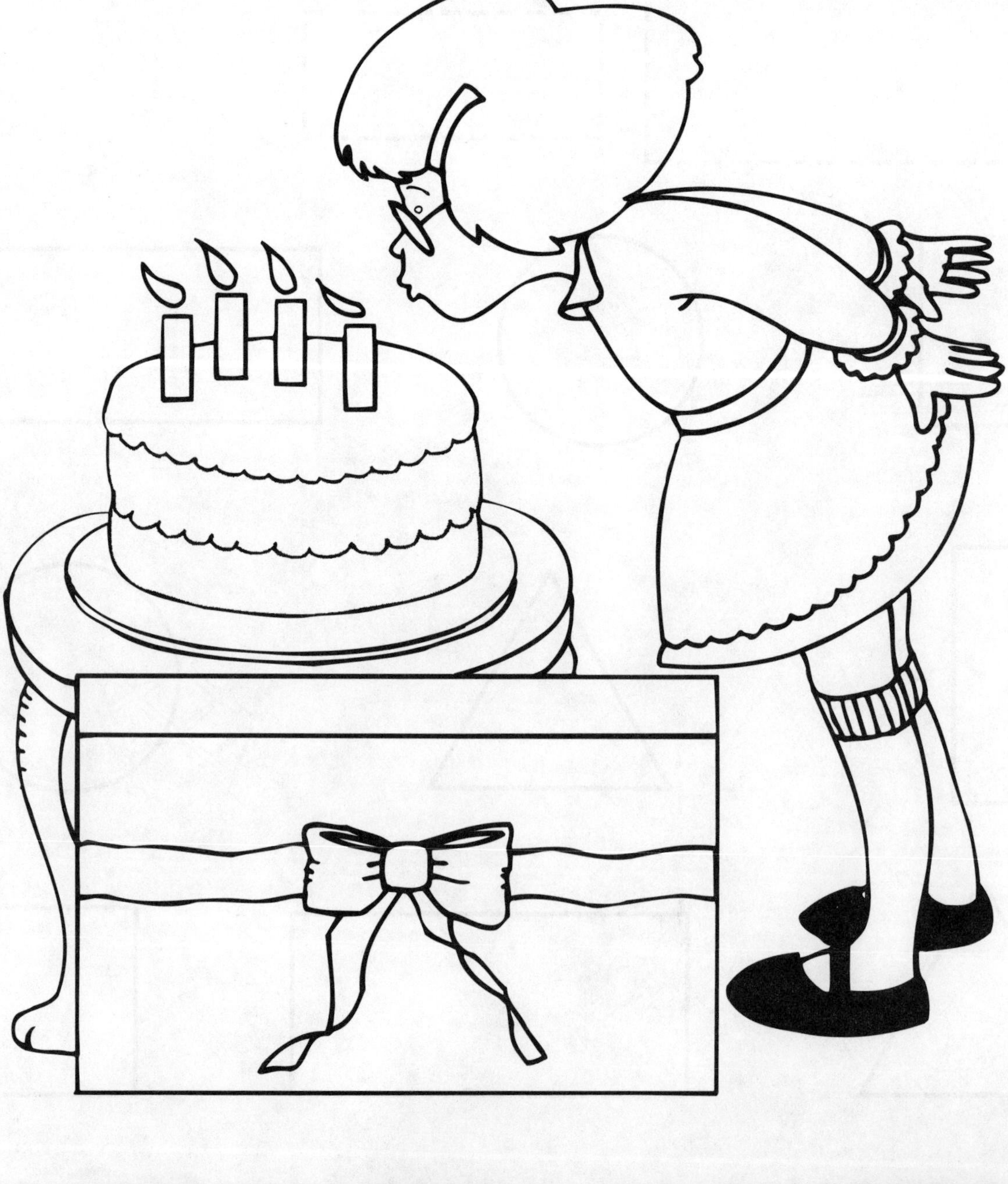

TRIANGLES

We see many **triangles** every day. **Triangles** have 3 sides. **Color** the **triangles**.

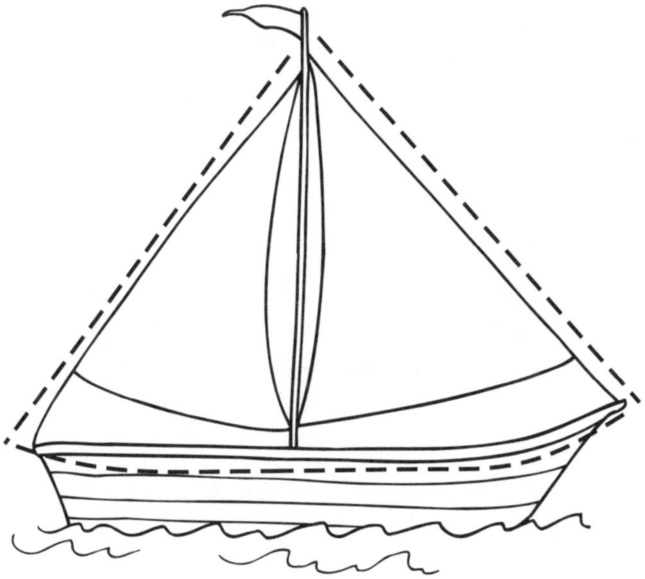

TRIANGLES

Triangles can be different sizes. **Color** the **triangles**.

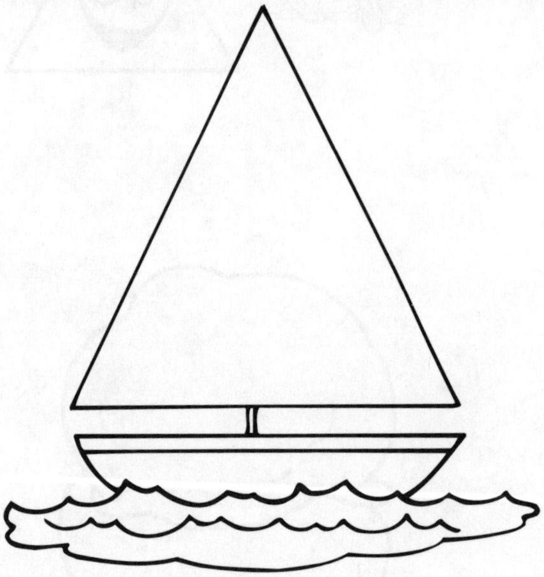

TRIANGLES

Trace the **triangles. Color** the **triangles.**

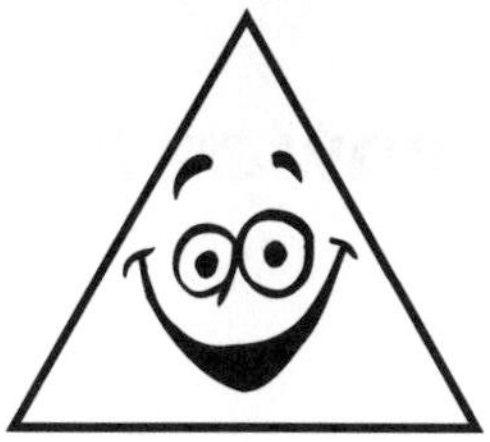

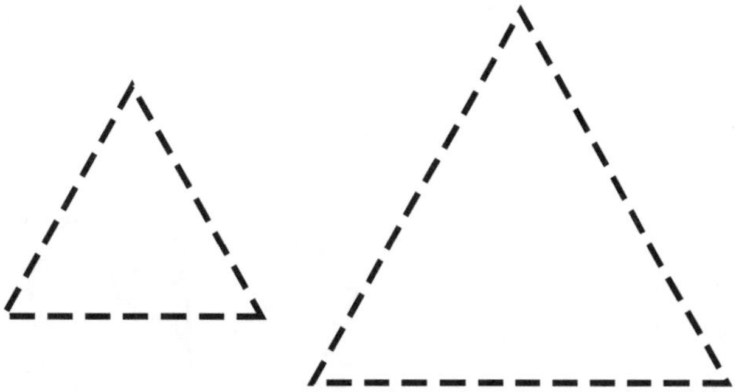

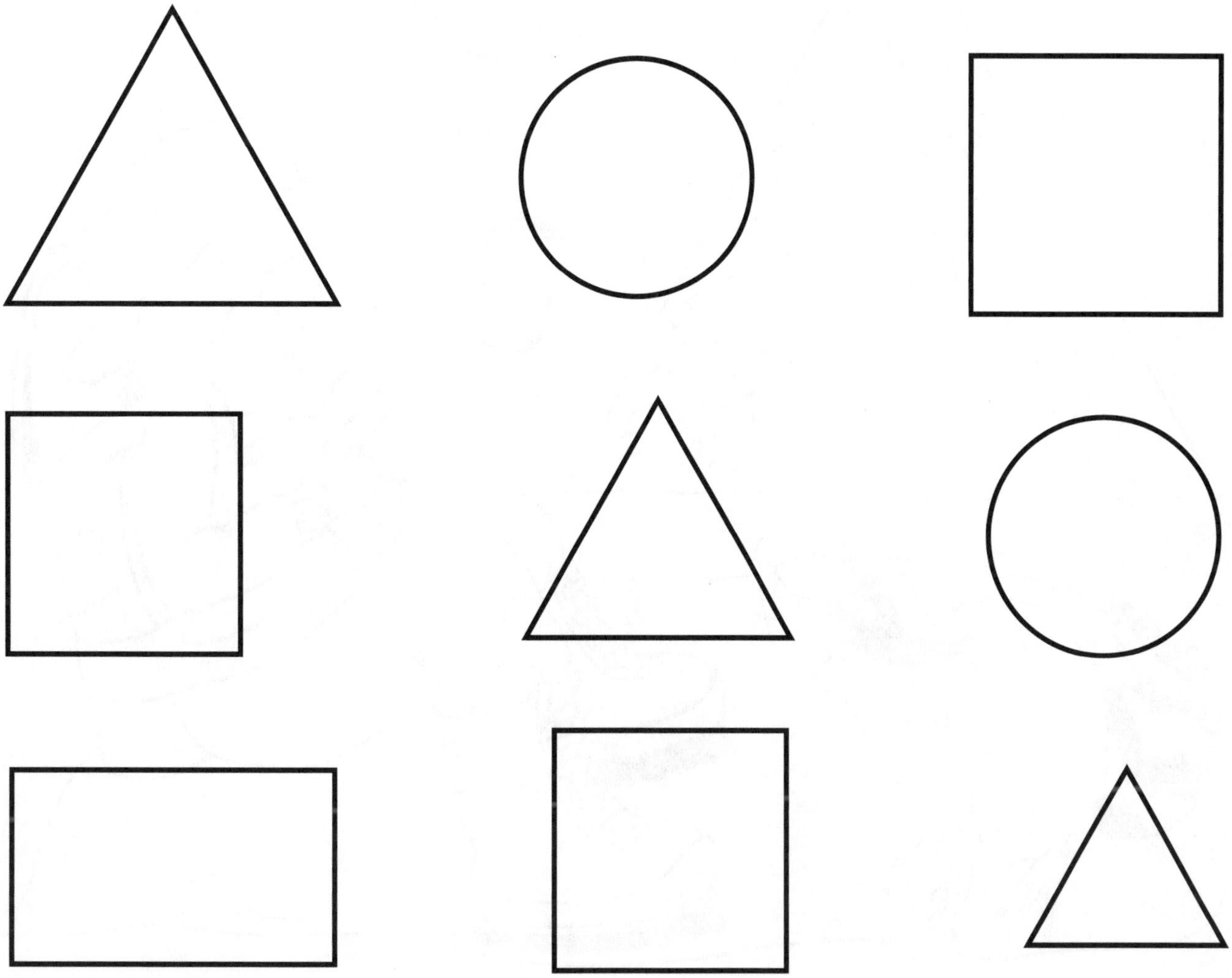

TRIANGLES

Draw an **X** on the things that have the **shape** of a **triangle**.

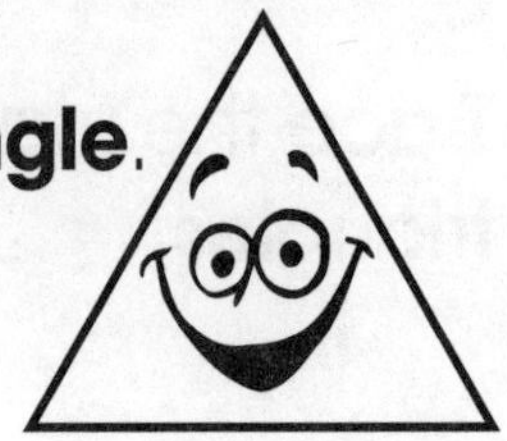

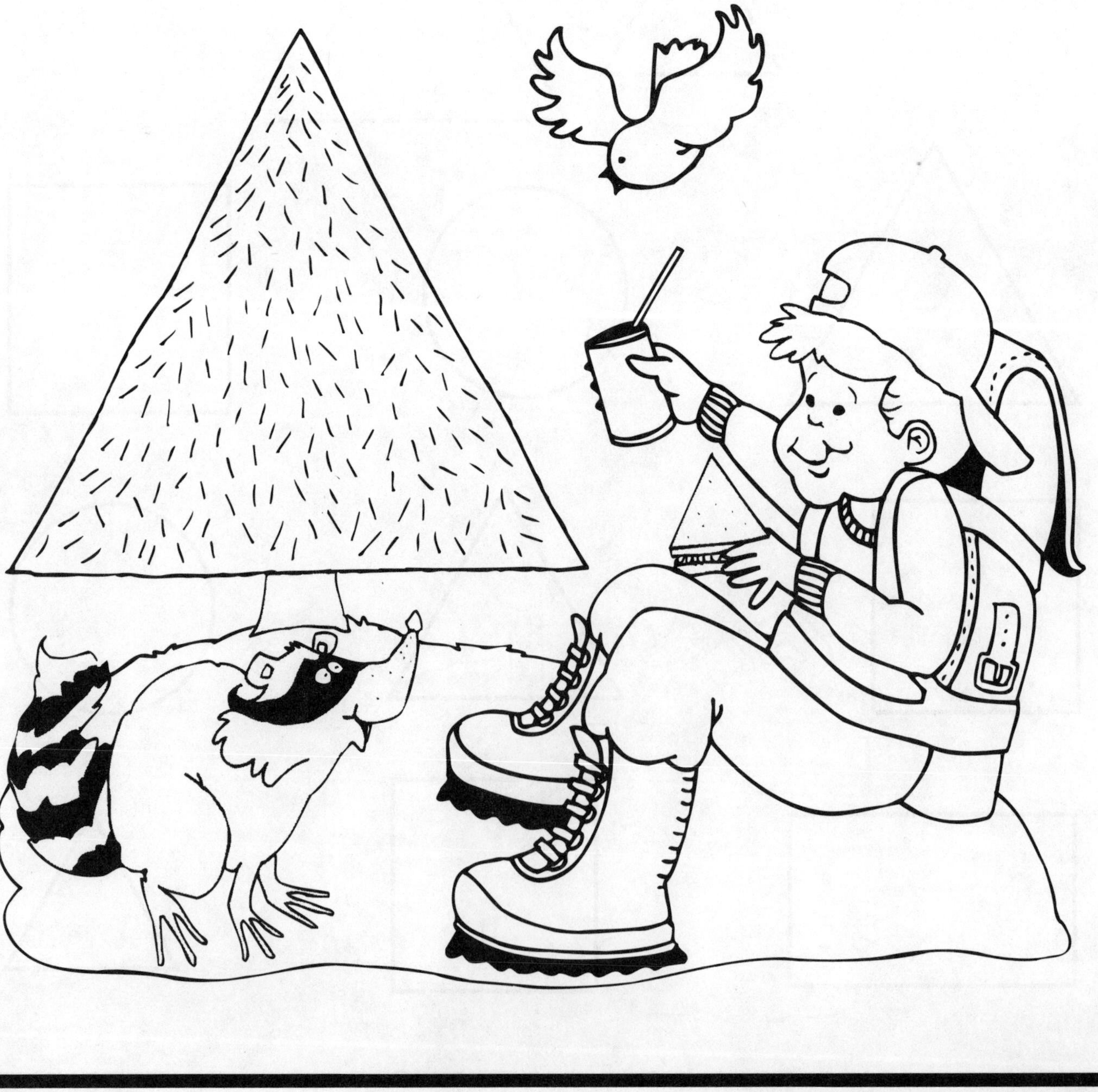

SHAPES

Color the **shapes** to finish this picture.

Color the ■'s **yellow**.
Color the ●'s **blue**.
Color the ▲'s **red**.
Color the ▬'s **green**.

SHAPE PATTERNS

Match the **shape patterns** on the **left** with the **shape patterns** on the **right**.

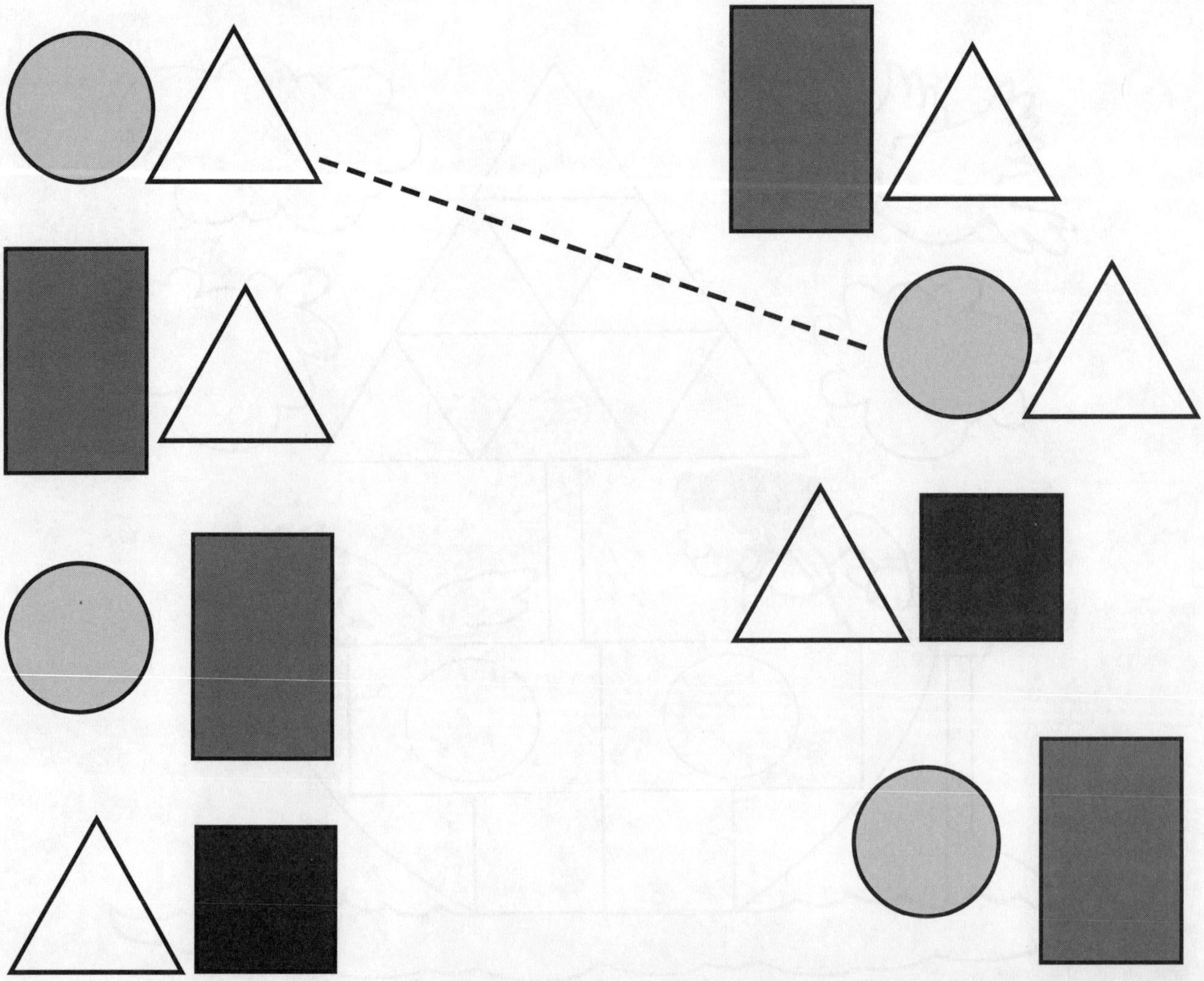

SHAPE PATTERNS

Look at the **shapes** in each row. **Draw** the next **shape** in the pattern.

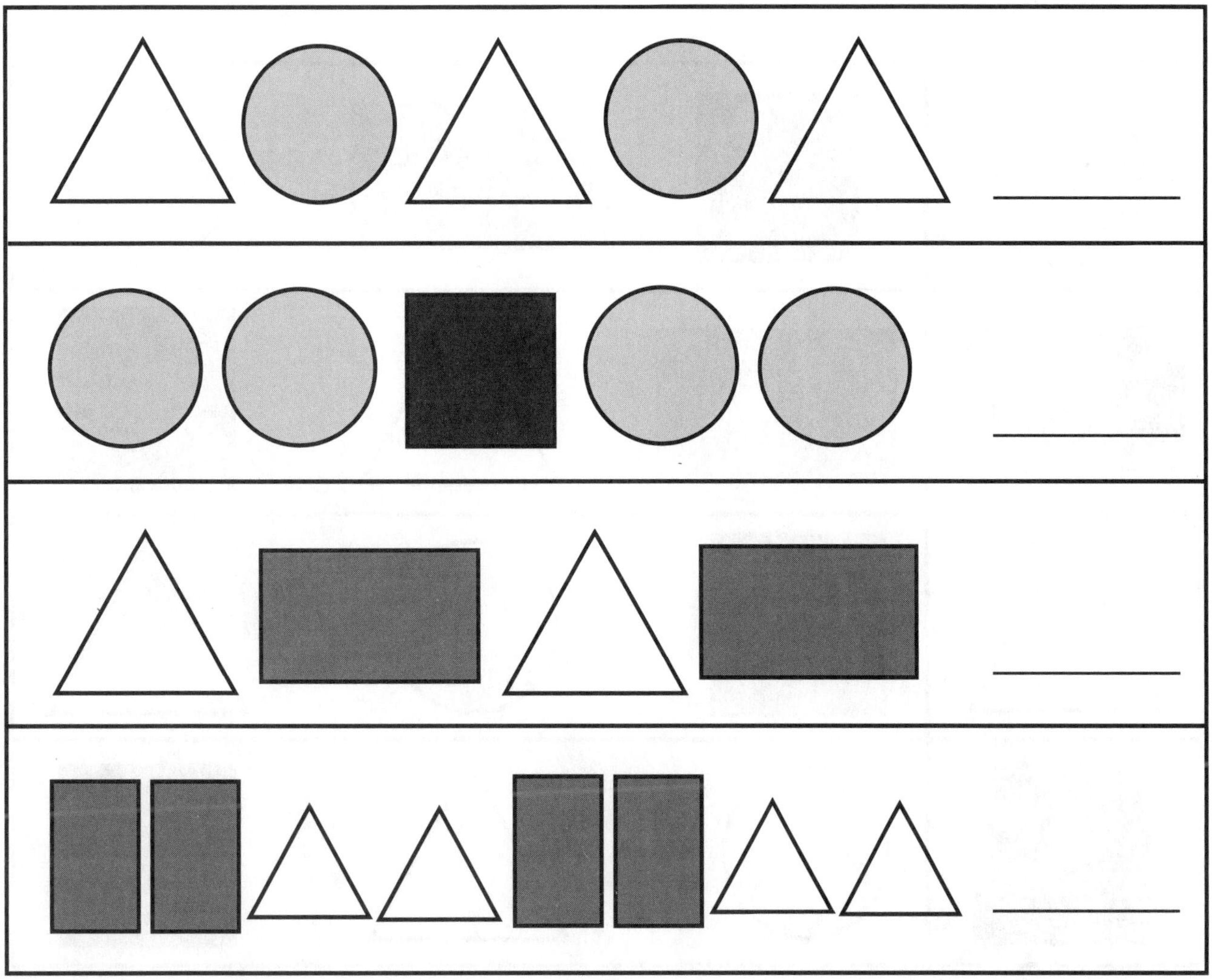

REVIEW SHAPES

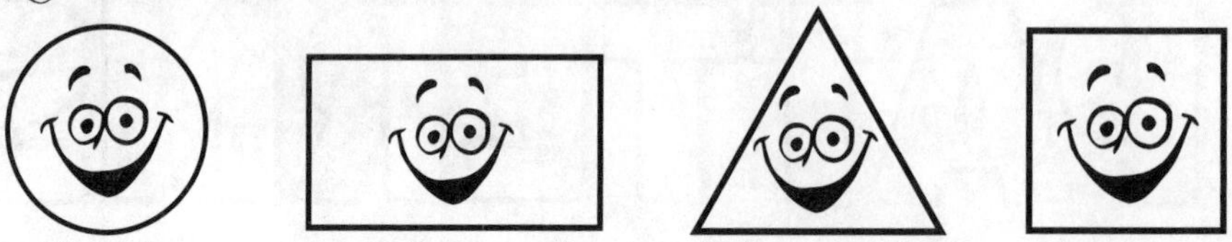

circle **rectangle** **triangle** **square**

Name the **shape** at the beginning of each row.
Circle the other **shape** in that row that is the same.

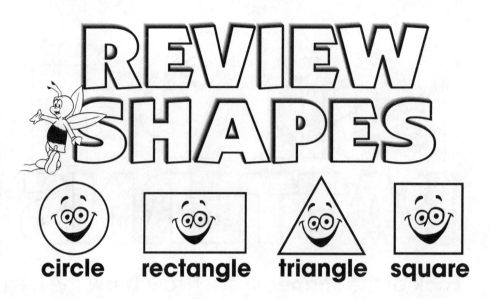

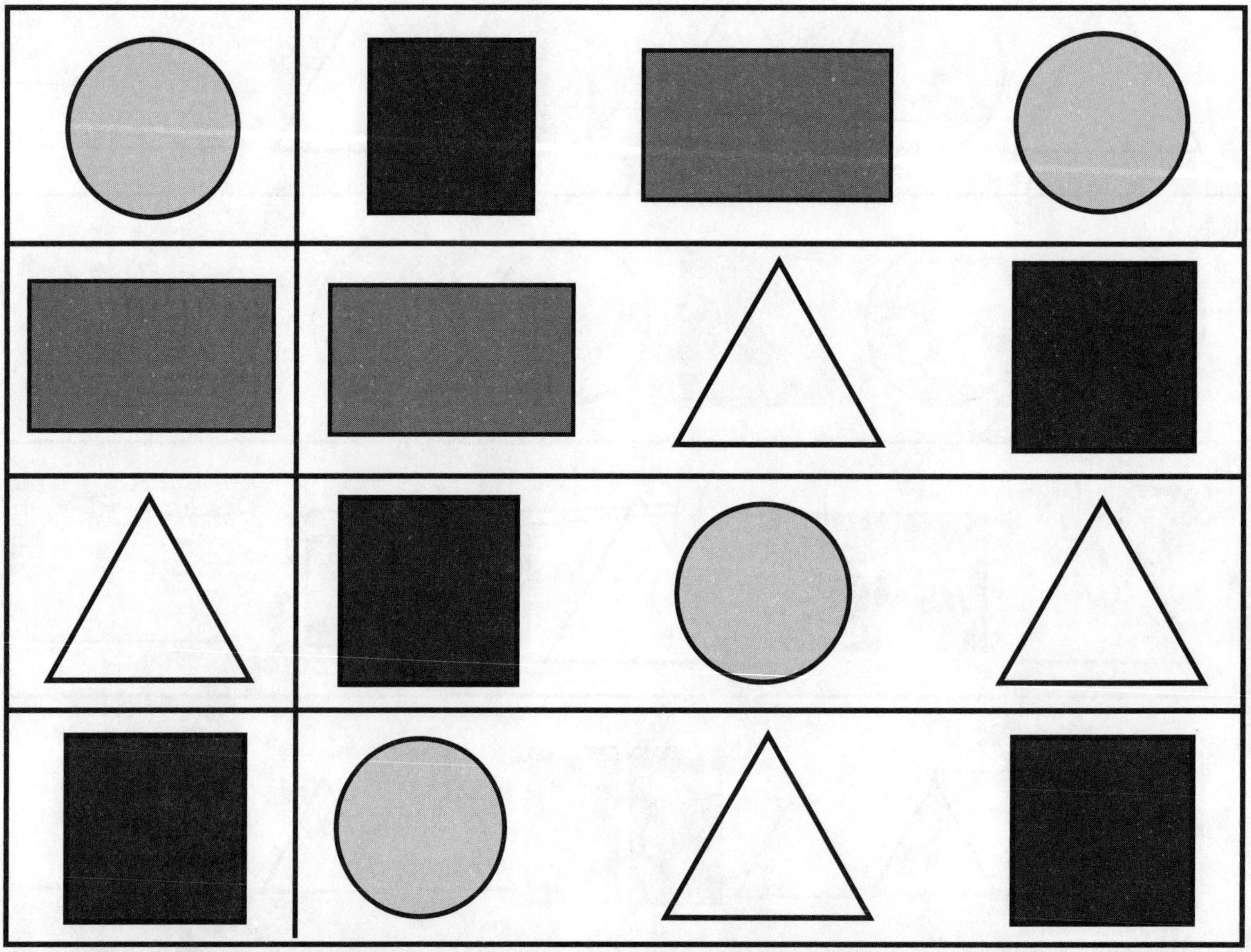

Look at all the **shapes**.

Color the ■'s **yellow**.

Color the ▲'s **red**.

Color the ●'s **blue**.

Color the ▬'s **green**.

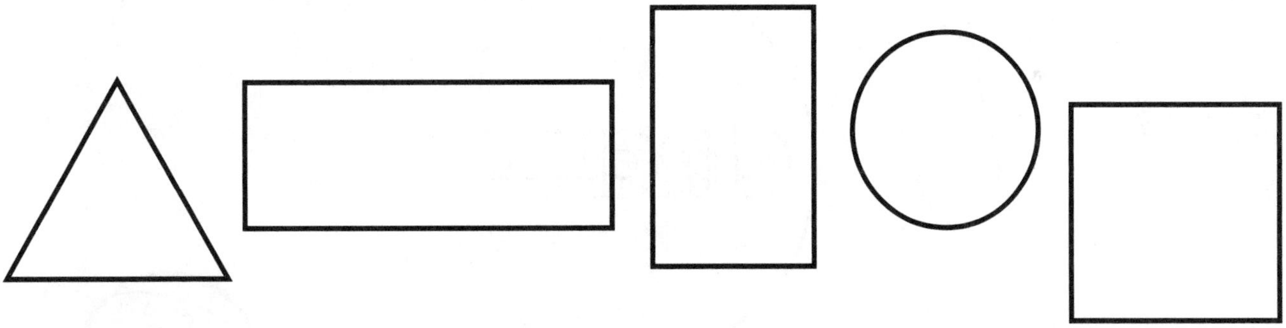

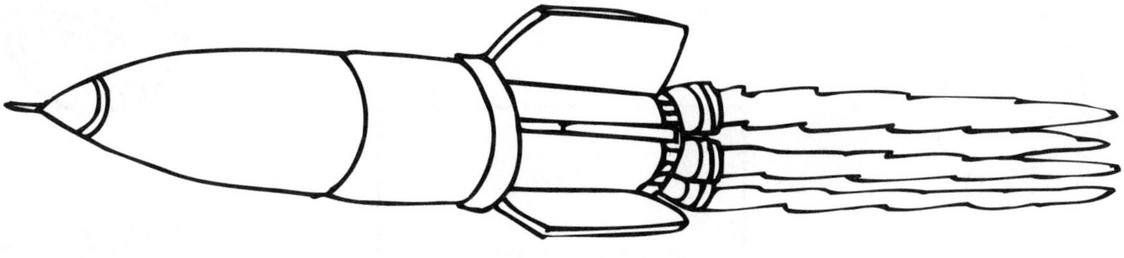

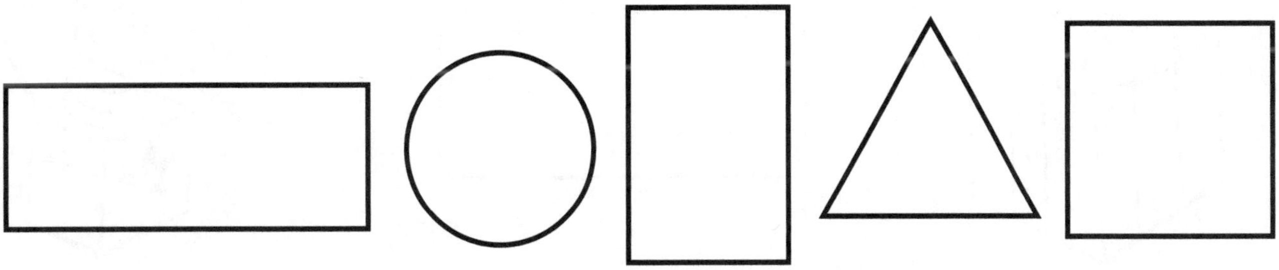

SORTING BY SHAPE

Draw a line from the **circle** to each thing that has the shape of a **circle**. **Draw** a line from the **square** to each thing that has the shape of a **square**.

SORTING BY SHAPE

Draw a line from the **rectangle** to each thing that has the shape of a **rectangle**. **Draw** a line from the **triangle** to each thing that has the shape of a **triangle**.

REVIEW SHAPES

Draw a **line** to the matching **shapes.**

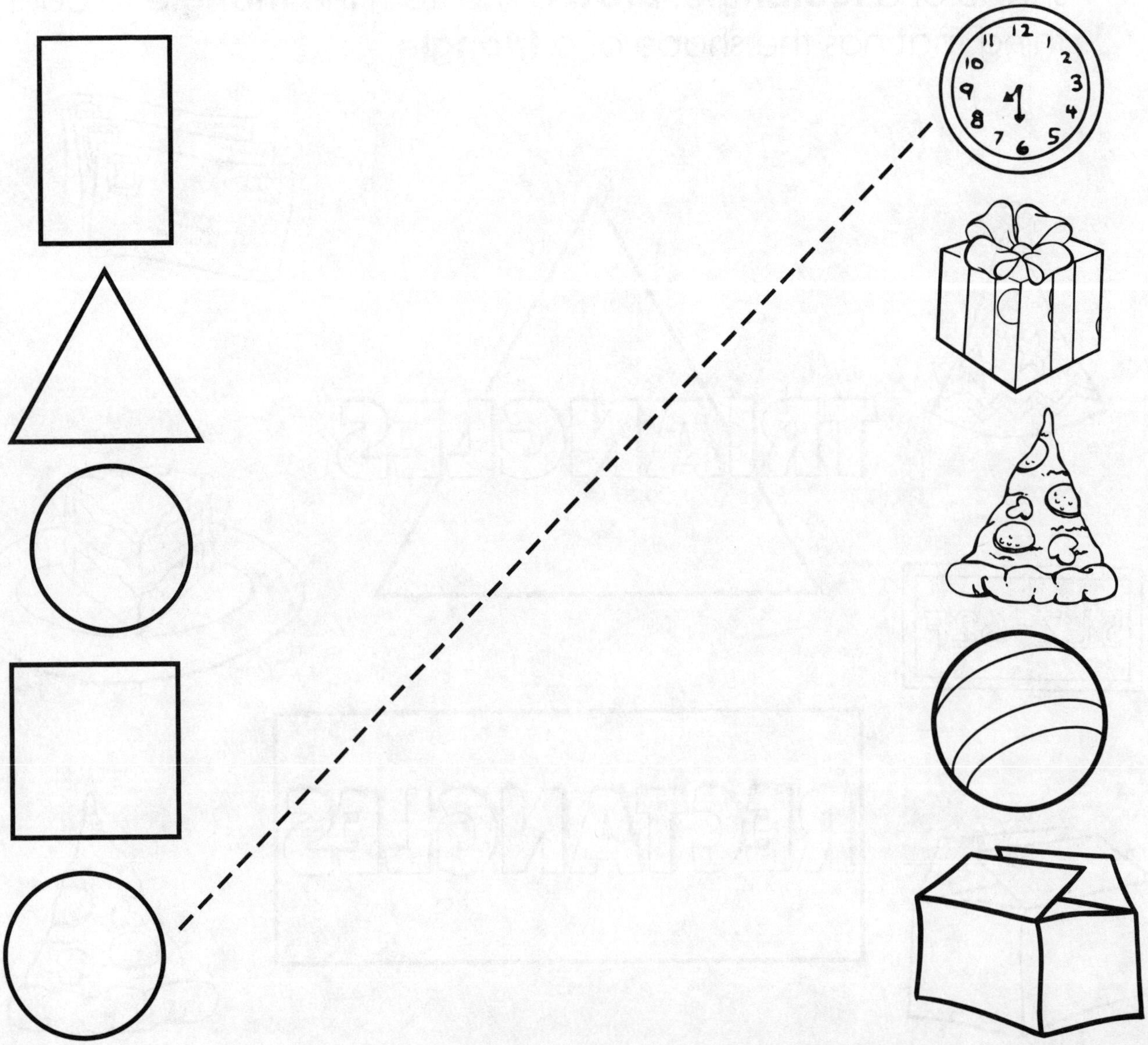

REVIEW SHAPES

Look at the **shapes**. **Draw** the **shape** that comes next in the pattern.

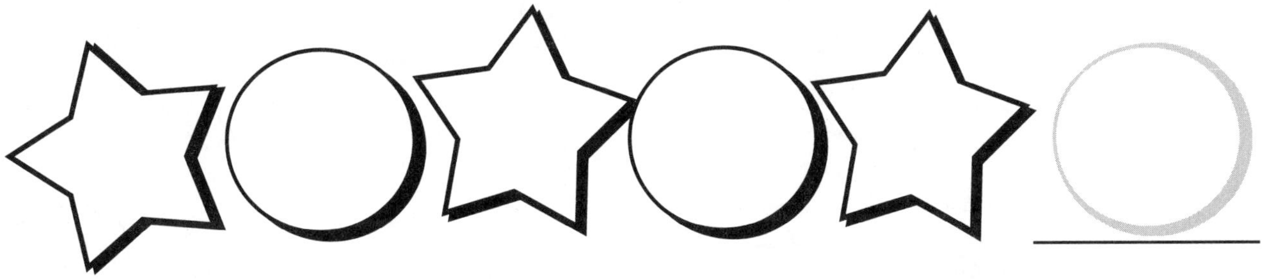

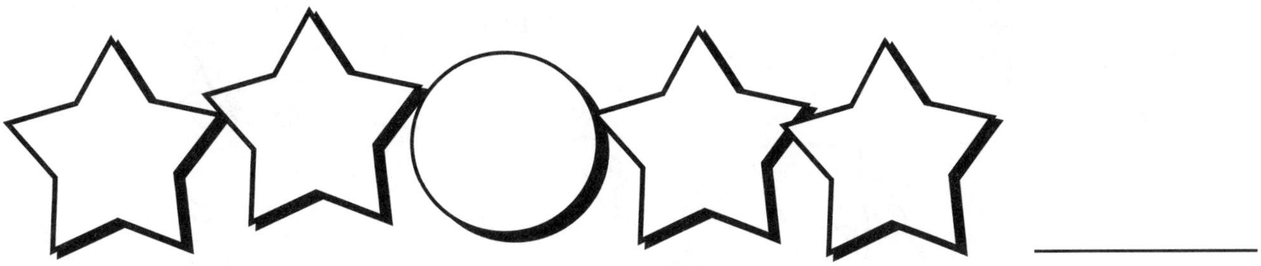

REVIEW COLORS AND SHAPES

Color each **square blue**. **Color** each **circle green**. **Color** each **triangle brown**. Then, finish the picture with your favorite colors!

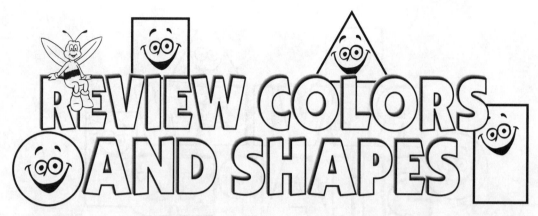

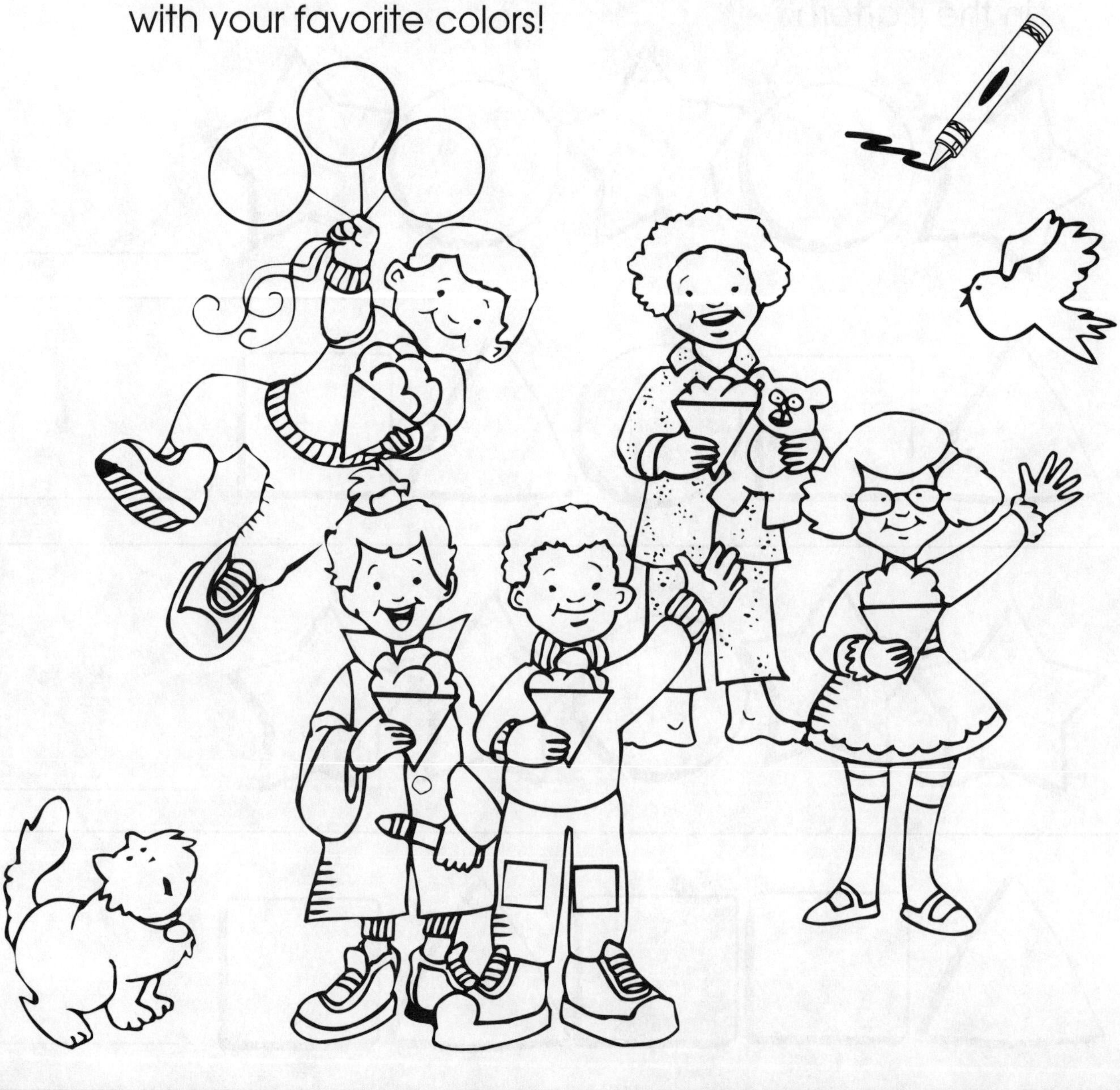

Some things are **big**. Some things are **small**. **Circle** the things that are **small**.

BIG

SMALL

Circle the things that are **small**.

Circle the things that are **big**.

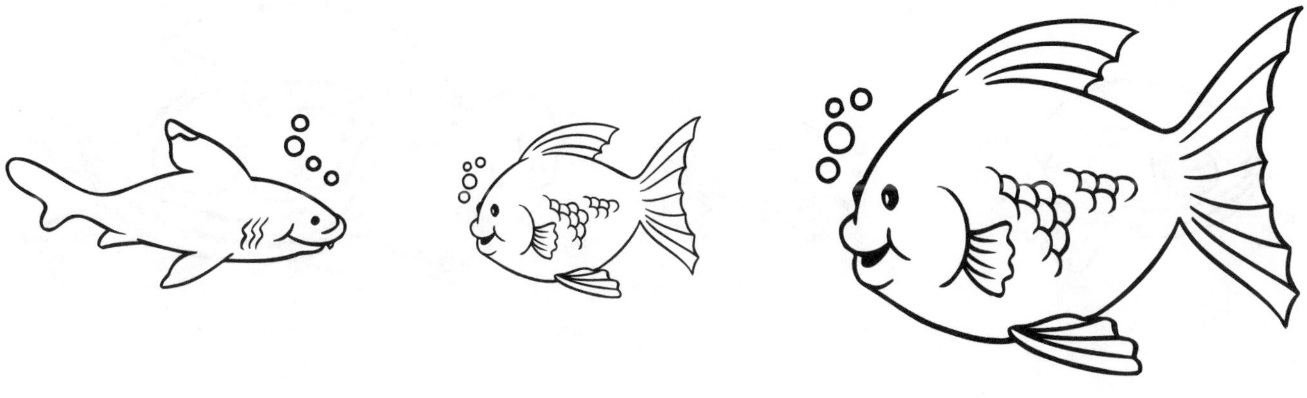

Which one is **big**? **Circle** the one that is **big**.
Color the pictures.

Look at the pictures in the box. **Color** the **small** pictures **green**. **Color** the **big** pictures **yellow**.

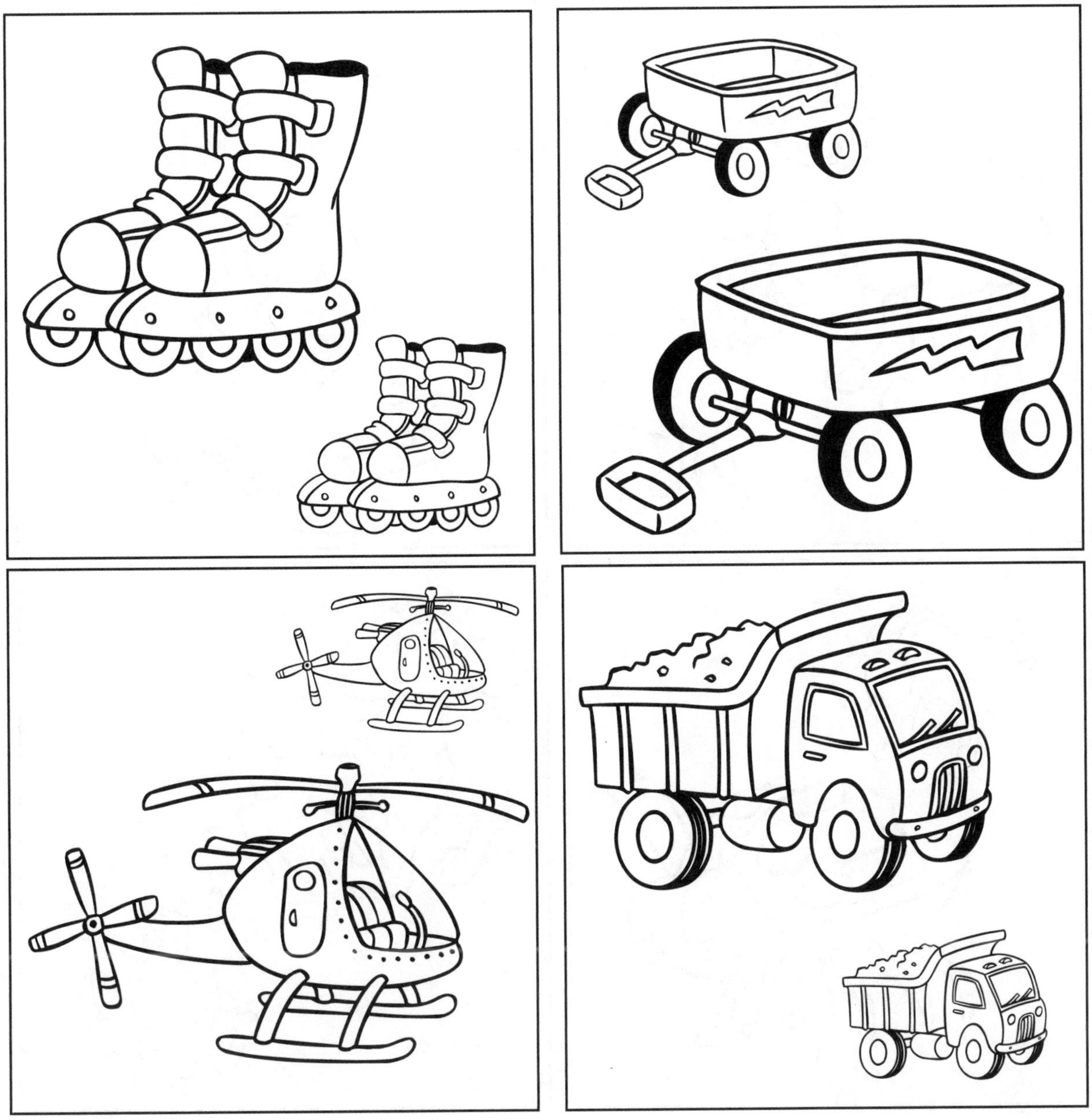

Look at the pictures in the box. **Color** the **small** pictures **red**. **Color** the **big** pictures **purple**.

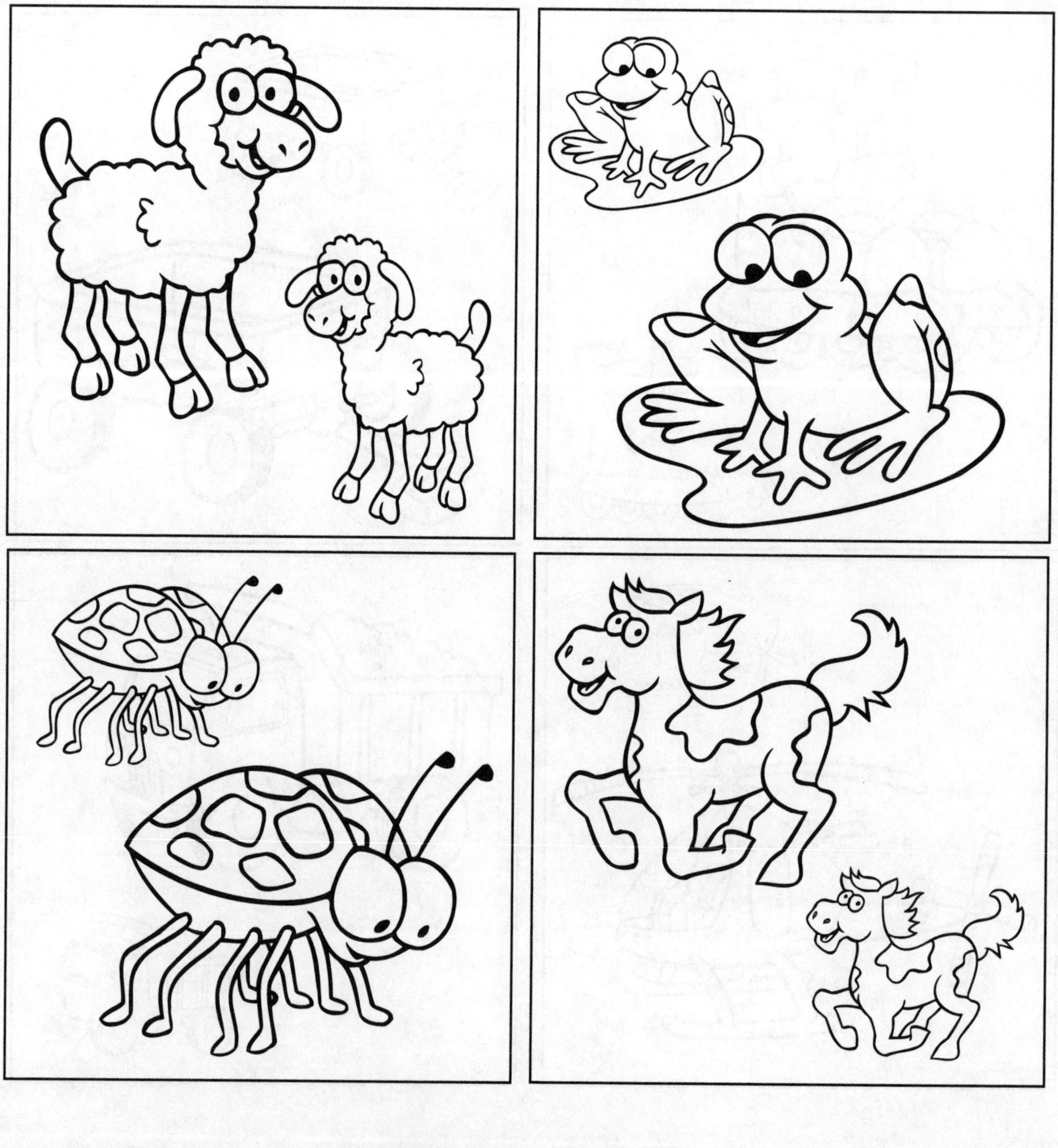

Circle the **biggest** thing. **Draw** an **X** on the **smallest** thing.

Circle the **smallest** thing. **Draw** an **X** on the **biggest** thing.

Color the pictures. **Cut out** the boxes. Put them in order from

SMALLEST
to
BIGGEST

Page is blank for cutting exercise on previous page.

Some things are **long**. Some things are **short**. **Circle** the things that are **long**.

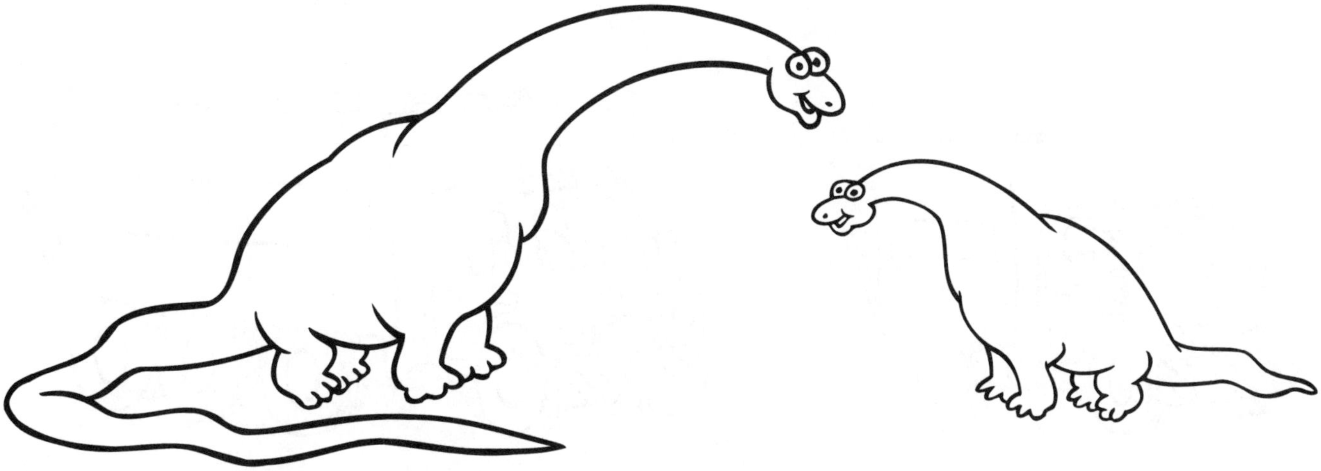

Which one is **long**? **Circle** the thing that is **long**. **Color** the pictures.

Look at the pictures in each box. **Circle** the things that are **short**. **Color** the pictures.

Which one is **short**? **Circle** the thing that is **short**. **Color** the pictures.

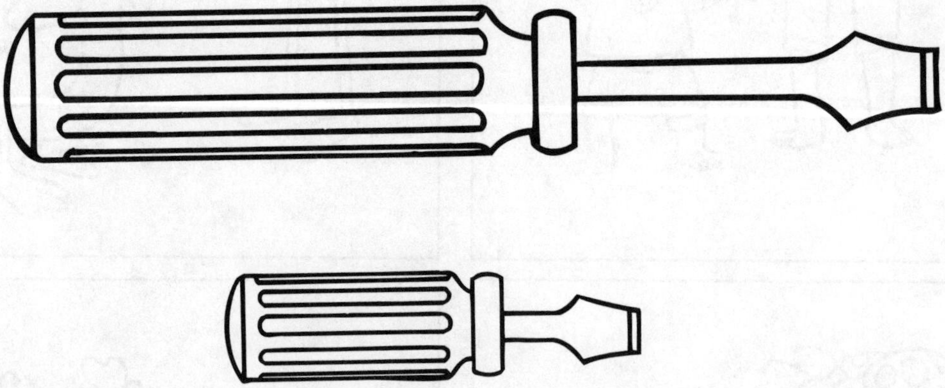

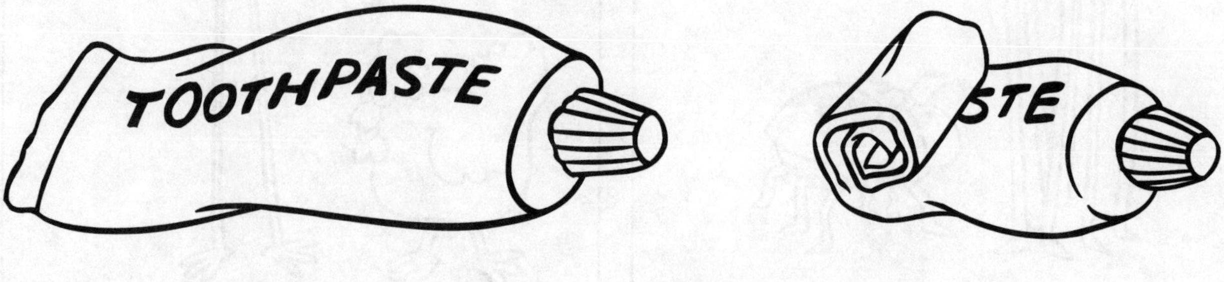

Circle the **longest** thing in each row.

LONG LONGER LONGEST

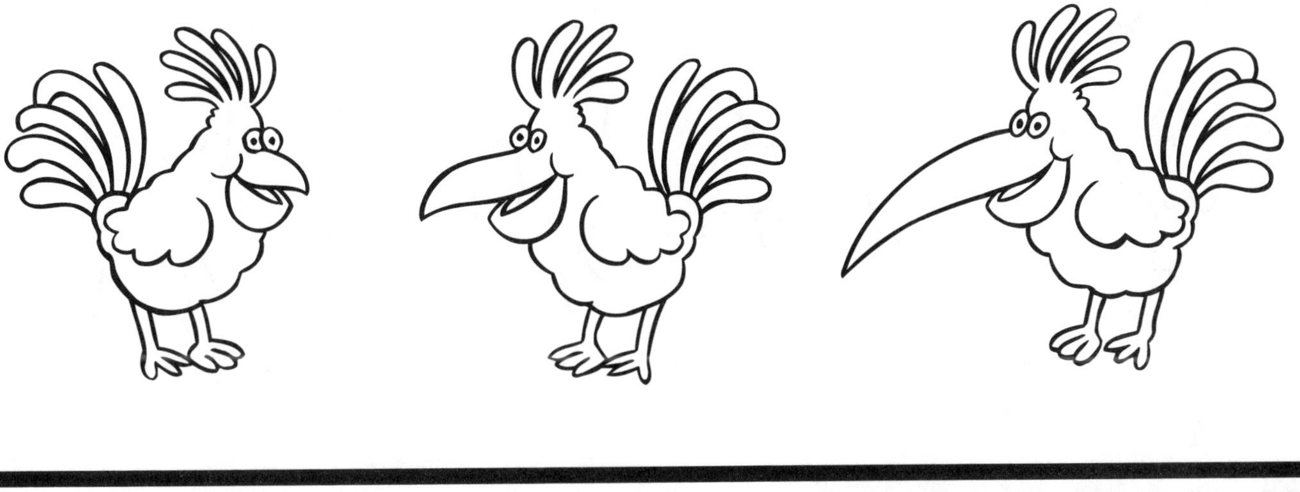

Circle the **shortest** thing in each row.

SHORT SHORTER SHORTEST

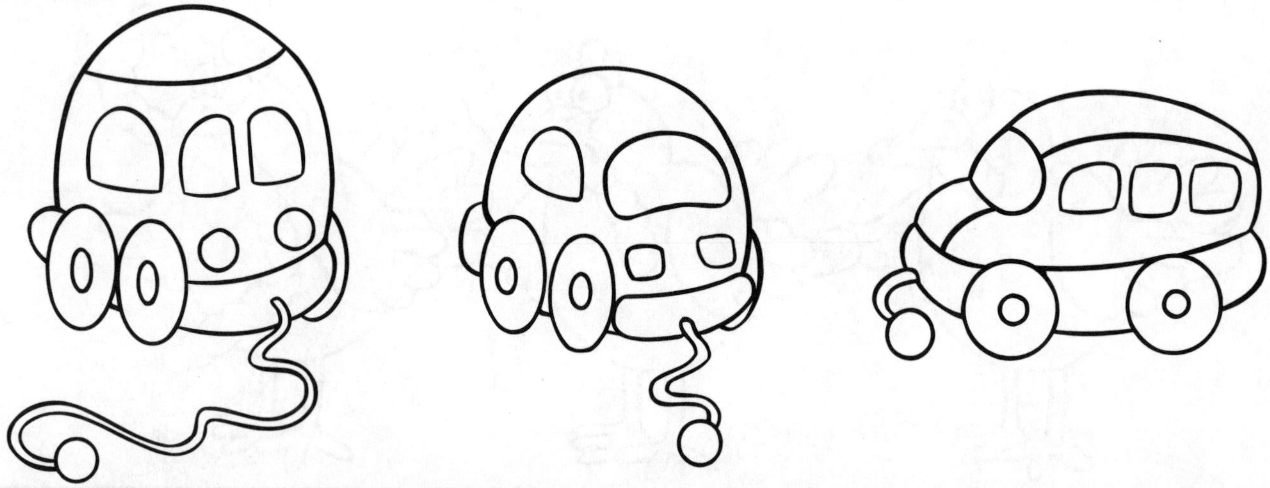

Circle the **longest** thing in each row. **Draw** an **X** on the **shortest** thing.

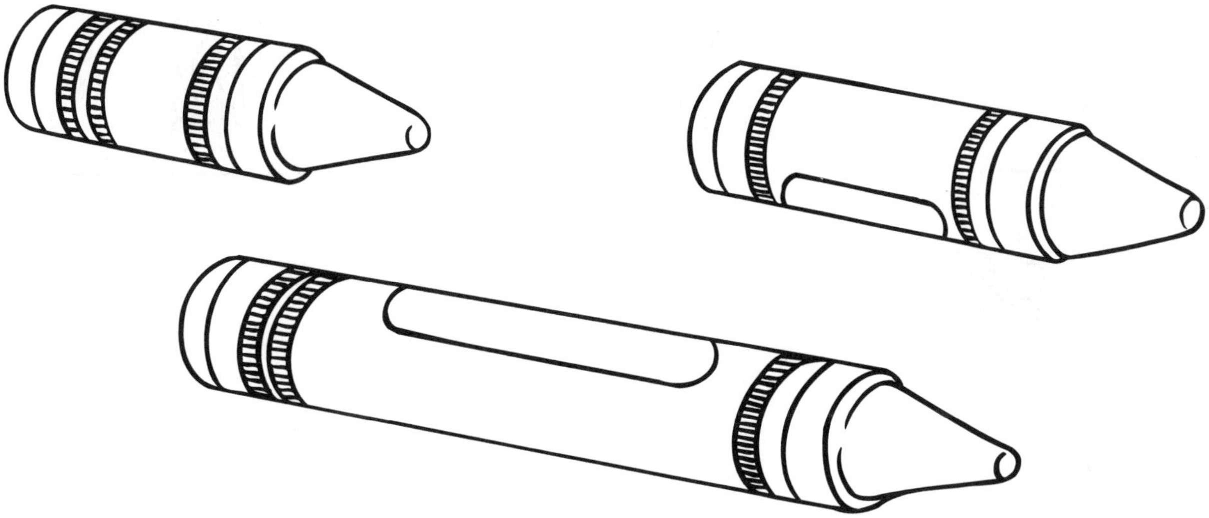

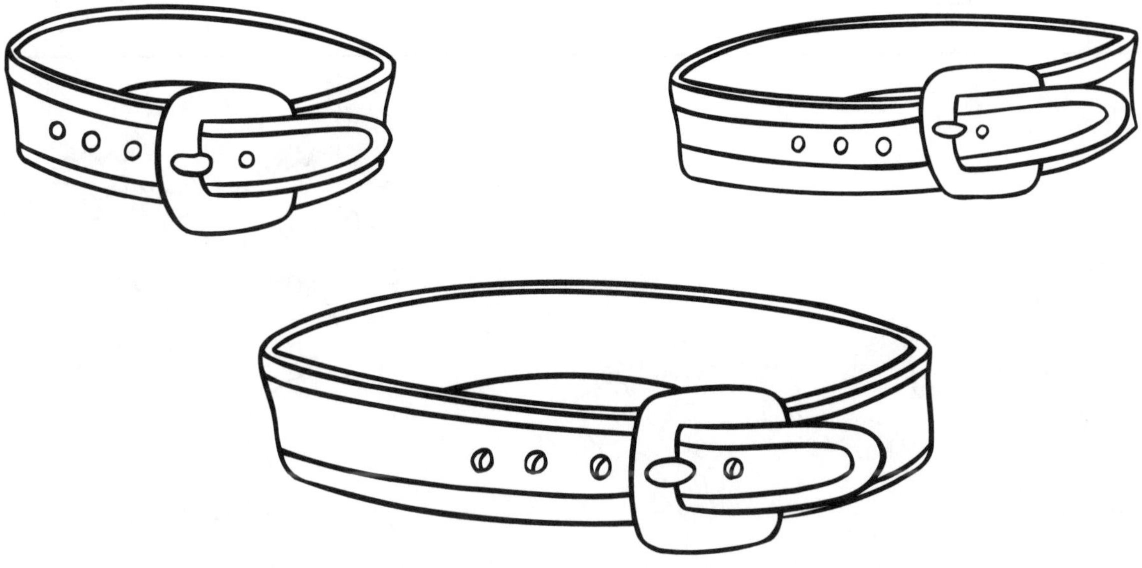

Some things are **tall**. Some things are **short**. **Circle** the things that are **short**.

Look at the pictures in each box. **Circle** the people who are **tall**. **Color** the pictures.

Circle the **tallest** thing in each row.

TALL TALLER TALLEST

Circle the **shortest** thing in each row.

SHORT SHORTER SHORTEST

Circle the **tallest** thing in each row. **Draw** an **X** on the **shortest** thing.

Color, **cut out** and **glue**. Put the goat going up the mountain.

UP

Do not cut.
Activity on other side.

Color, **cut out** and **glue**. Put the bunny going **down** the slide.

DOWN

Do not cut.
Activity on other side.

Color and **cut out** the **children**. **Glue** one child **up** at the **top** of the slide. **Glue** the other child **down** at the **bottom** of the slide.

UP AND DOWN

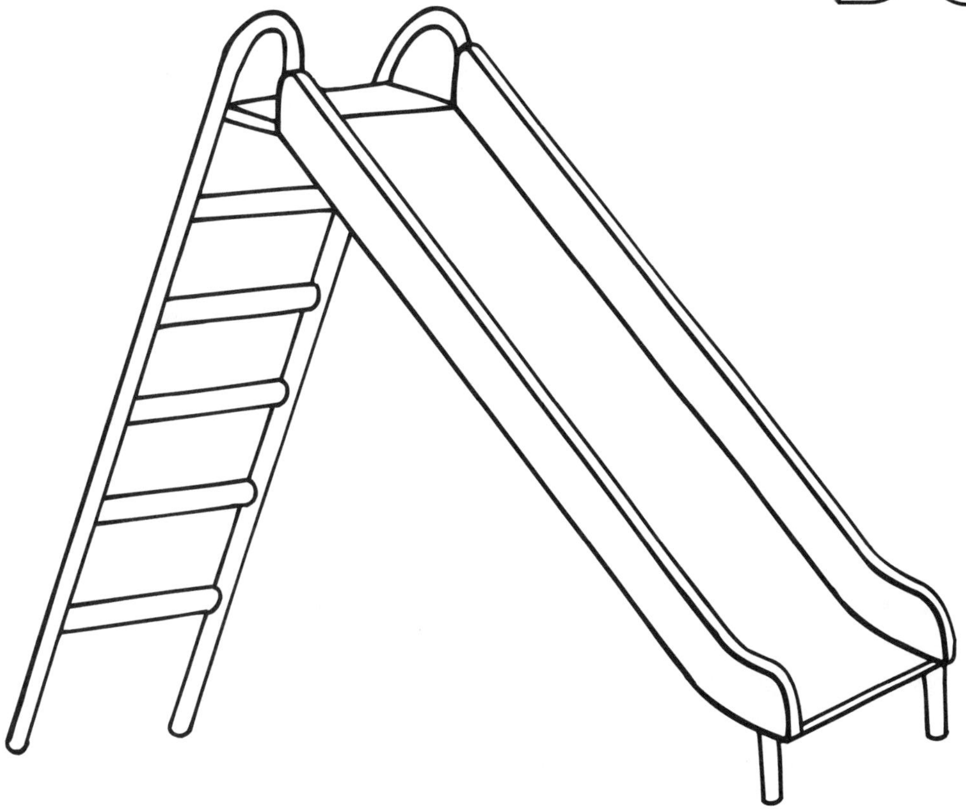

Page is blank for cutting exercise on previous page.

Color, **cut out** and **glue**. Put the school bell on top of the schoolhouse.

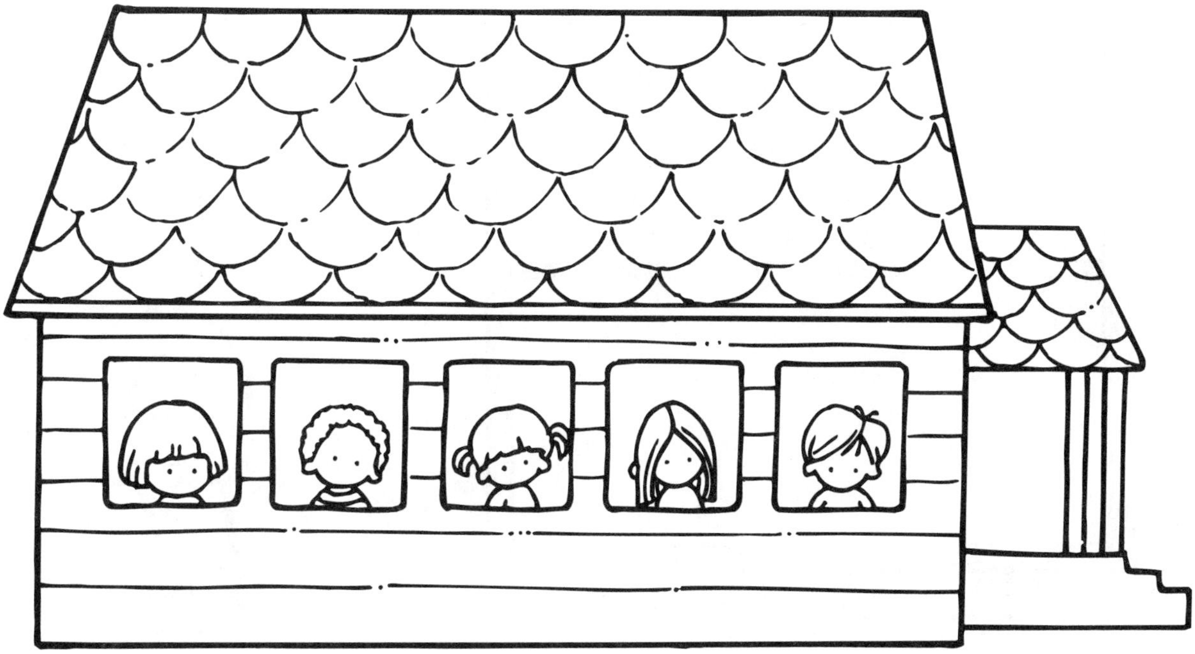

Do not cut.
Activity on other side.

Color, **cut out** and **glue**. Put the drum on the bottom shelf.

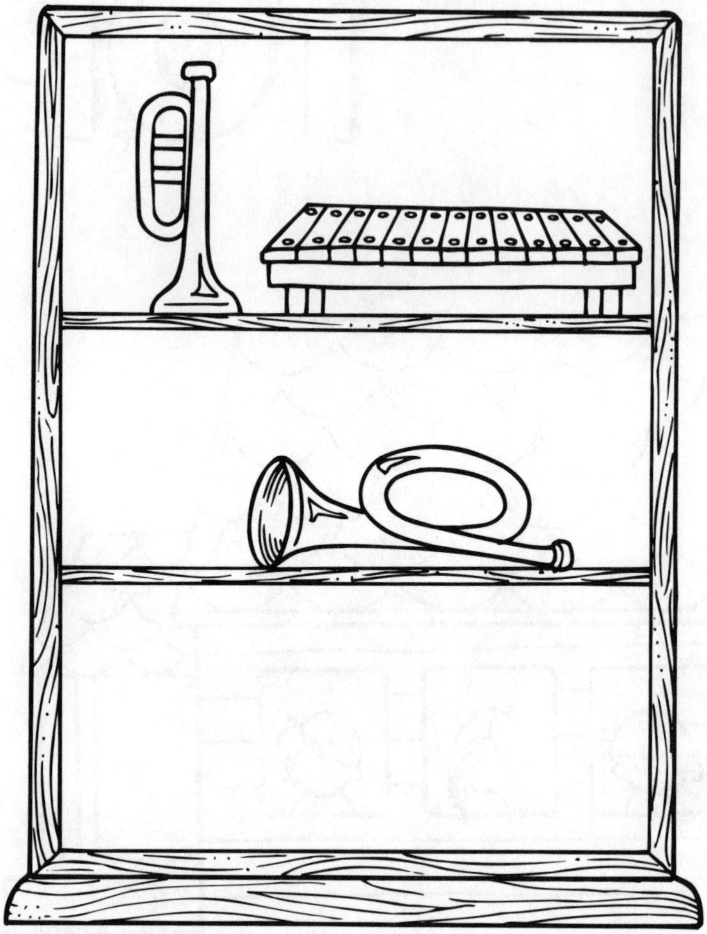

BOTTOM

Do not cut.
Activity on other side.

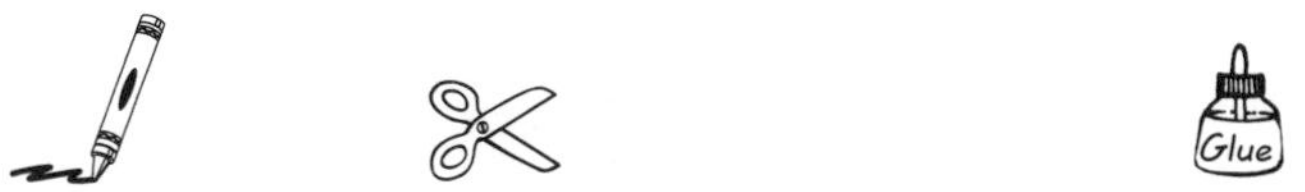

Color and **cut out** the balls. **Glue** one ball on the **top** stair. **Glue** the other ball on the **bottom** stair.

TOP AND BOTTOM

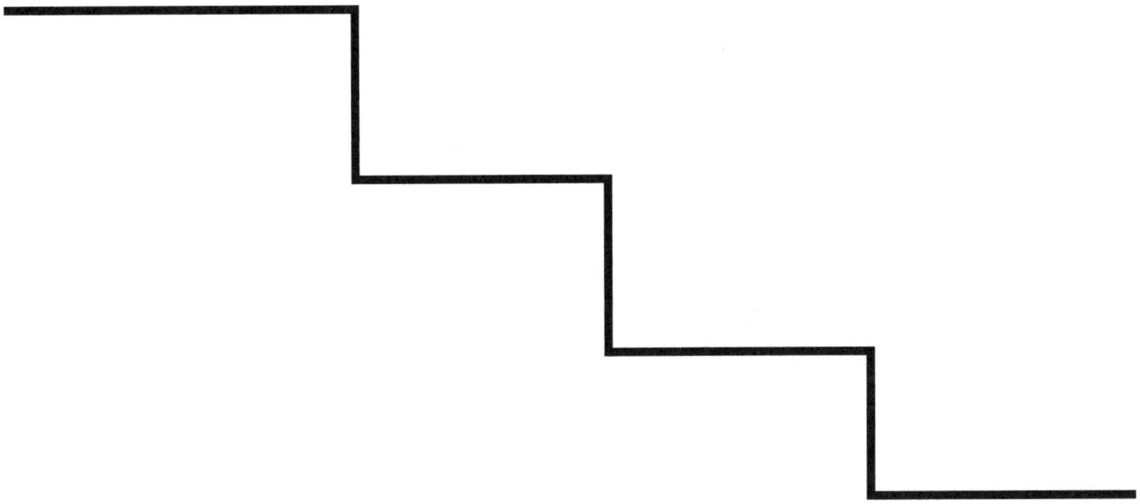

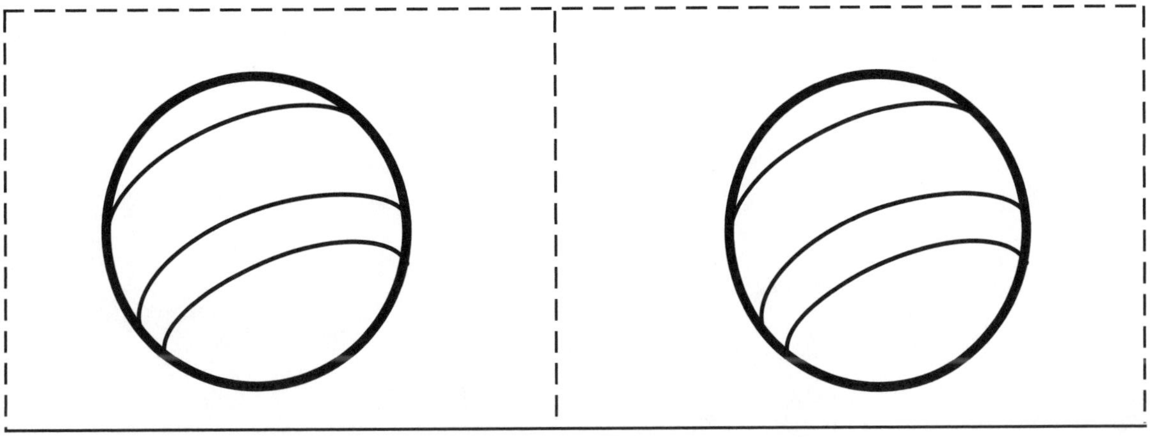

Page is blank for cutting
exercise on previous page.

Color, **cut out** and **glue**. Put the teddy bear **on** the bed.

Do not cut.
Activity on other side.

Color, **cut out** and **glue**. Put the lamp shade on the lamp that is **off**.

OFF

Do not cut.
Activity on other side.

Color and **cut out** the bears. **Glue** one bear **on** the box. **Glue** the other bear **off** the box.

ON AND OFF

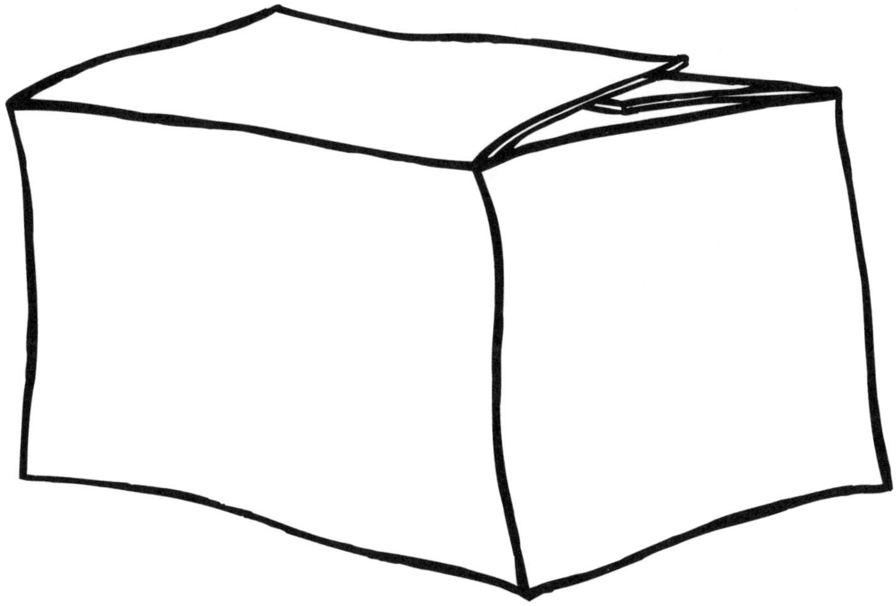

Page is blank for cutting exercise on previous page.

Color, **cut out** and **glue**. Put the plane **over** the cloud.

OVER

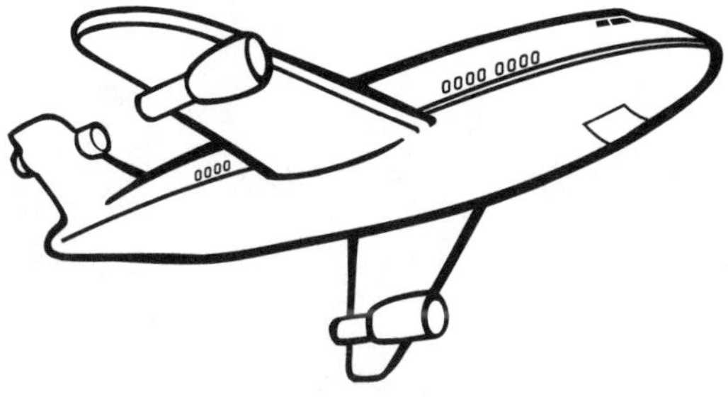

Do not cut.
Activity on other side.

Color, **cut out** and **glue**. Put the bear **under** the beehive.

UNDER

Do not cut.
Activity on other side.

Color and **cut out** the birds. **Glue** one bird **over** the rainbow. **Glue** the other bird **under** the rainbow.

OVER AND UNDER

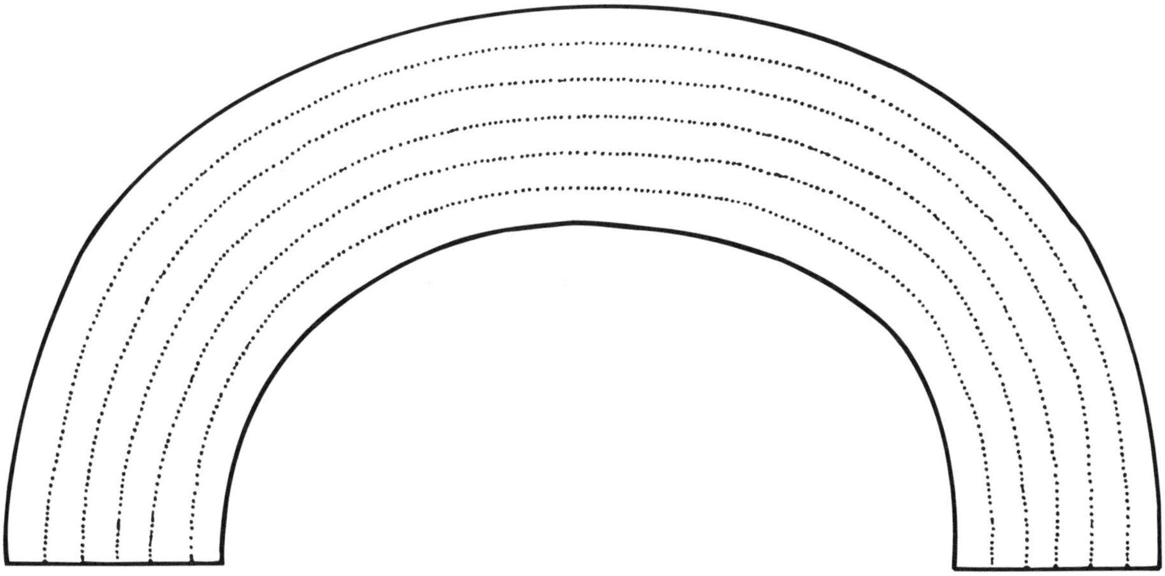

Page is blank for cutting exercise on previous page.

Color, **cut out** and **glue**. Put the mouse **inside** the mouse hole.

INSIDE

Do not cut.
Activity on other side.

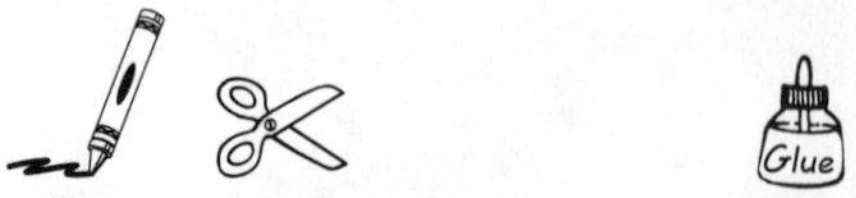

Color, **cut out** and **glue**. Put the bat **outside** the bat cave.

OUTSIDE

Do not cut.
Activity on other side.

Color, **cut out** and **glue**. Put the rows of flowers in **front** of the house.

FRONT

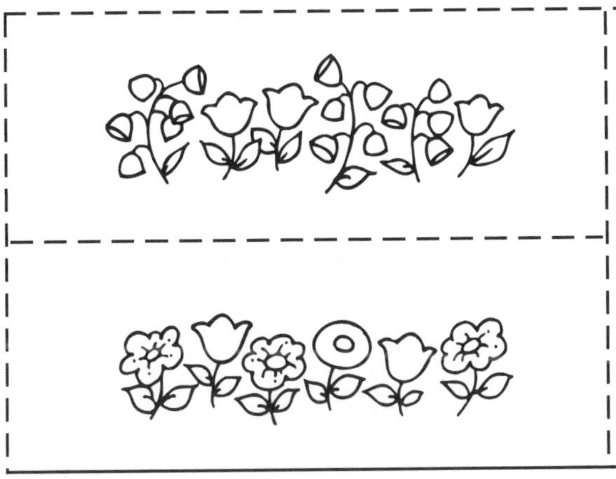

Do not cut.
Activity on other side.

Color, **cut out** and **glue**. Put the toy into the **back** of the wagon.

BACK

Do not cut.
Activity on other side.

Color, **cut out** and **glue**. Put the rocket **below** the moon.

BELOW

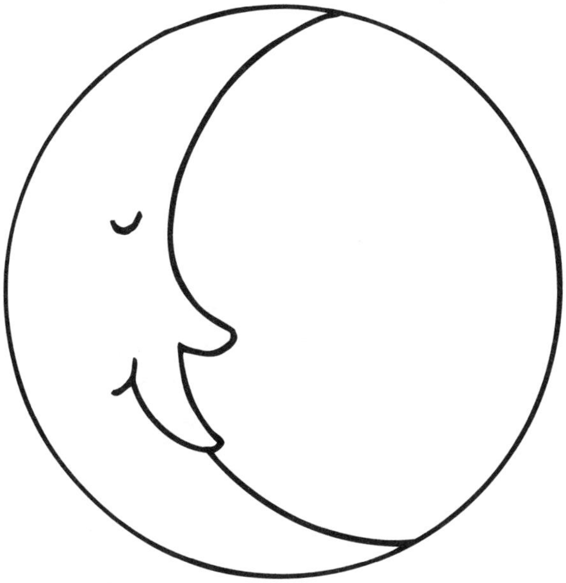

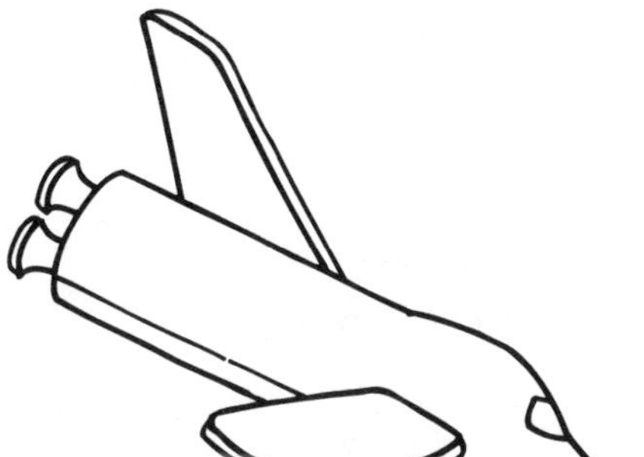

Do not cut.
Activity on other side.

Color, **cut out** and **glue**. Put the spaceship **above** the stars.

ABOVE

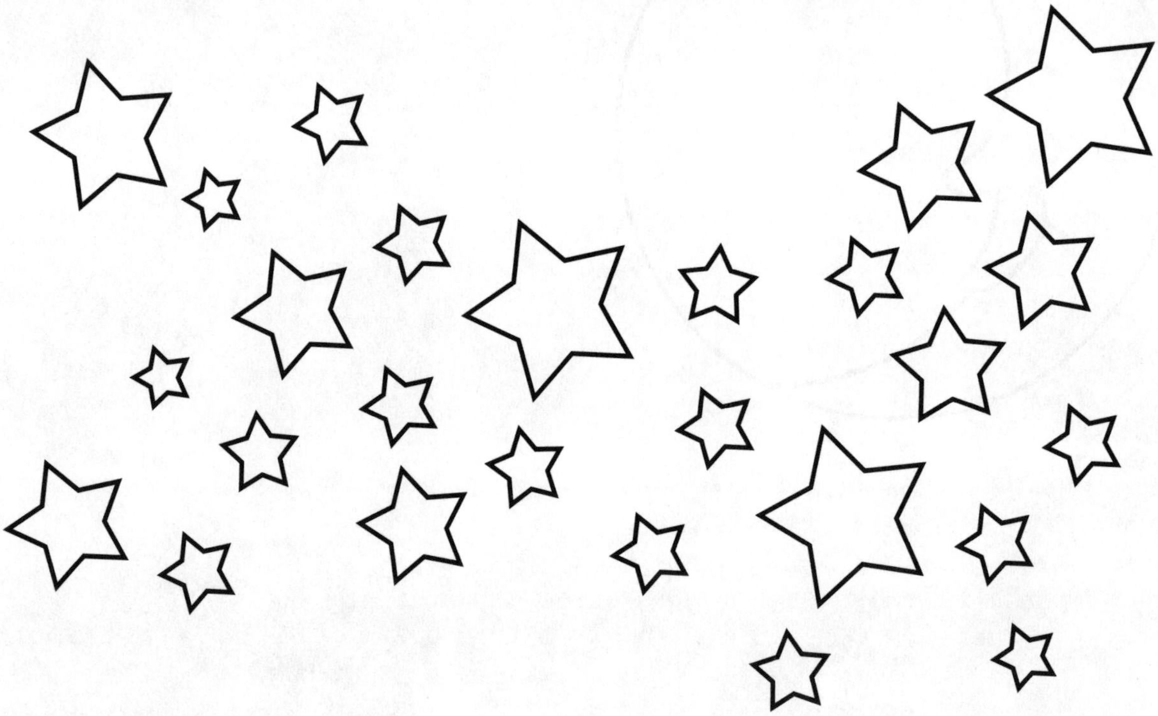

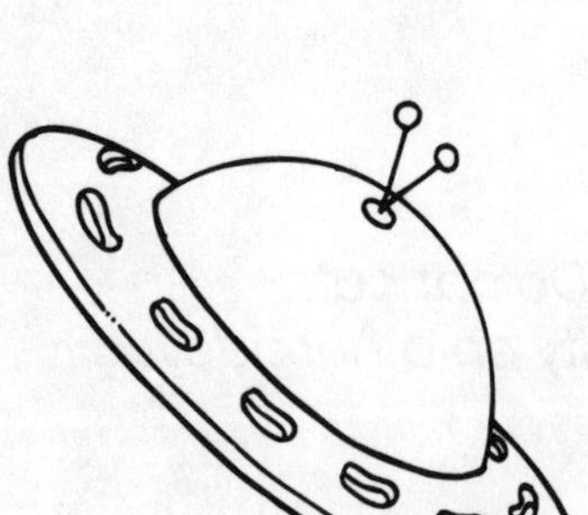

Do not cut.
Activity on other side.

Which tea cup is **nearest** to the teapot? **Color** the picture.

NEAREST

Which skunk hit the ball the **farthest**? **Color** the picture.

FARTHEST

Color, **cut out** and **glue**. Put the chicken **beside** the barn.

BESIDE

Do not cut.
Activity on other side.

Color, **cut out** and **glue**. Put the cart **behind** the horse.

BEHIND

Do not cut.
Activity on other side.

Color, **cut out** and **glue**. Put the basket of fruit **between** the trees.

BETWEEN

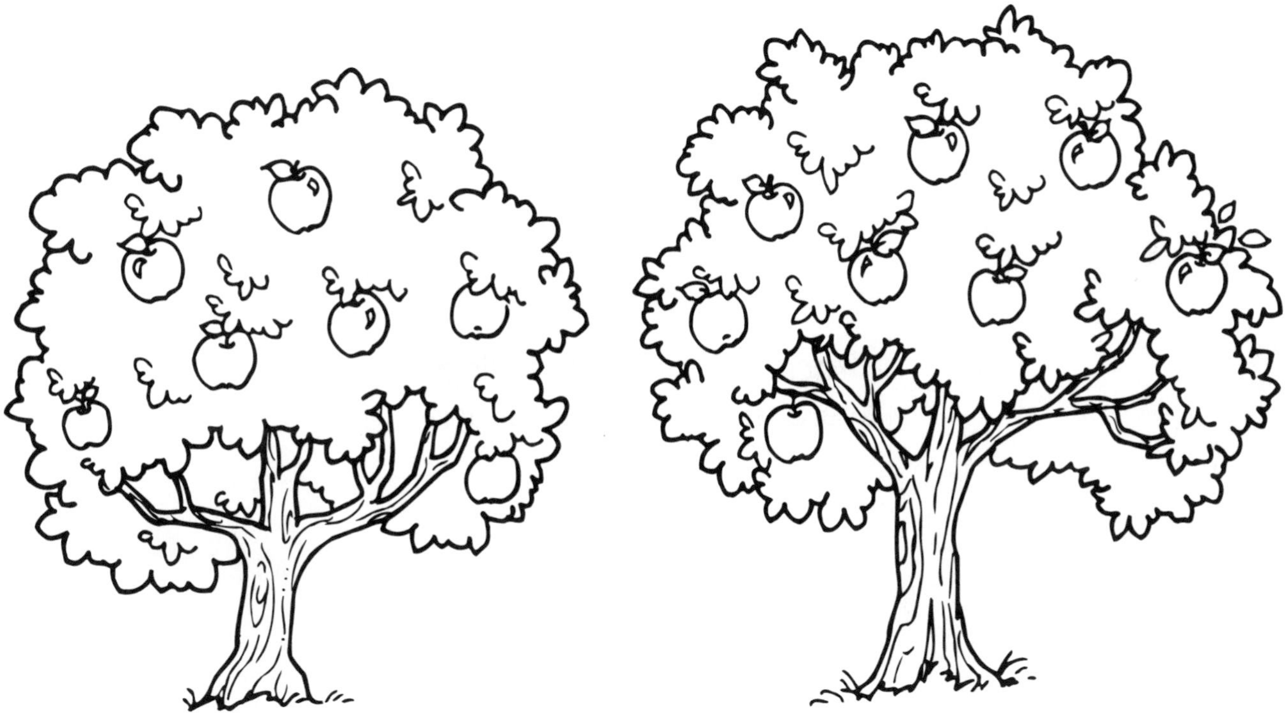

Do not cut.
Activity on other side.

Page is blank for cutting exercise on previous page.

Color, **cut out** and **glue**. Put the ballerina's slipper on her **right** foot.

RIGHT

Do not cut.
Activity on other side.

Color, **cut out** and **glue**. Put the mitt on the baseball player's **left** hand.

LEFT

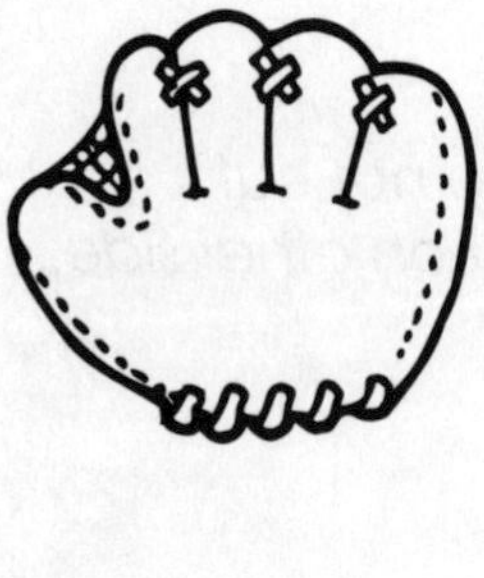

Do not cut.
Activity on other side.

Draw a line to match the **things that go together**.

MATCH

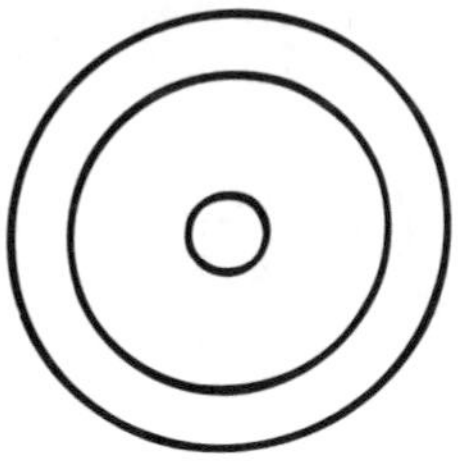

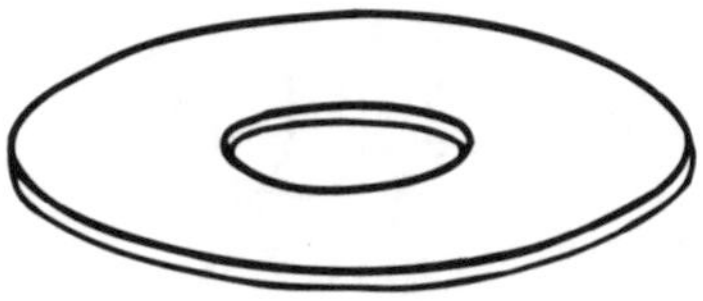

Things That Go Together

Draw a line to match the **things that go together**.

MATCH

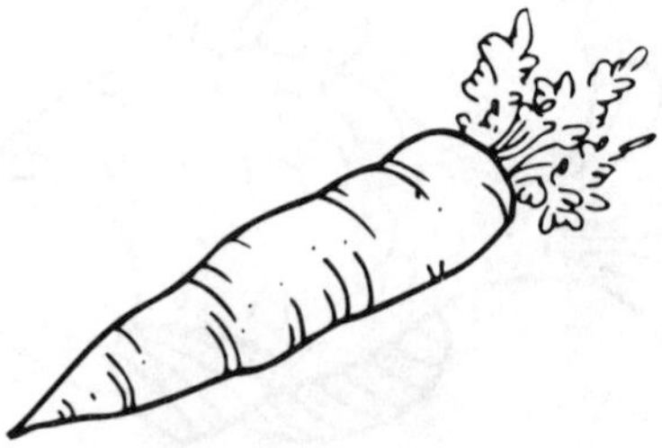

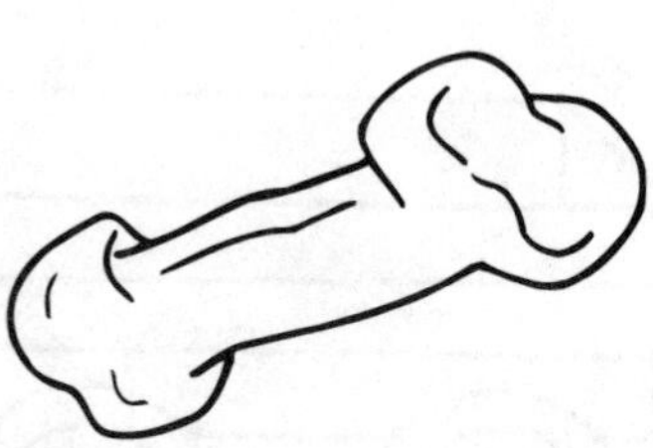

Look at the pictures below. **Draw** a picture to show something else that can go with each group.

GROUPS

Things for **Warm** Weather

Things for **Cold** Weather

Things for **Rainy** Weather

WHERE DOES IT GO?

Help put things in the right place in the house. **Cut out** the pictures at the **bottom** of the page. **Glue** the kitchen things in the kitchen. **Glue** the bedroom things in the bedroom.

WHAT BELONGS?

Color the pictures in each row that belong together.
Draw an **X** on the one that **does not** belong.

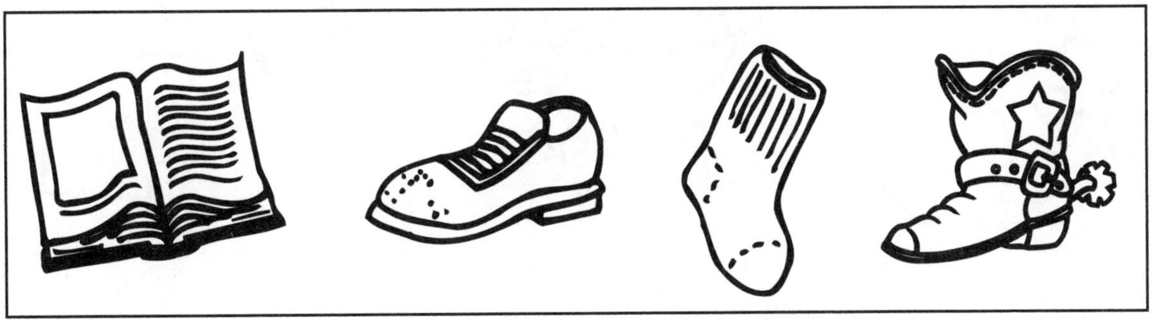

MATHEMATICS READINESS

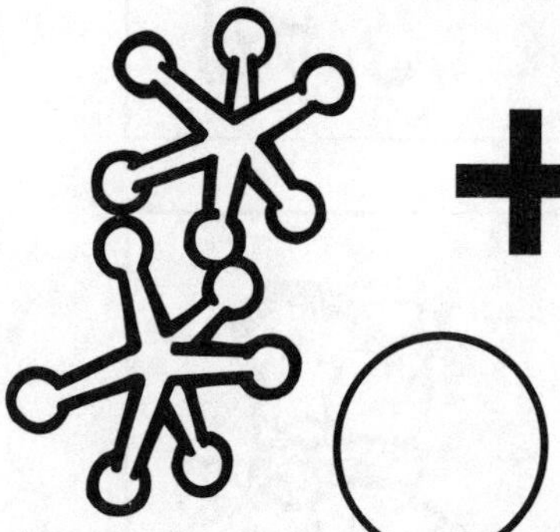 +  = 4

Draw a **line** from each animal to its home.

MATCH

Look at the pictures in each box. **Draw** a line from each animal to its home.

MATCH

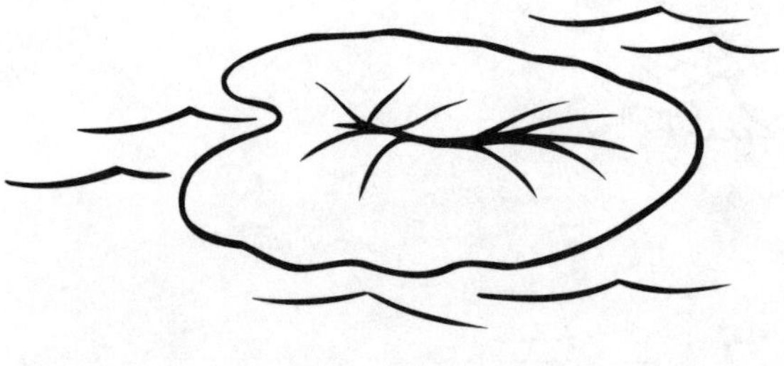

Look at the pictures in each box. **Draw** a **line** to match each thing at the **top** to the thing at the **bottom**. **Color** the pictures.

ONE-TO-ONE

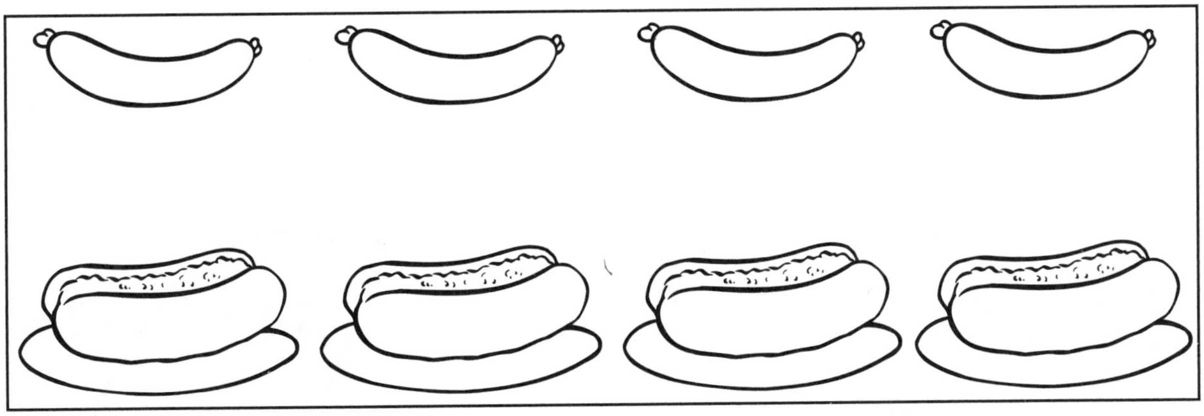

Look at the animals. **Draw** a ball for **each** animal. **Color** the pictures.

ONE-TO-ONE

SAME NUMBER

Each pond has the **same number** of ducks in it. **Color** the ducks.

Draw kites so that Sue will have the **same number** as Billy.

Match the pictures. **Circle** the group that has **more**.

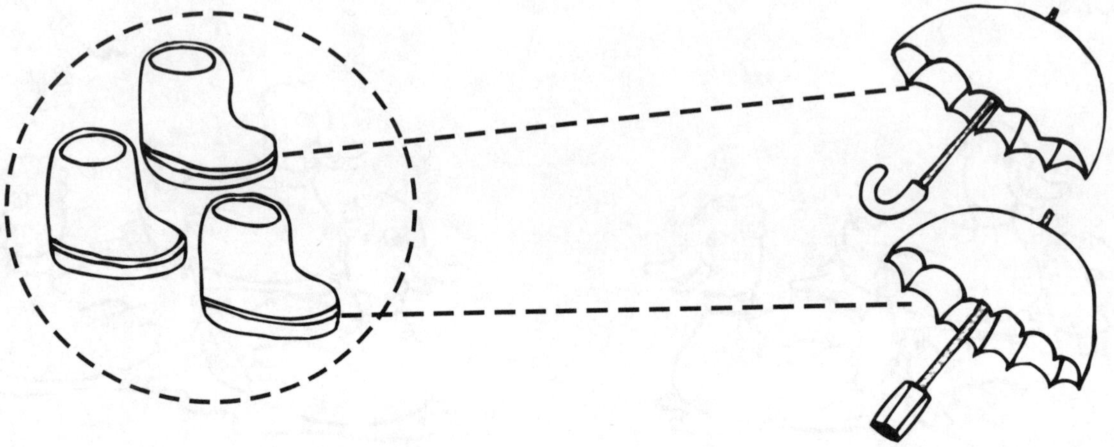

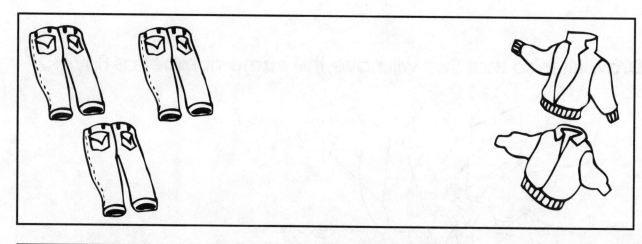

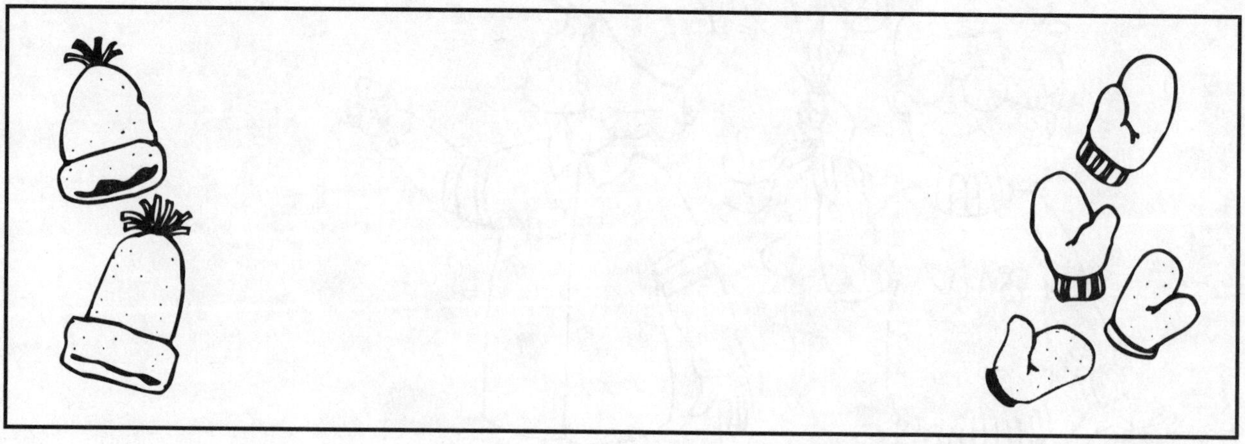

Look at the pictures in each box. **Circle** the group that has **more**. **Color** the pictures.

Match the pictures. **Circle** the group that has **fewer**.

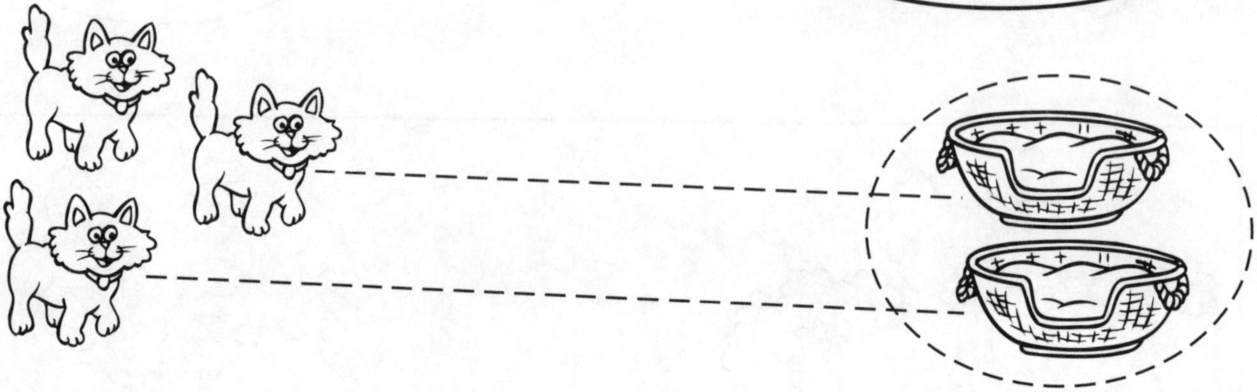

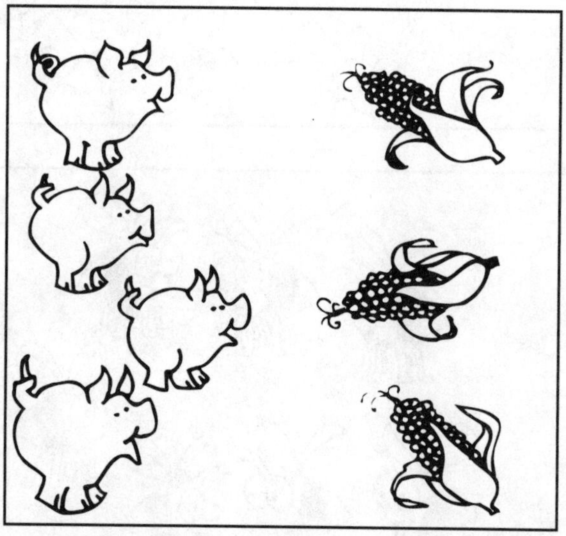

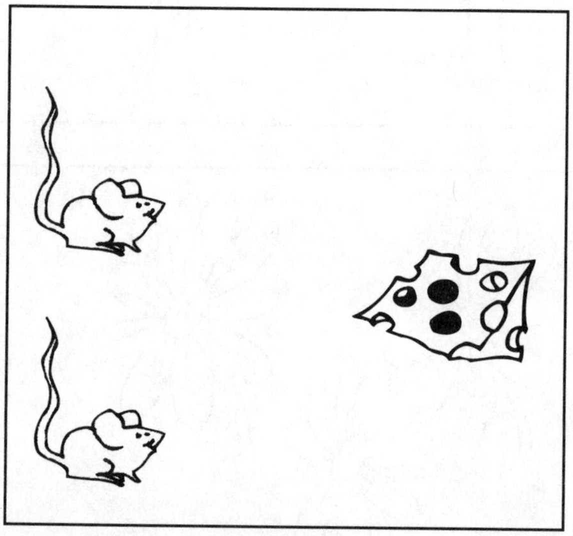

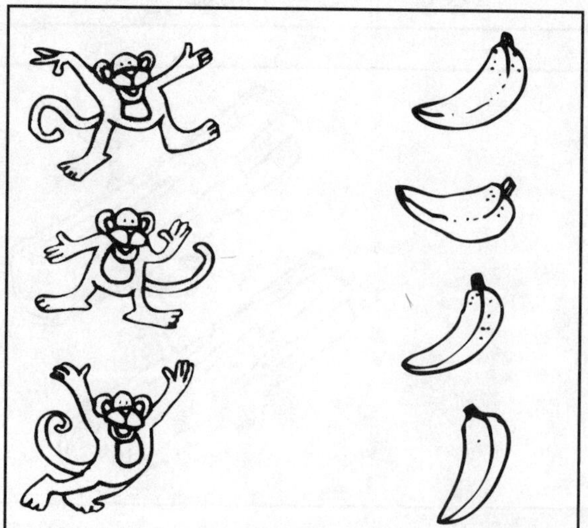

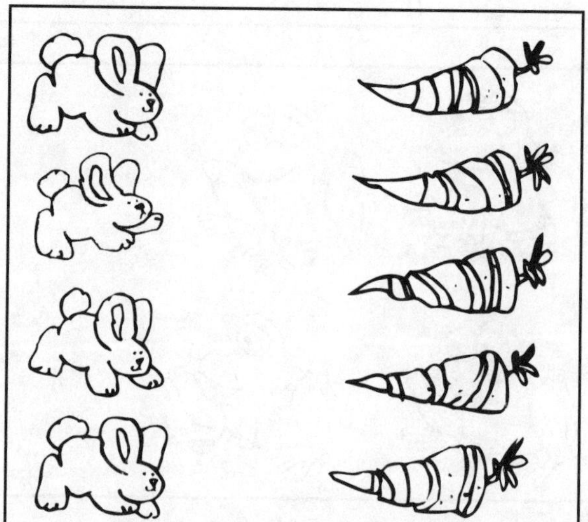

Look at the pictures in each box. **Circle** the group that has **fewer**. **Color** the pictures.

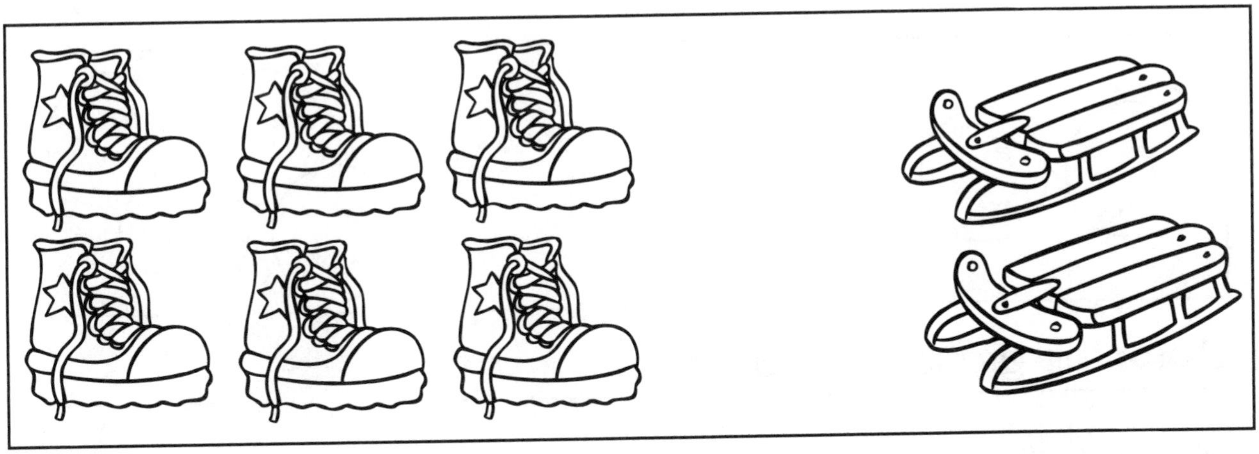

MORE and FEWER

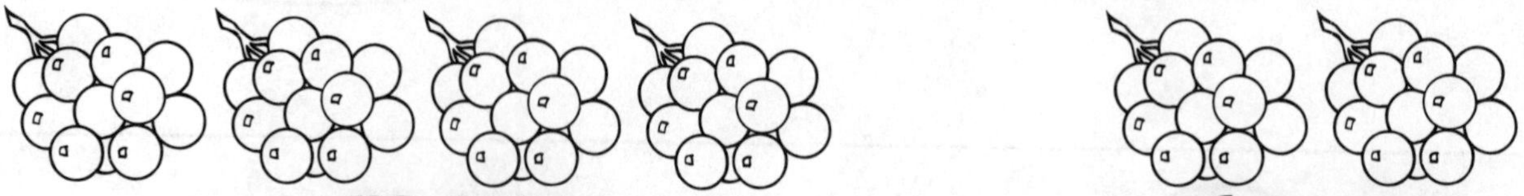

more fewer

1. **Color** the group that has **more**.

2. **Color** the group that has **fewer**.

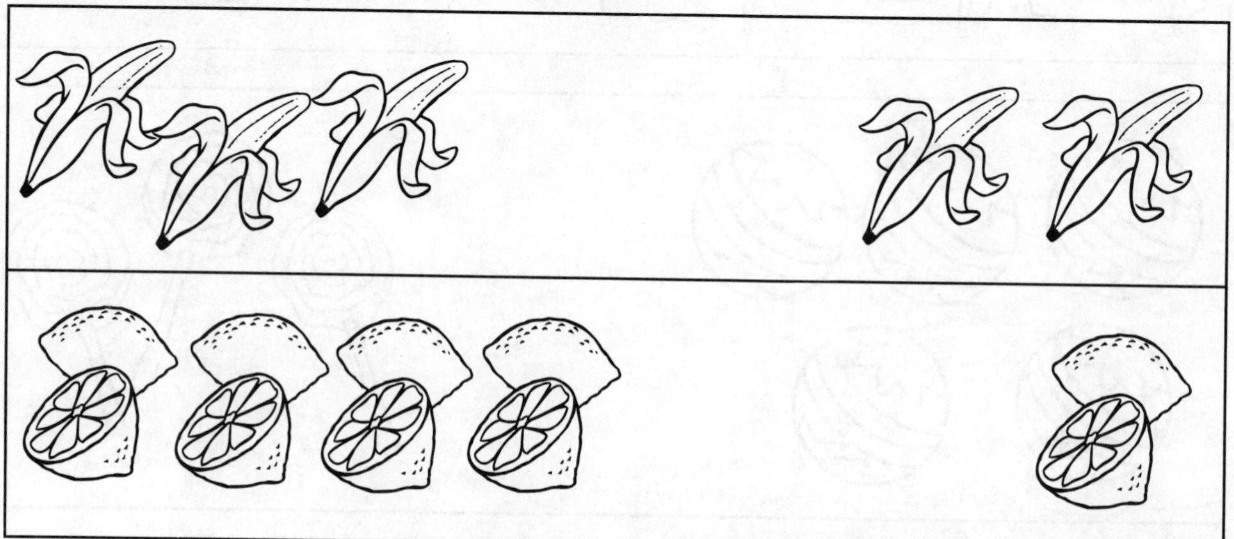

What happened **before**? **Circle** the **small** picture that shows what happened **before** the pictures in the boxes.

Look at the pictures. Which happened **first** in each row?
Circle the picture that shows what happened **first**.

Circle the thing that happened **first** in each row.

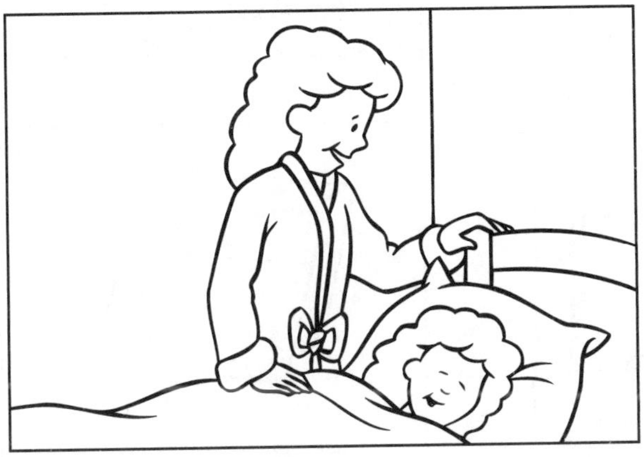

What comes **next**? **Look** at the big pictures. **Circle** the small picture that shows what would happen **next**.

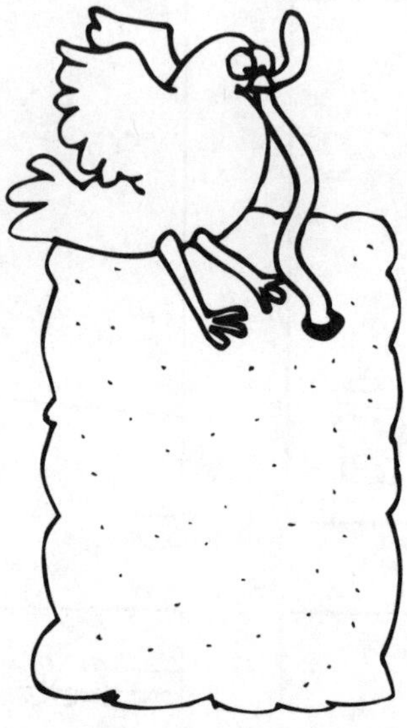

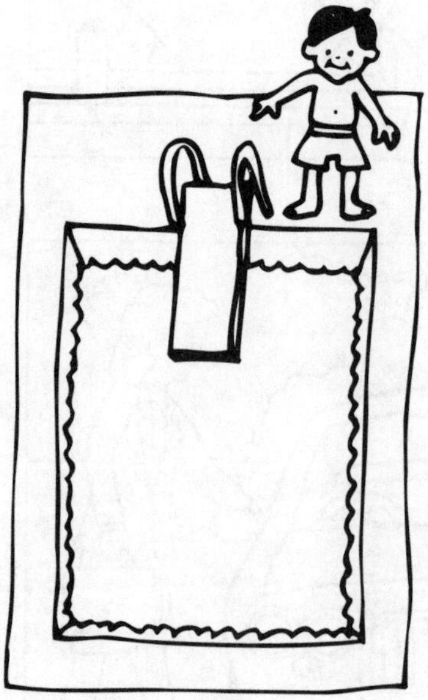

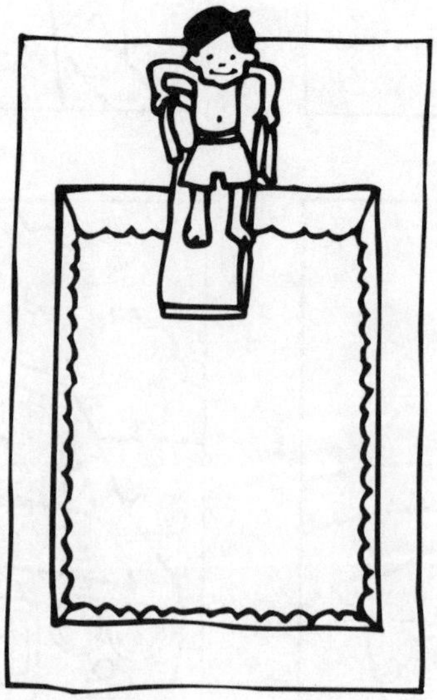

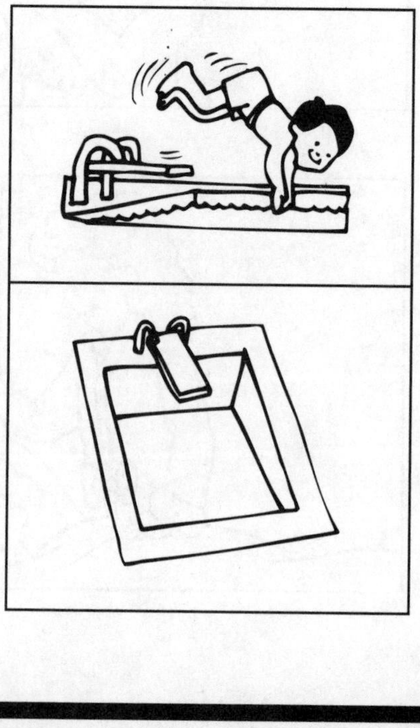

Draw a line from the picture on the left to the picture which happens **next**.

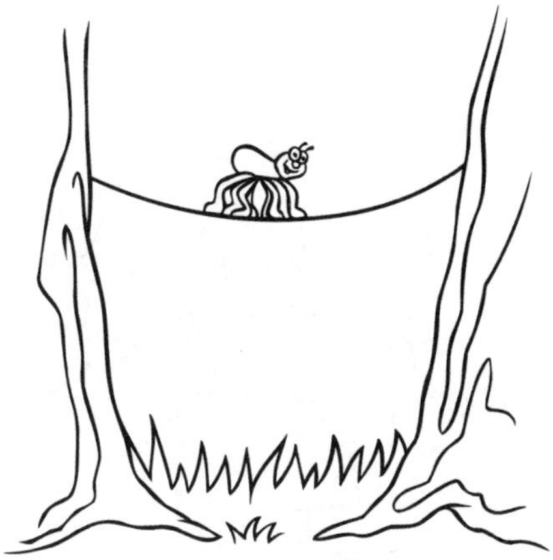

Look at the pictures. What happened **first**? What happened **second**? What happened **third**? **Draw** a line from the correct word to the picture.

first

second

third

Cut out the pictures and **glue** them to show what happened **first**, **second** and **third**.

FIRST SECOND THIRD

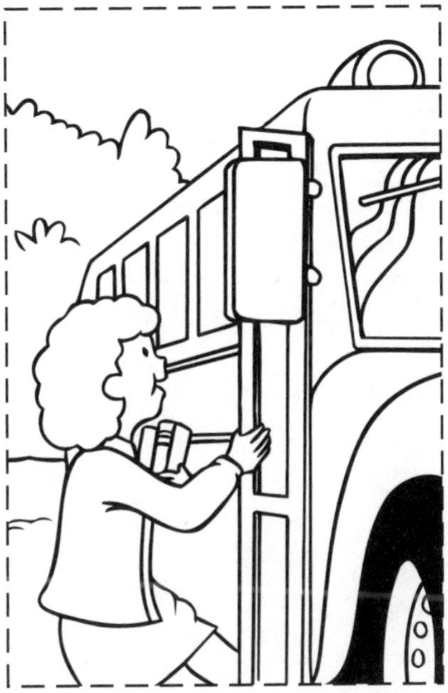

Page is blank for cutting exercise on previous page.

How does a plant grow? **Cut out** the pictures. **Glue** the pictures in the boxes to show what happens **first**, **second** and **third**.

FIRST SECOND THIRD

Page is blank for cutting
exercise on previous page.

Write **1**, **2** and **3** in the boxes to show what happens **first**, **second** and **third**.

FIRST SECOND THIRD

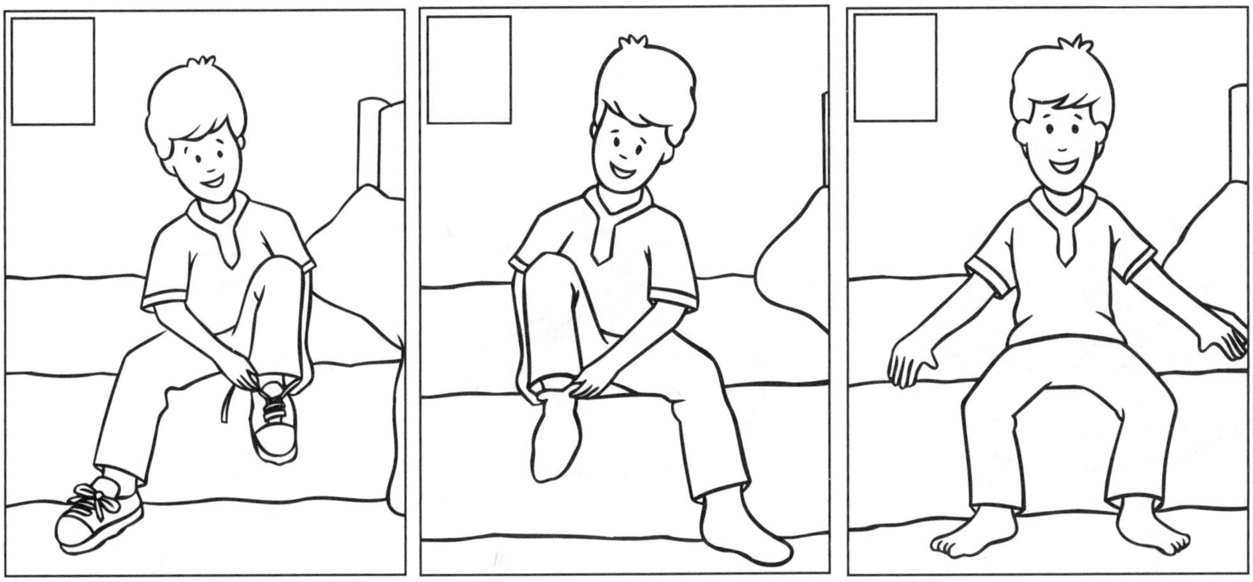

REVIEW

Circle the picture that shows what comes **next**.

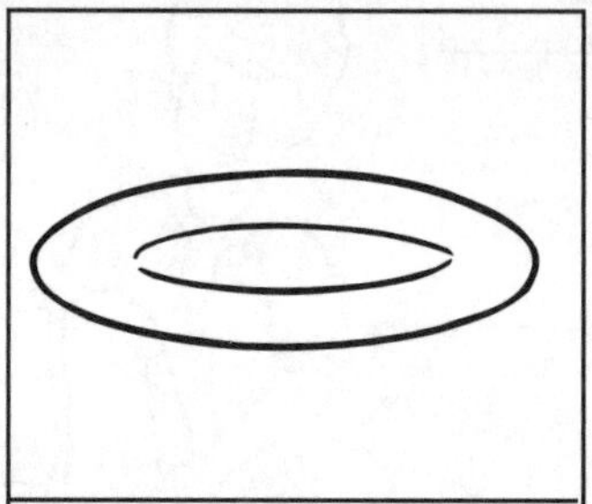

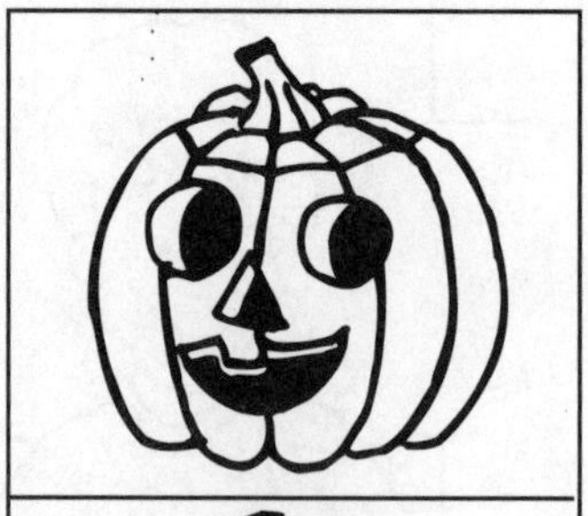

Some things take a **little time**. Some things take **a lot of time**. **Color** each picture that takes **more** time.

Color the picture that would take **more** time to do.

Circle the picture in each row that takes **more** time.

Circle the picture in each row that takes **more** time.

When you eat an ice-cream cone, it is gone in **a short time**. **Color** the picture of the job which takes **less time to do**.

Color the picture of the job which takes **less time to do**.

NUMBERS 0-10

NUMBER 0

This is 0.

Color the number. **Color** the word.

0

ZERO

NUMBER 1

This is 1.

Color the number. **Color** the word.
Color the rest of the picture.

NUMBER 1

Count and **color**.

Color 1 red, **1** blue and **1** green. **Circle** each group of **1**.

NUMBER 1

1 ball is colored.

Color 1 ball.

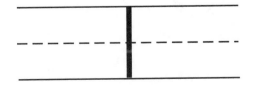

Trace the number. **Write** the number on the line **one** time.

1

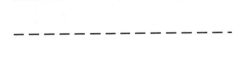

NUMBER 2

This is 2.

Color the number. **Color** the word.
Count and **color** the rest of the picture.

TWO

NUMBER 2

Count and **color**. **Color** the flowers: **2 red**, **2 purple** and **2 yellow**.

Circle each  with a **2**.

NUMBER 2

2 fish are colored.

Color 2 fish.

Trace the number. **Write** the number on the lines **two** times.

2

NUMBERS 1 AND 2

Circle groups of **1**. **Color** each group of **2**.

1

2

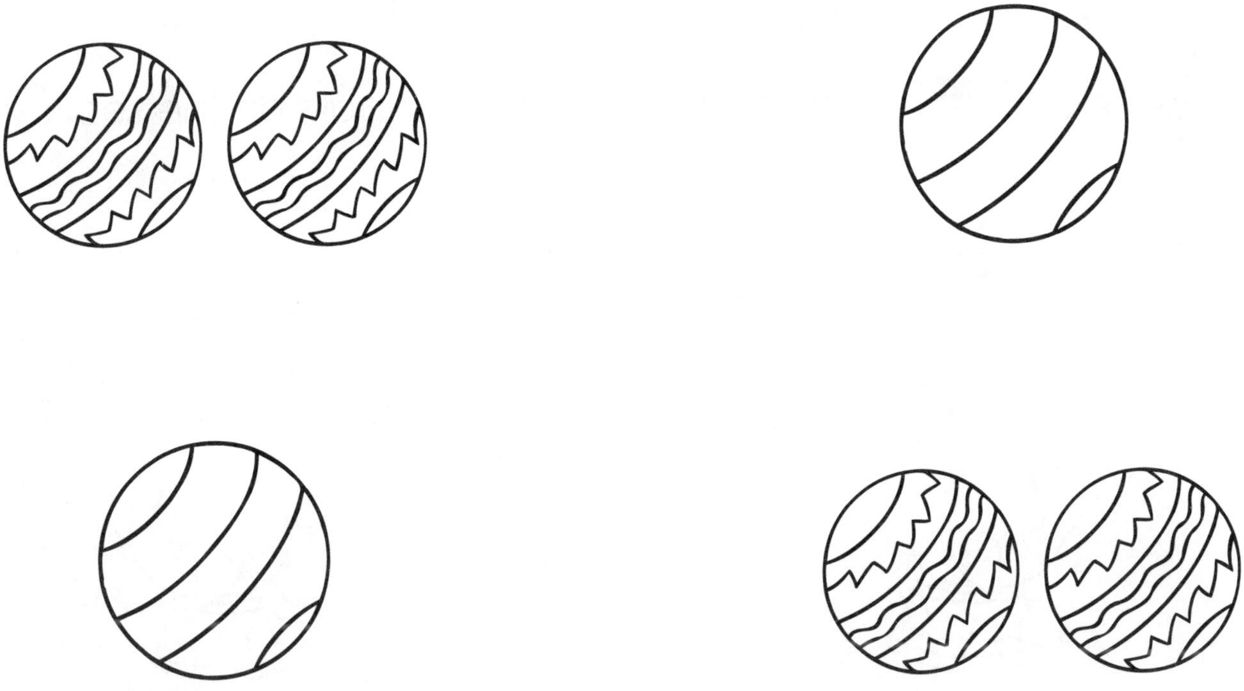

NUMBERS 1 AND 2

Write the numbers **1** and **2**.

1 1

2 2

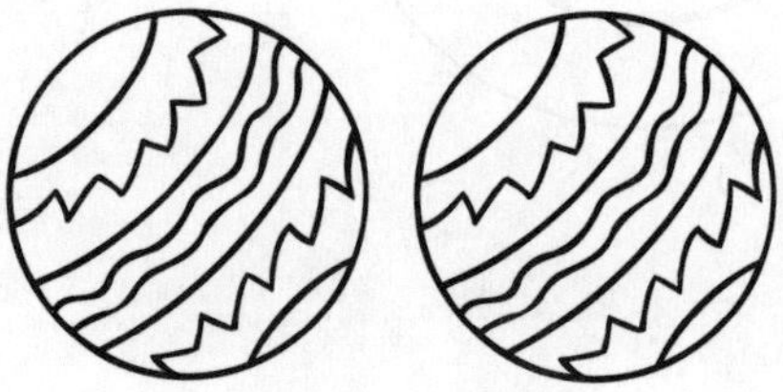

Draw 1 ball on the seal's nose.

Draw 2 balls on the seal's nose.

NUMBER 3

This is 3.

Color the number. **Color** the word.
Count and **color** the rest of the picture.

NUMBER 3

Count and **color** the pictures. **Circle** each group of **3**.

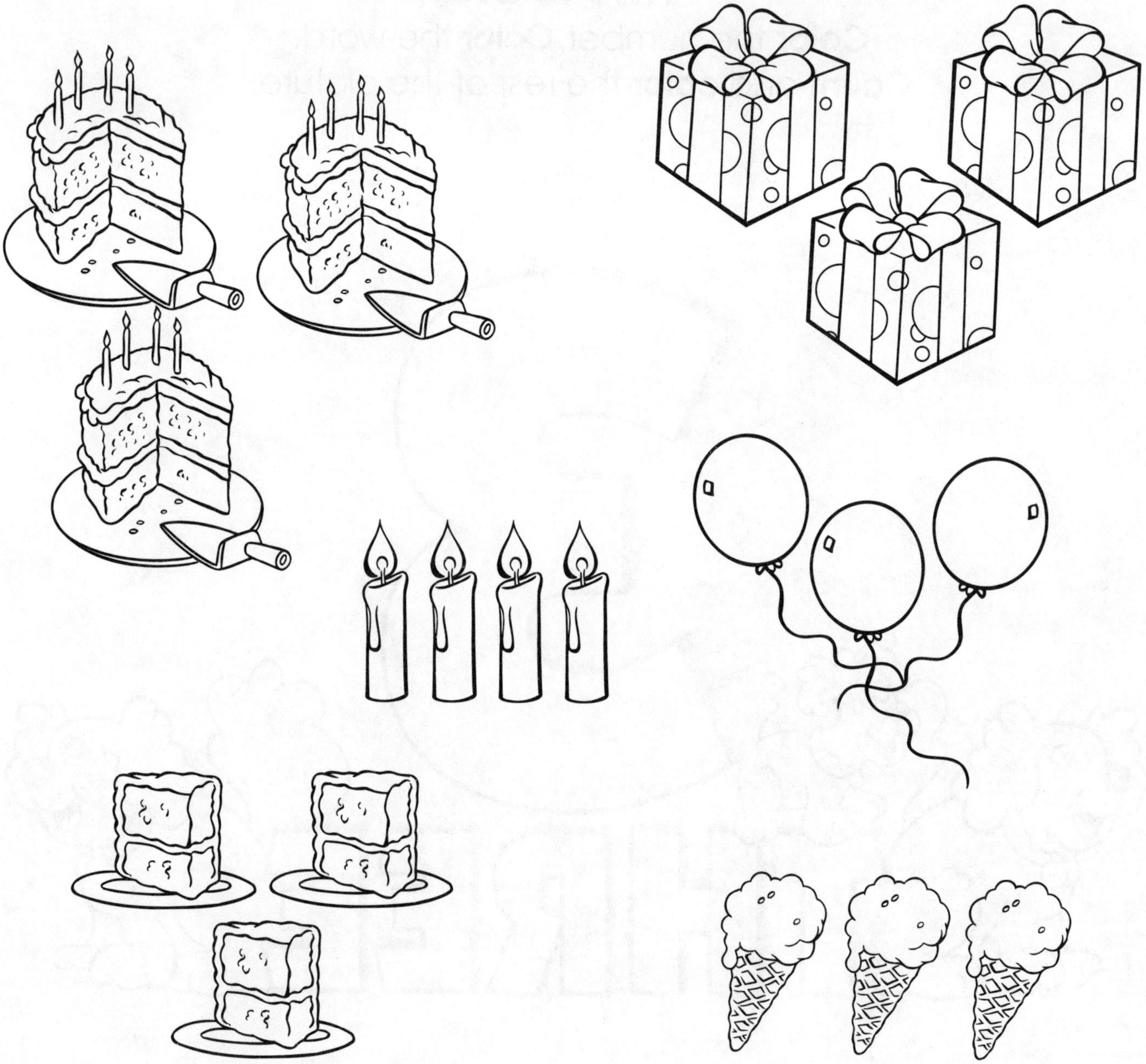

NUMBER 3

3 birds are colored.

Color 3 birds.

Trace the number. **Write** the number on the lines **three** times.

3

NUMBER 4

This is 4.

Color the number. **Color** the word.
Count and **color** the rest of the picture.

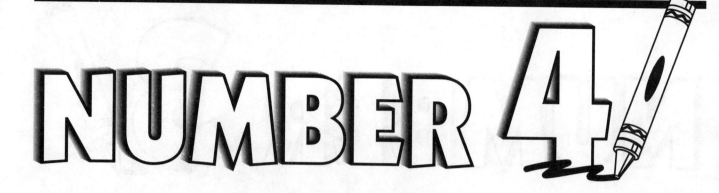

NUMBER 4

Circle each group of **4**. **Color** the picture.

NUMBER 4

4 cats are **colored**.

Color 4 cats.

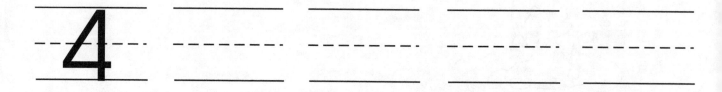

Trace the number. **Write** the number on the lines **four** times.

4

NUMBERS 3 AND 4

Circle groups of **3**. **Color** each group of **4**.

3

4

NUMBERS 3 AND 4

Write the numbers **3** and **4**.

3 3

4 4

Draw 3 scoops of ice cream on the cone.

Draw 4 scoops of ice cream on the cone.

NUMBER 5

This is 5.

Color the number. **Color** the word.
Count and **color** the rest of the picture.

5

FIVE

NUMBER 5

Count and **color** each picture. **Circle** each group of **5**.

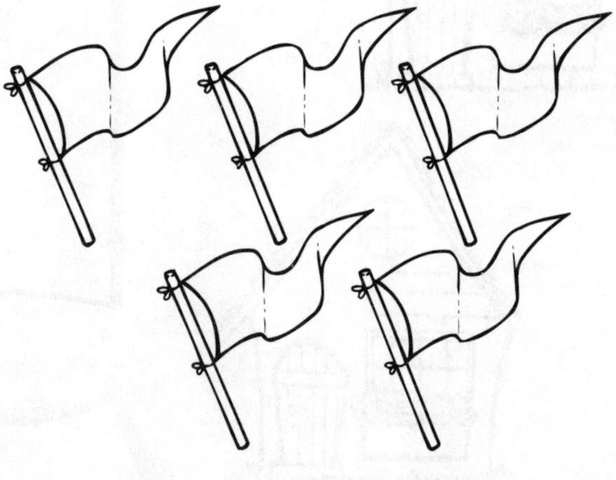

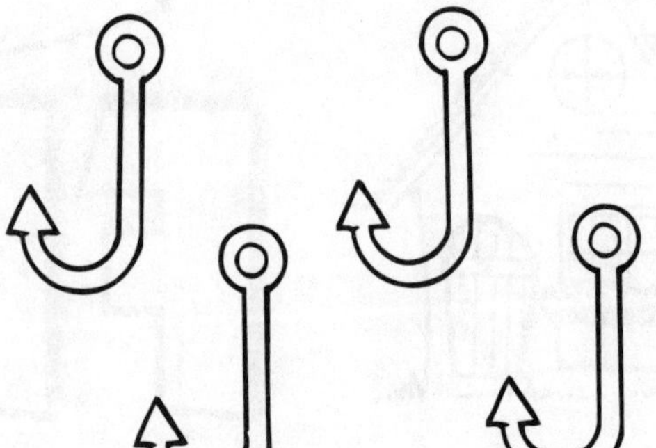

NUMBER 5

5 dogs are **colored**.

Color 5 dogs.

Trace the number. **Write** the number on the lines **five** times.

5

Review

NUMBERS 0-5

How Many?

Circle the number of things below. **Color** the pictures.

1 2 3

2 3 4

3 4 5

1 2 3

Review NUMBERS 0-5

How Many?

Circle the number of things below. **Color** the pictures.

2 3 4

3 4 5

1 2 3

3 4 5

Review NUMBERS 0-5

Count each group of fruit. **Write** the number in the box.
Color the fruit, too.

How many?

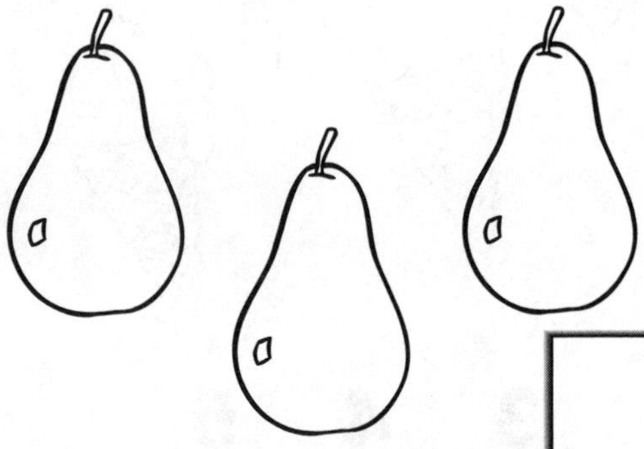

How many?

How many?

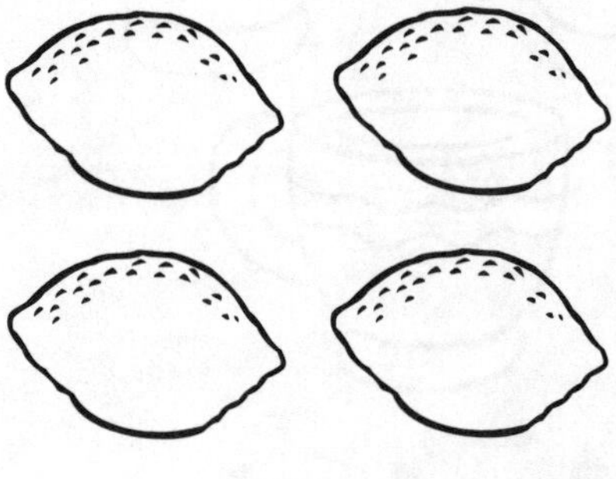

How many?

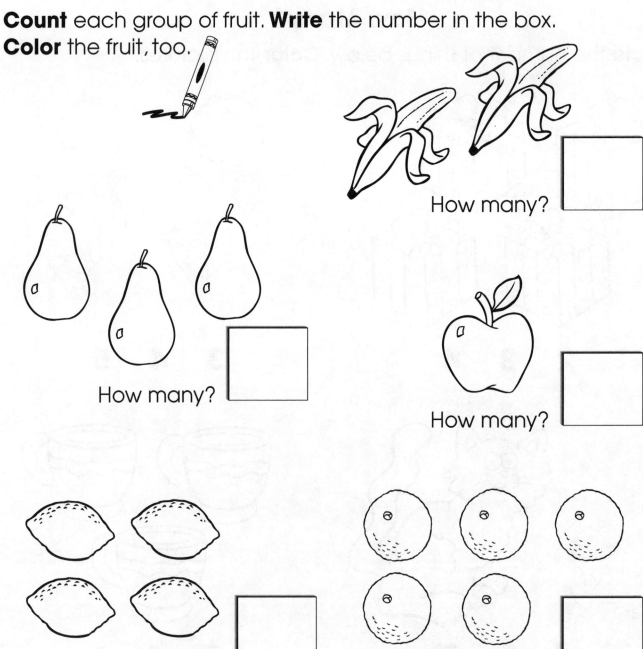

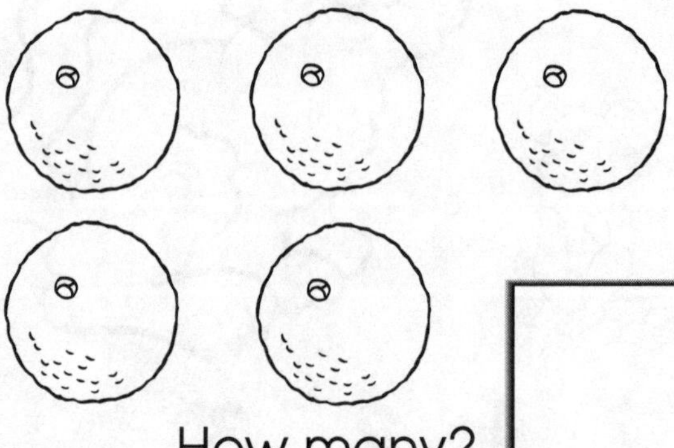

How many?

Review

NUMBERS 0-5

Count and **color** each group of animals. **Cut out** and **glue** the numbers.

1	2	3	4	5

Page is blank for cutting exercise on previous page.

NUMBER 6

This is 6.

Color the number. **Color** the word.
Count and **color** the rest of the picture.

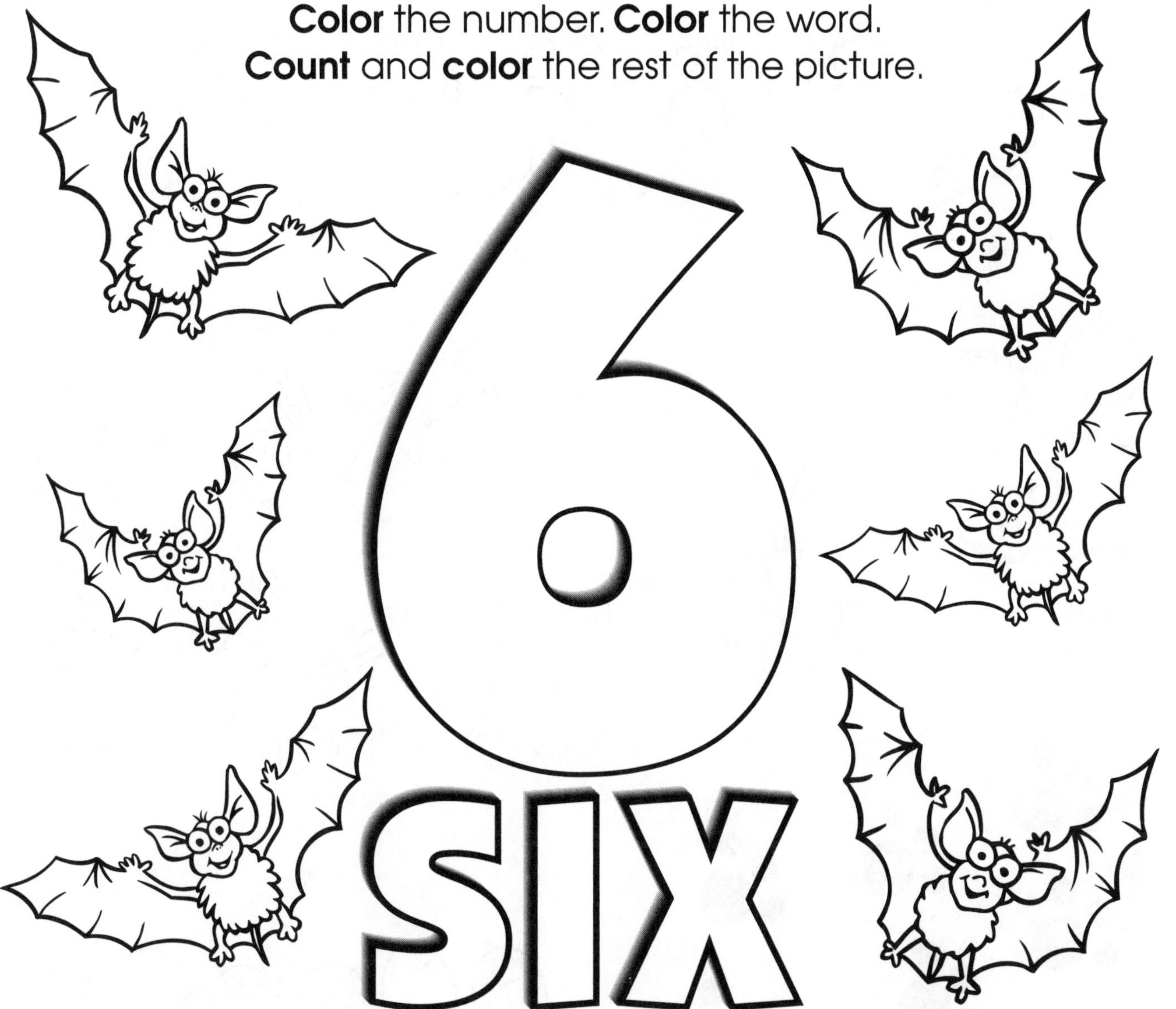

NUMBER 6

Count and **color** each picture. **Circle** each group of **6**.

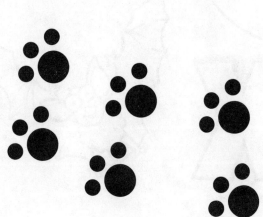

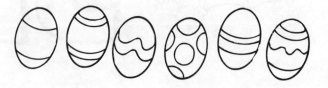

NUMBER 6

Circle each group of **6**.

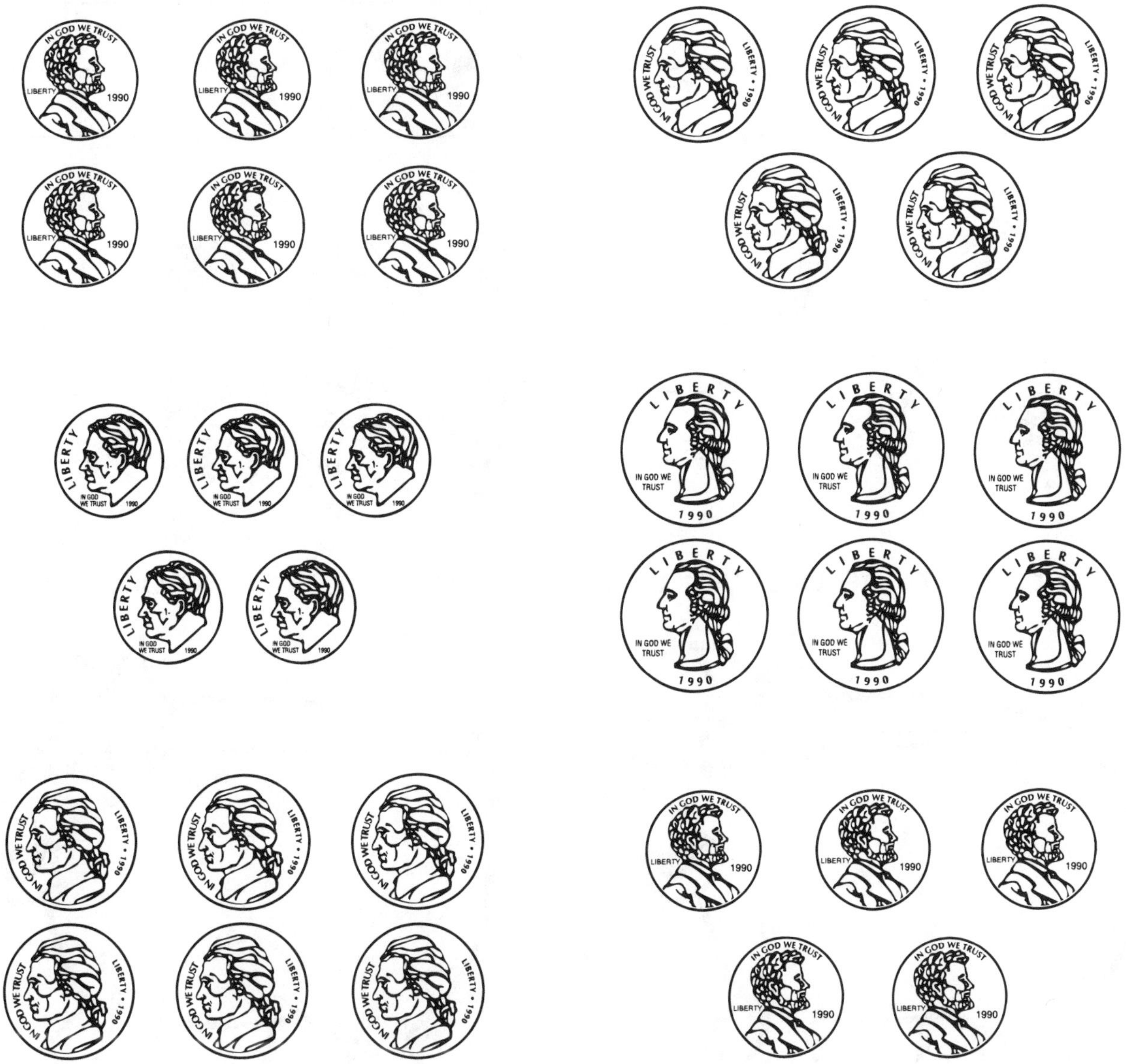

NUMBERS 5 AND 6

Write the numbers **5** and **6**.

5 5

6 6

Draw 5 coins in the piggy bank.

Draw 6 coins in the piggy bank.

NUMBER 7

This is 7.

Color the number. **Color** the word.
Count and **color** the rest of the picture.

NUMBER 7

Count and **color** each picture. **Circle** each group of **7**.

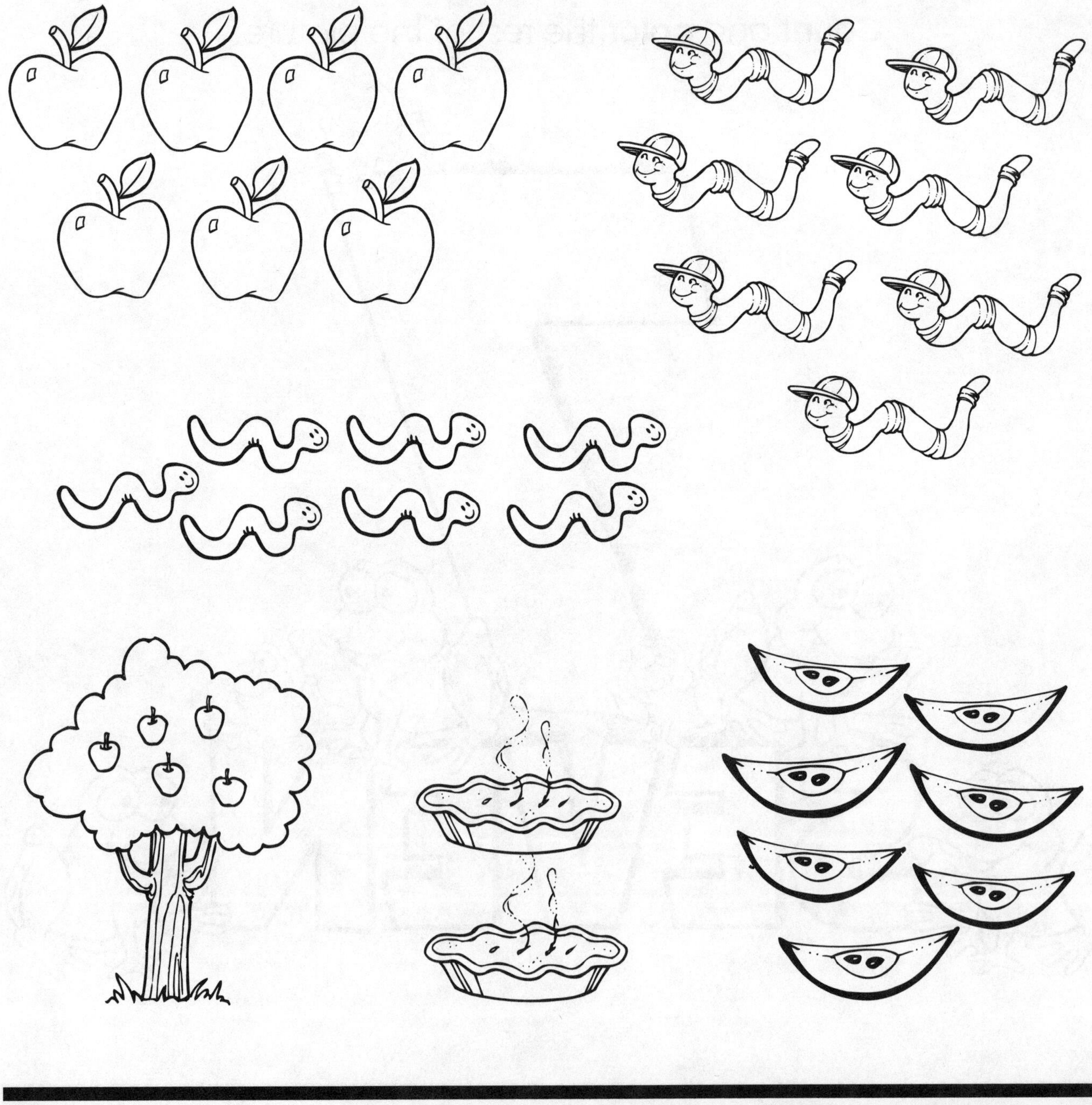

NUMBER 7

Write the number **7**.

7 7

Count and **color**.

Draw 7 peas on the plate.

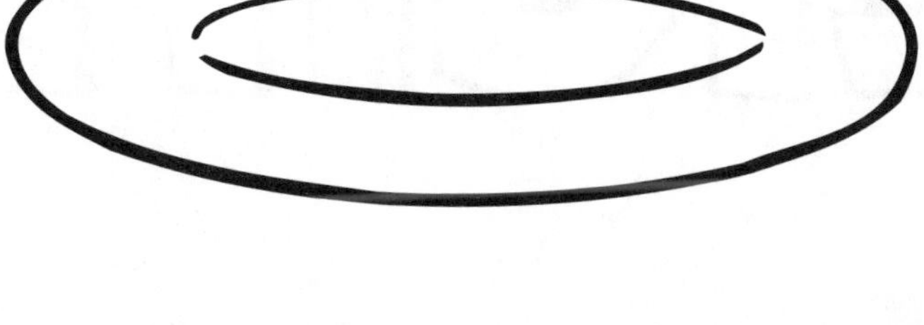

NUMBER 8

This is 8.

Color the number. **Color** the word.
Count and **color** the rest of the picture.

NUMBER 8

Color the spaces: **8 = yellow**  **= red** **eight = green**

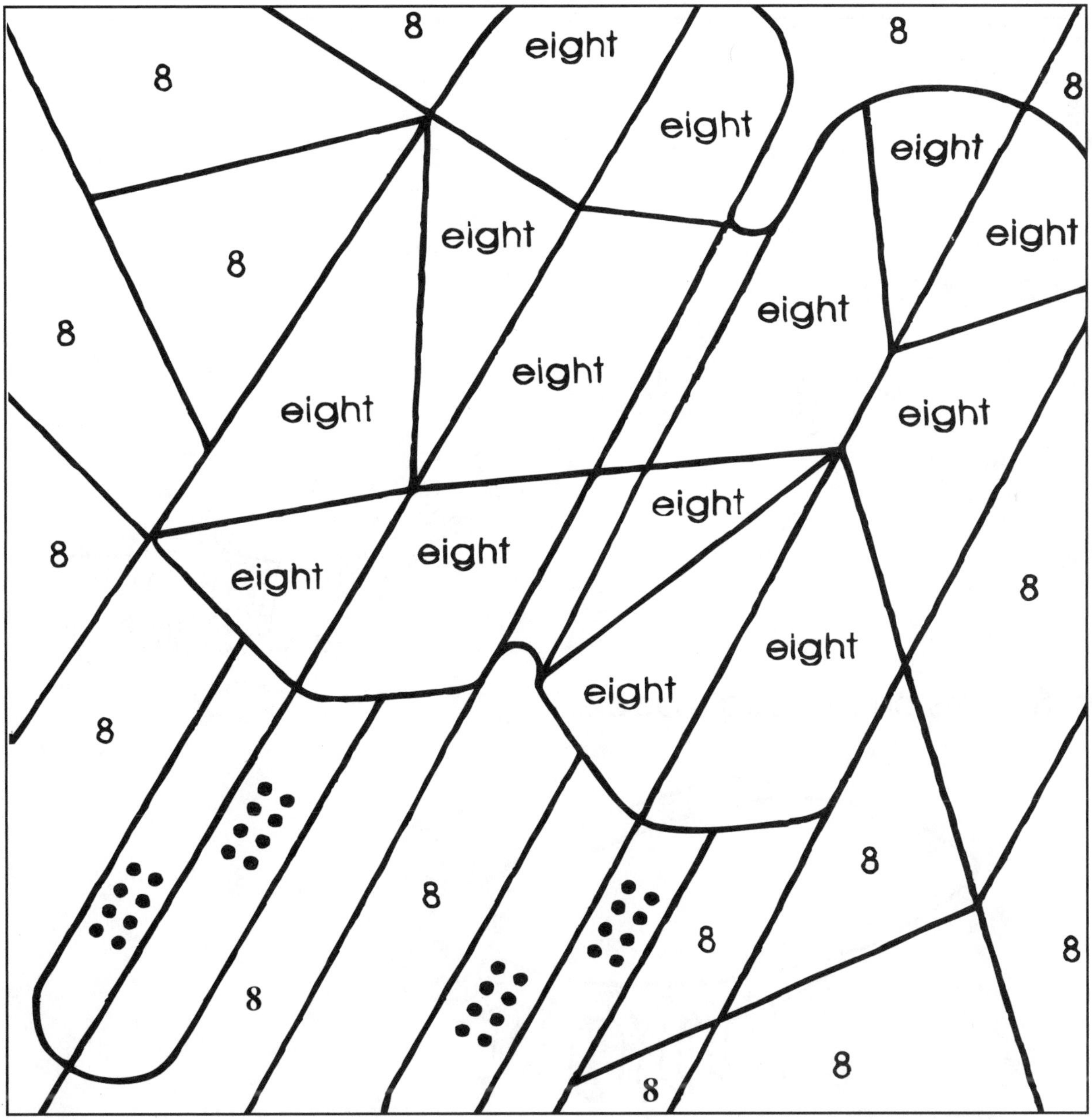

NUMBER 8

Write the number **8**.

8 8

Count and **color**.

Draw 8 spots on the bug's back.

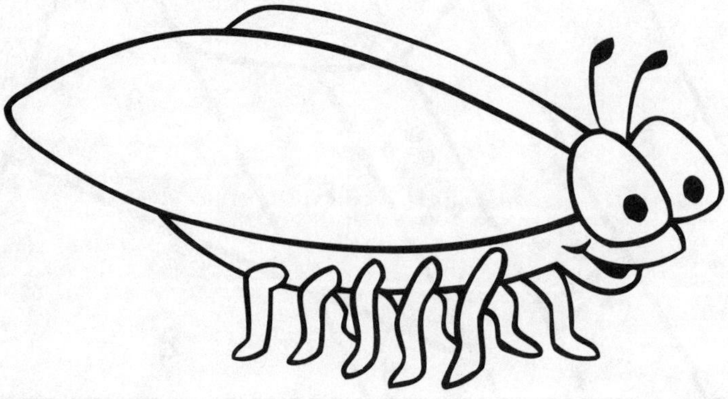

NUMBERS 7 AND 8

Circle groups of **7**. **Color** each group of **8**.

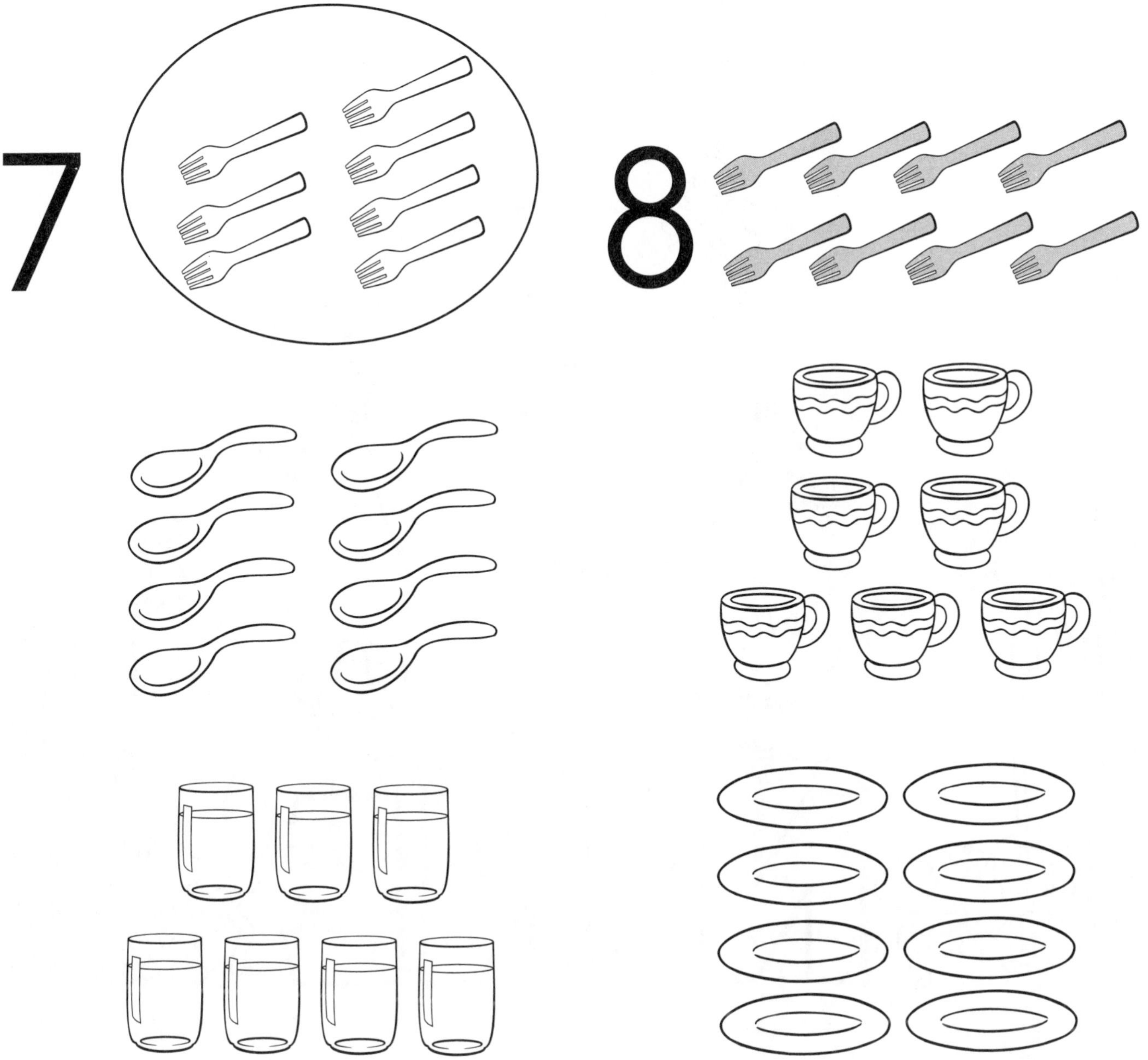

NUMBER 9

This is 9.

Color the number. **Color** the word.
Count and **color** the rest of the picture.

NUMBER 9

Count and **color** each picture. **Circle** each group of **9**.

NUMBER 9

Write the number **9**.

9 9

Count and **color**.

Draw 9 ice-cream scoops on the cones.

NUMBER 10

This is 10.

Color the number. **Color** the word.

Count and **color** the rest of the picture.

NUMBER 10

Where are the **10**'s? **Circle** the **10**'s with **red**. **Color** the picture.
How many 's ?

NUMBER 10

Write the number **10**.

10 10

Count and **color**.

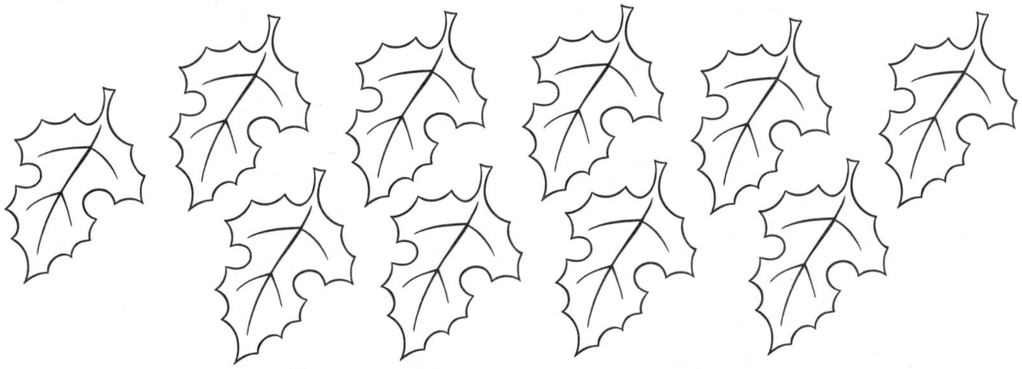

Draw 10 triangles on the snake's back.

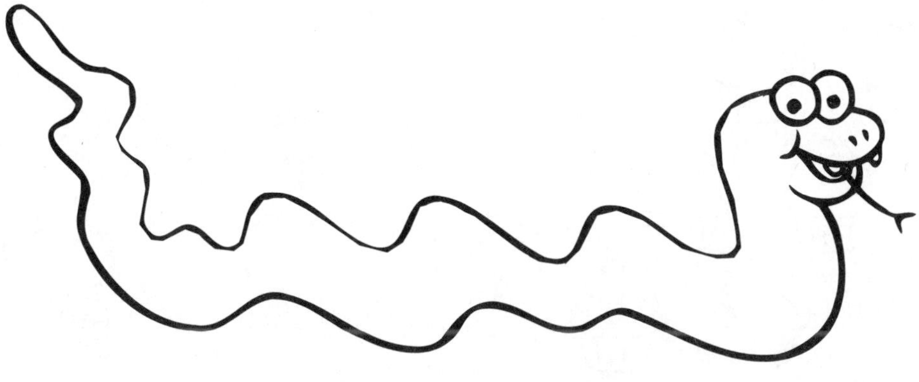

NUMBERS 9 AND 10

Circle groups of **9**. **Color** each group of **10**.

9

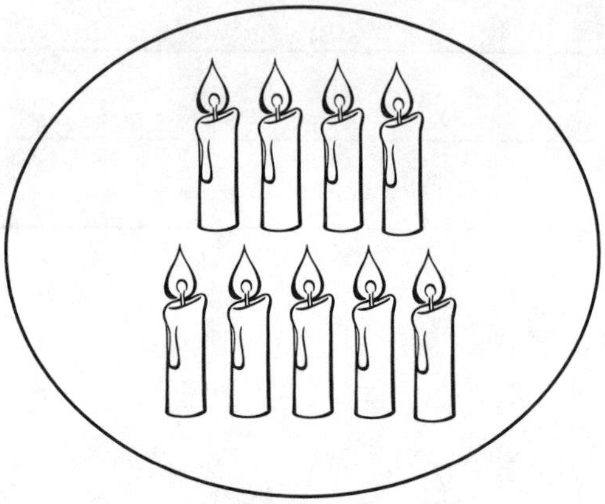

10

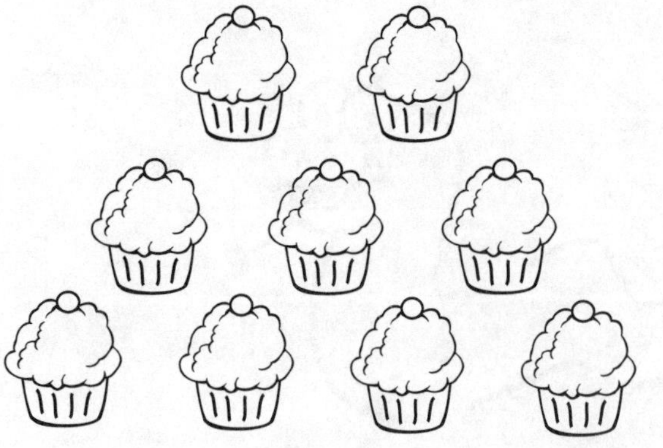

Review NUMBERS 0-10

Count the pictures in each group. **Circle** the number. **Color** the pictures.

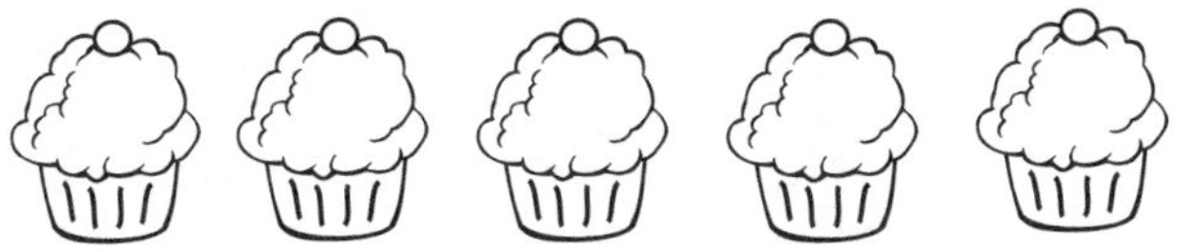

8 3 5

2 6 1

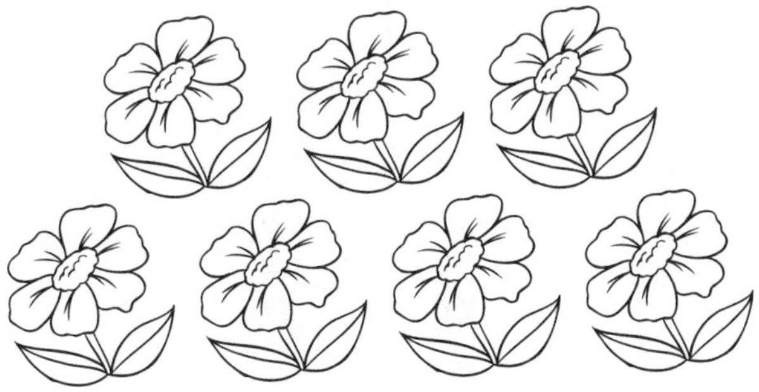

3 7 9

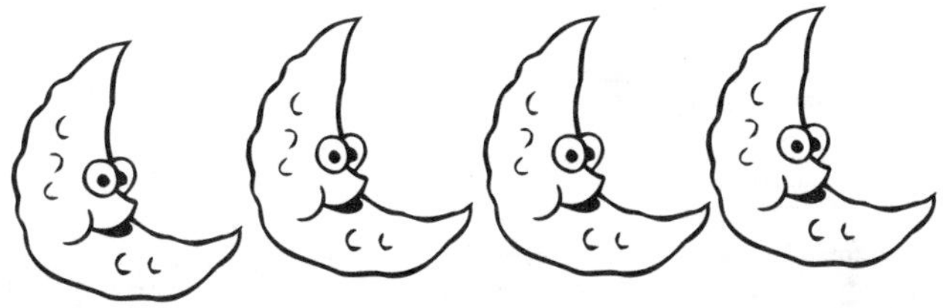

6 8 4

3 8 2

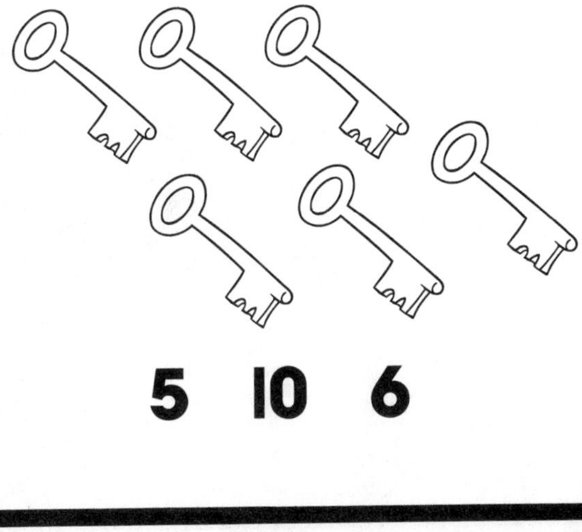

5 10 6

Review NUMBERS 0-10

Count the pictures in each group. **Circle** the number. **Color** the pictures.

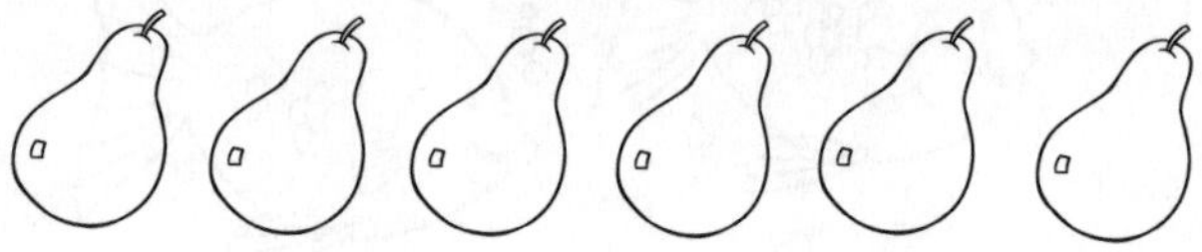

5 4 6

3 7 10

2 9 8

6 4 1

4 5 7

3 8 9

Review NUMBERS 0-10

Too Many Objects

Draw an **X** on the extra things in each row.

2 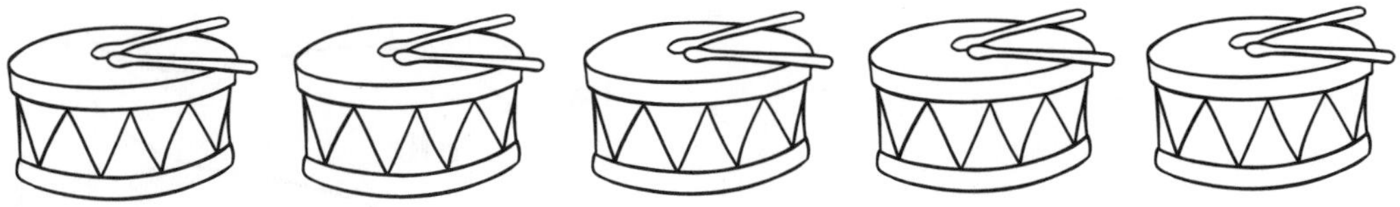

5 

10 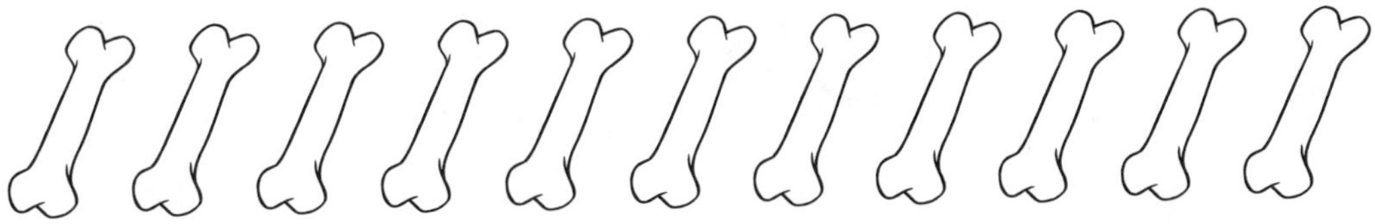

6 

1 

7 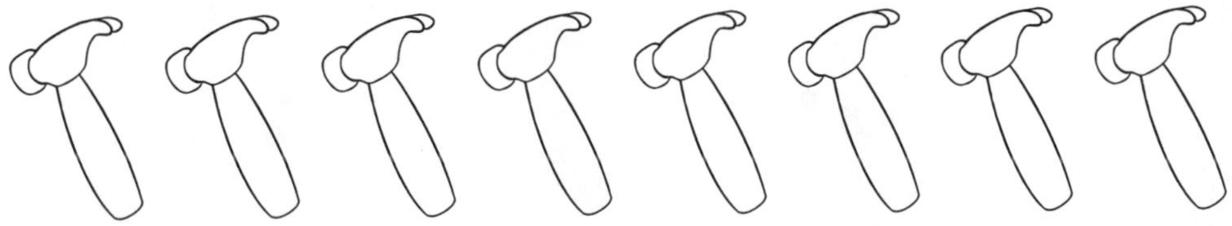

Review NUMBERS 0-10

Connect the dots from **1** to **10**. **Color** the picture.

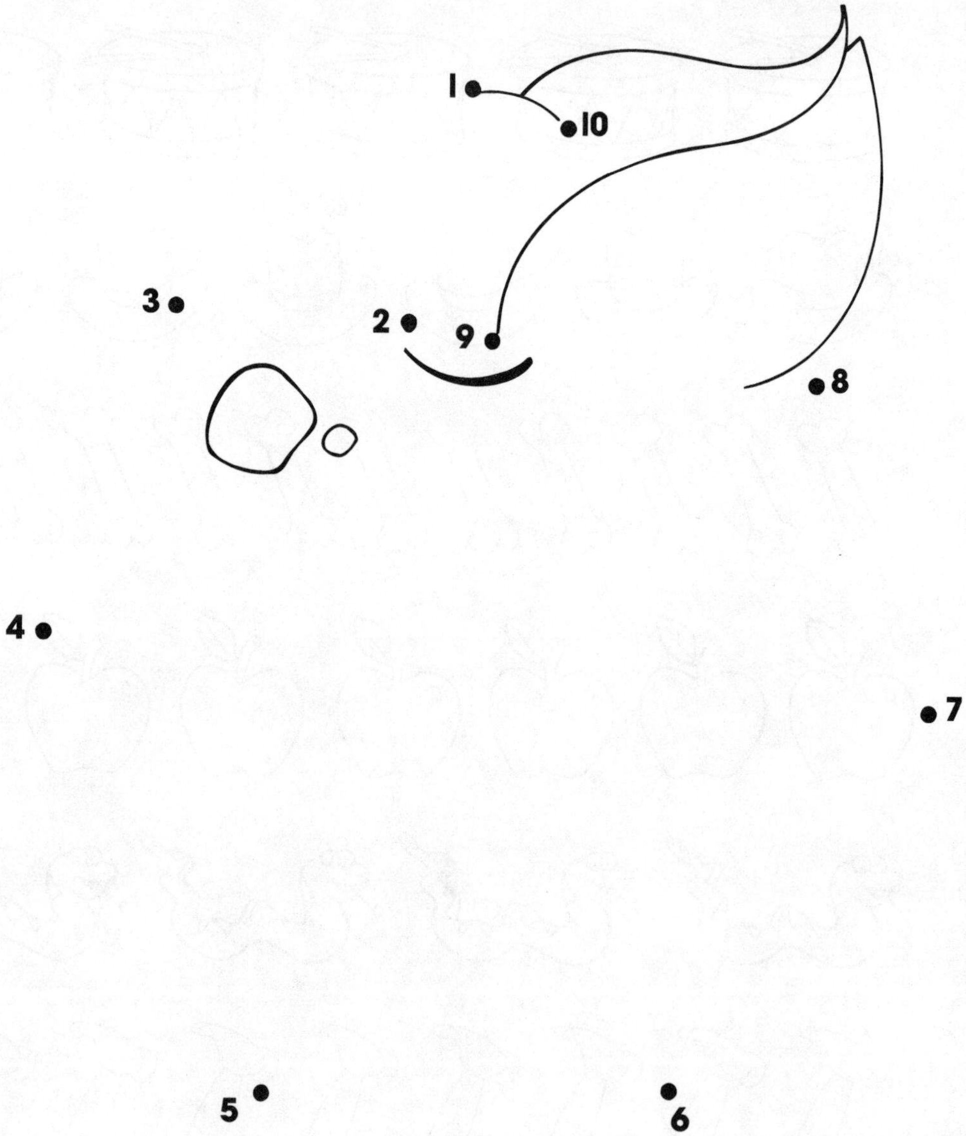

Review
NUMBERS 0-10

Connect the dots from **1** to **10**. **Color** the picture.

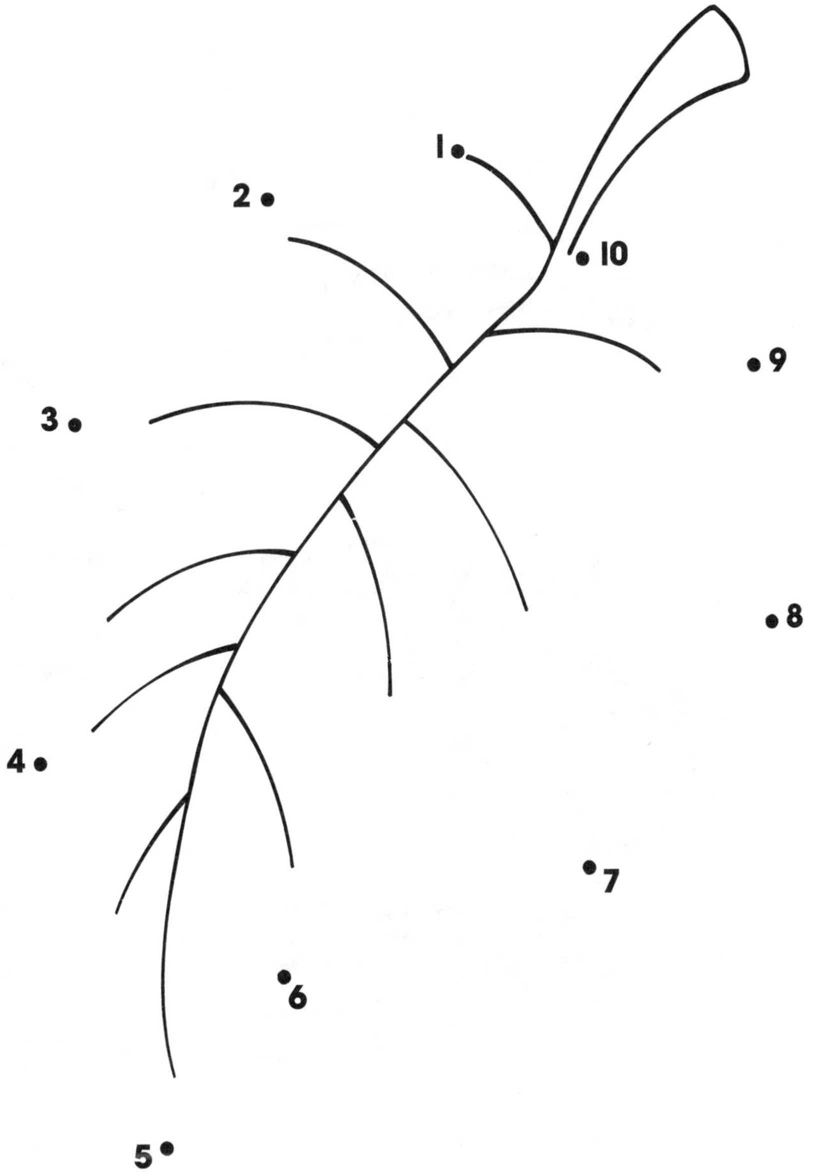

Review NUMBERS 0–10

Connect the dots from **1** to **10**. **Color** the picture.

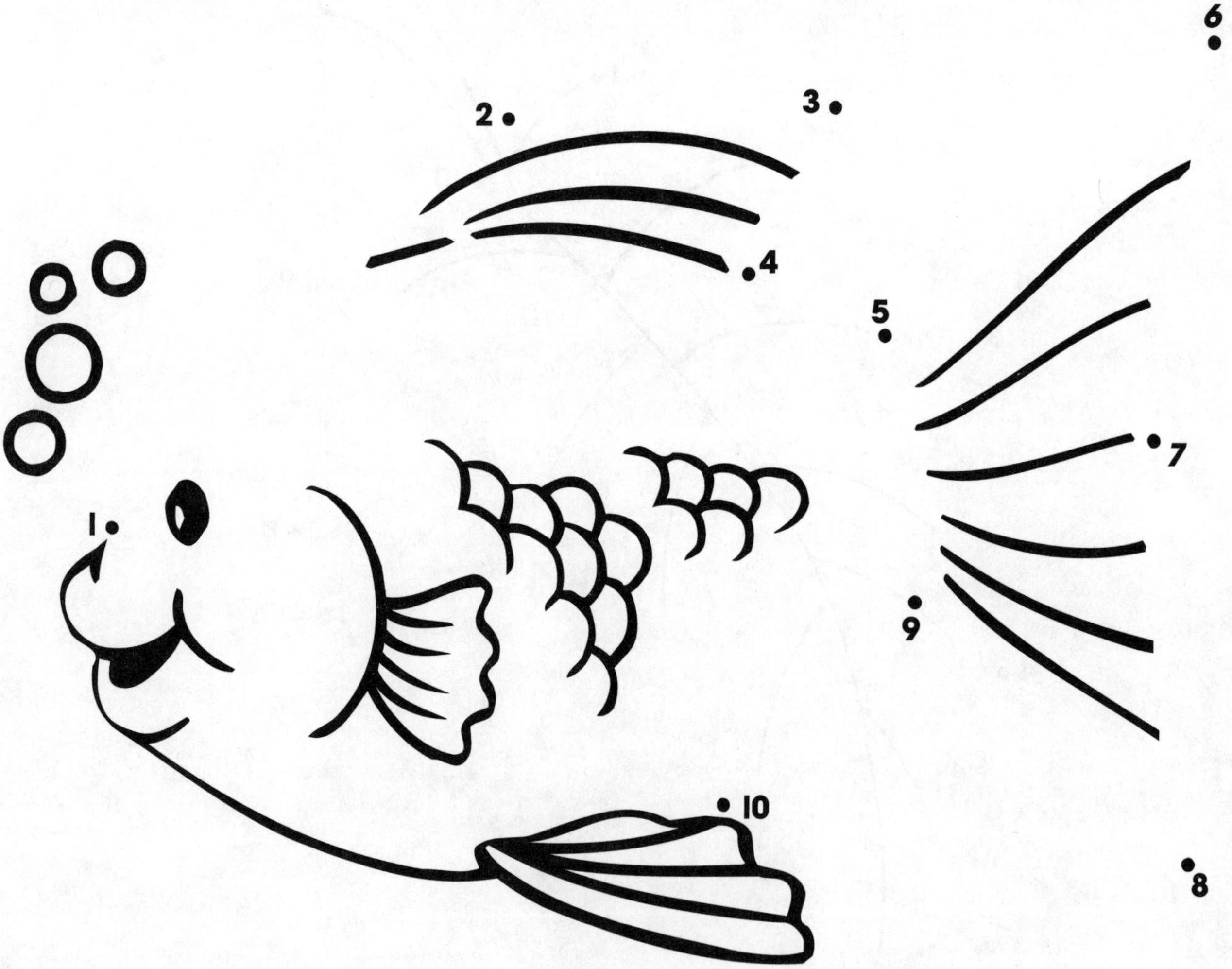

Review NUMBERS 0-10

Connect the dots from **1** to **10**. **Draw** and **color** a picture on Teddy's shirt.

READING READINESS

Color the pictures in each row that are the **same**.

Color the pictures in each row that are the **same**.

Color the pictures in each row that are the **same**.

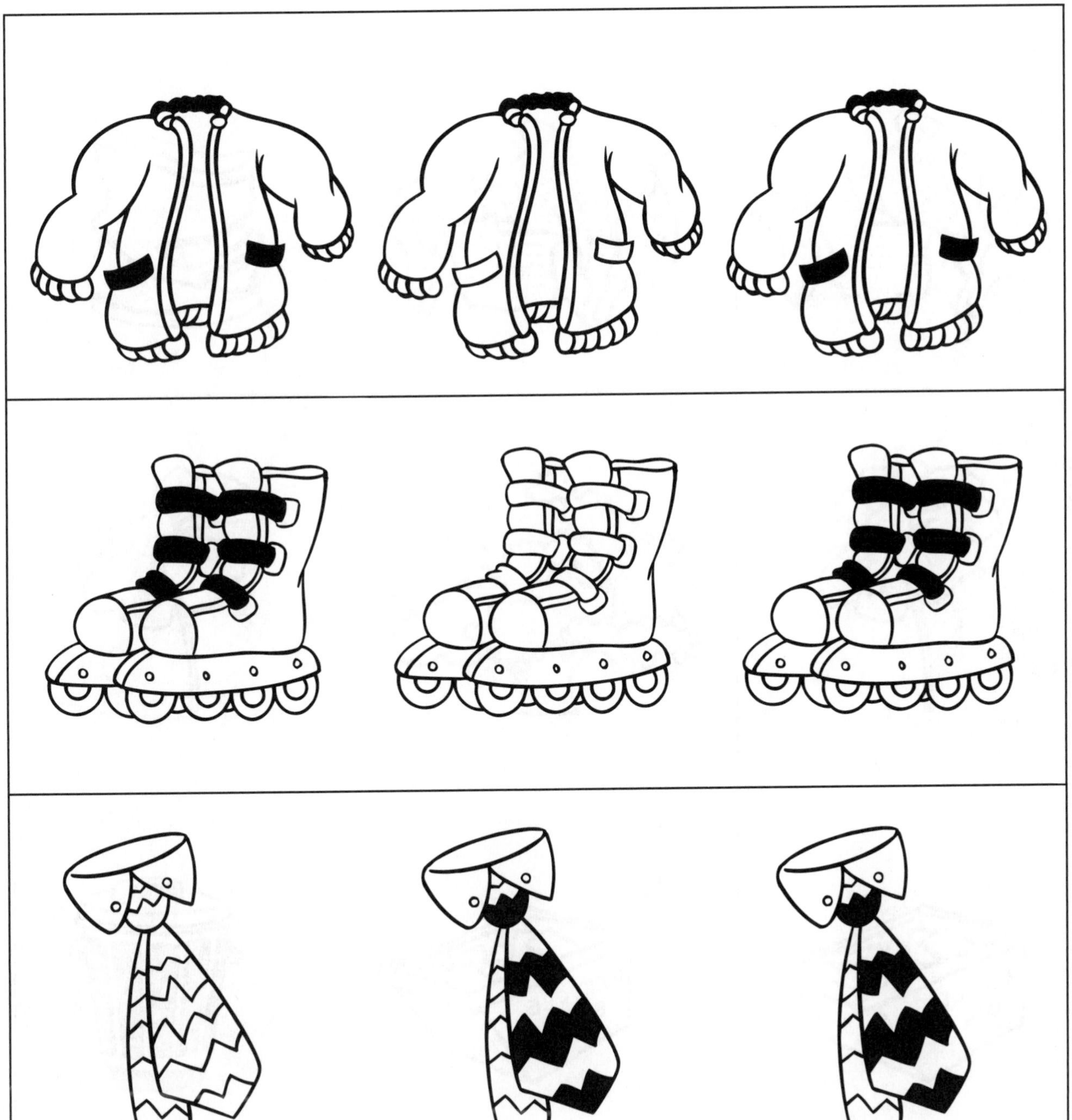

Circle each picture that is the **same** as the **first** picture in the row.

1. **Cut out** the picture cards below.
2. Put the cards in a bag. Shake the bag.
3. Pull out two cards.
4. If the pictures are the **same**, keep them.
5. If the pictures are **not the same**, put them back in the bag and try again.

Page is blank for cutting exercise on previous page.

Color the **picture** in each row that is **different**.

DIFFERENT

Circle the **picture** in each row that is **different**.

Circle the puzzle piece in each row that is **different**.

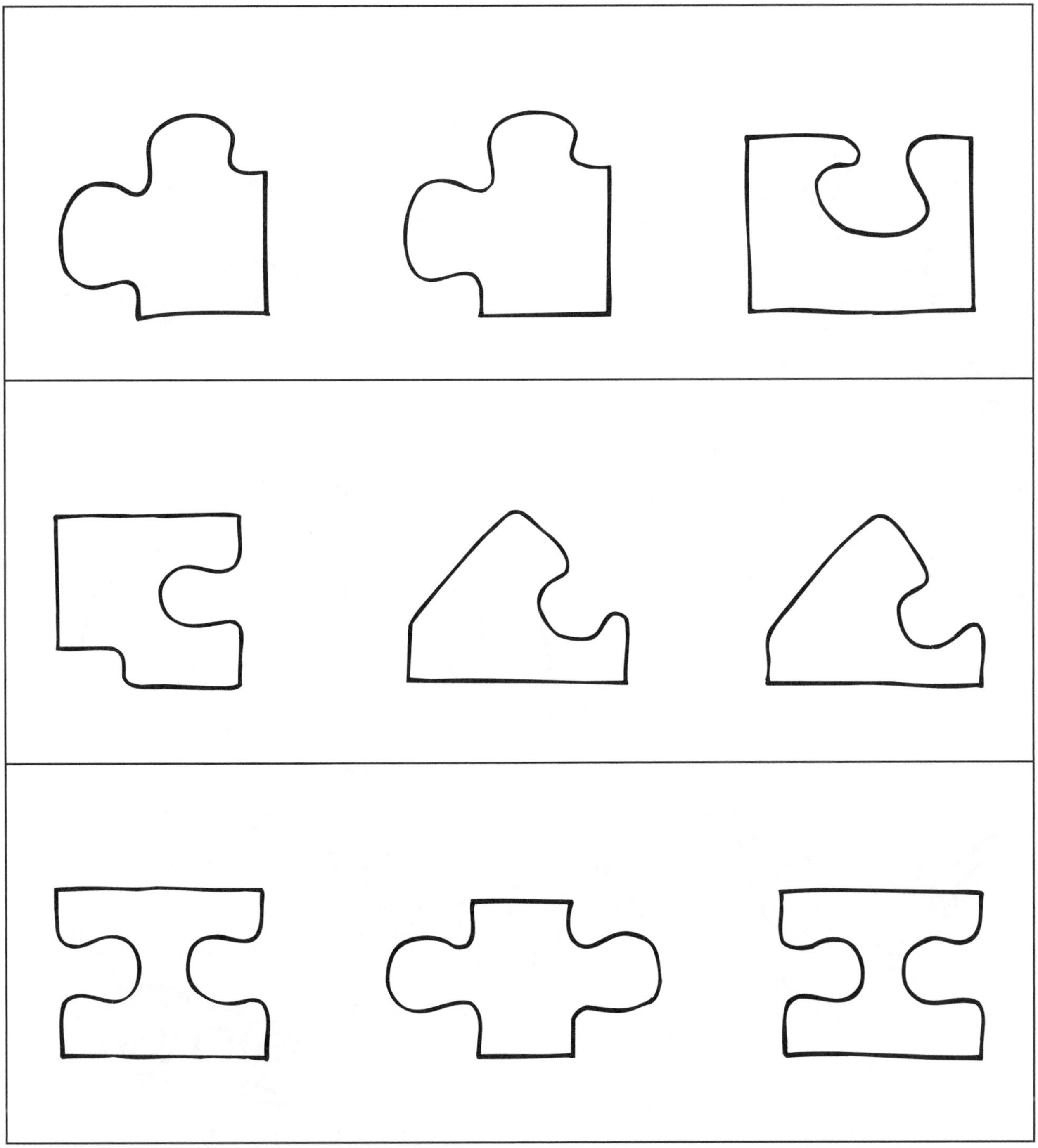

Circle the **picture** in each row that is **different**.

DIFFERENT

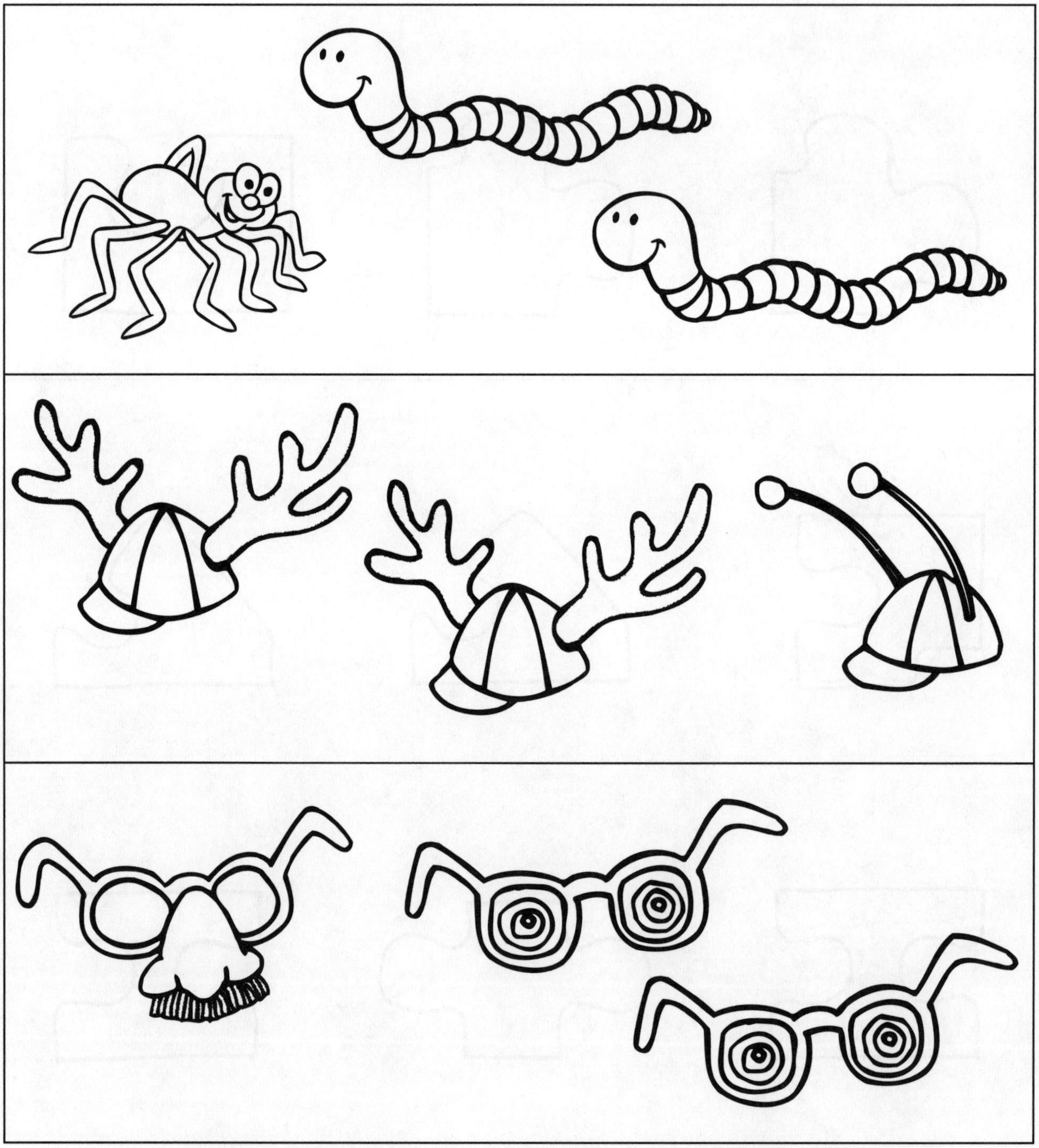

Look at the picture in each box. **Circle** the picture of the thing it **comes from**.

COMES FROM

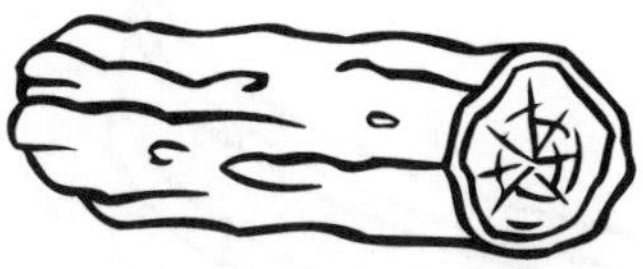		

Look at the pictures of the musical instruments. **Draw** the missing parts.

WHAT IS MISSING?

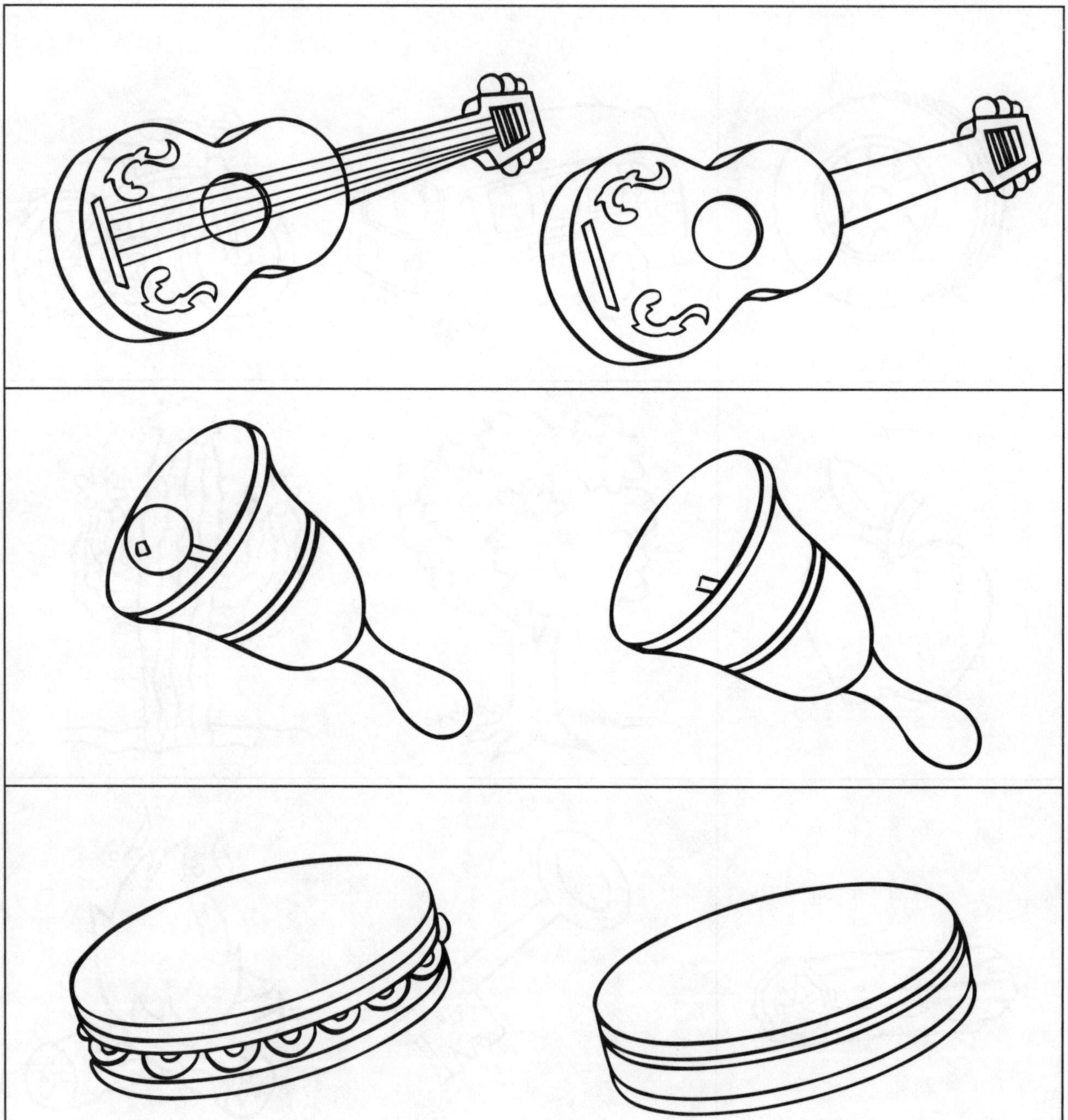

Play a matching game with cookies!

1. **Cut out** the cards.
2. Put the cards letter side down on the tray. Mix them up.
3. Turn over two cards at a time. If they match, keep the cards. If not, put them back on the tray.
4. Play until no cards are left.

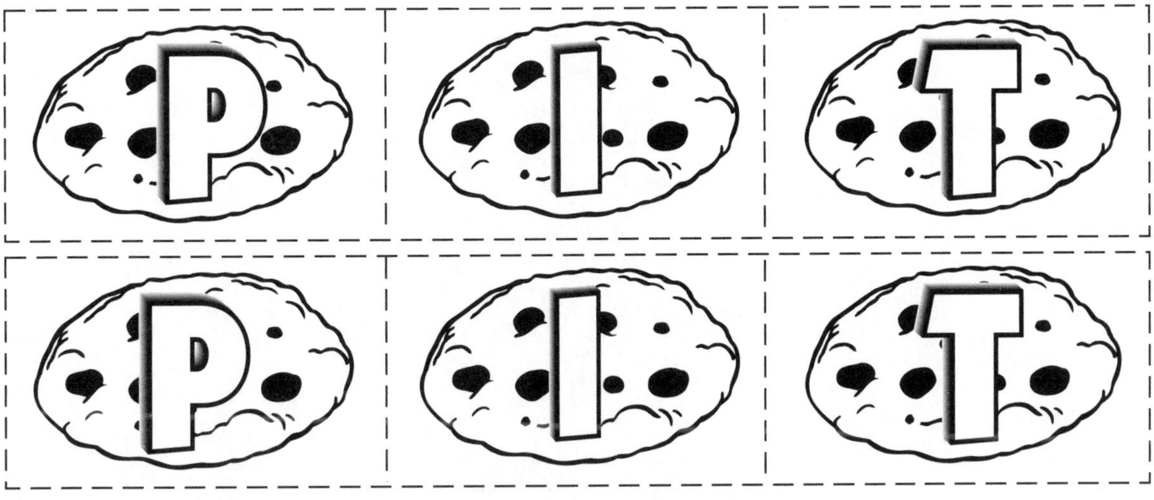

Page is blank for cutting exercise on previous page.

Look at the letters below. **Draw** an **X** on the letter in each row that is **different**.

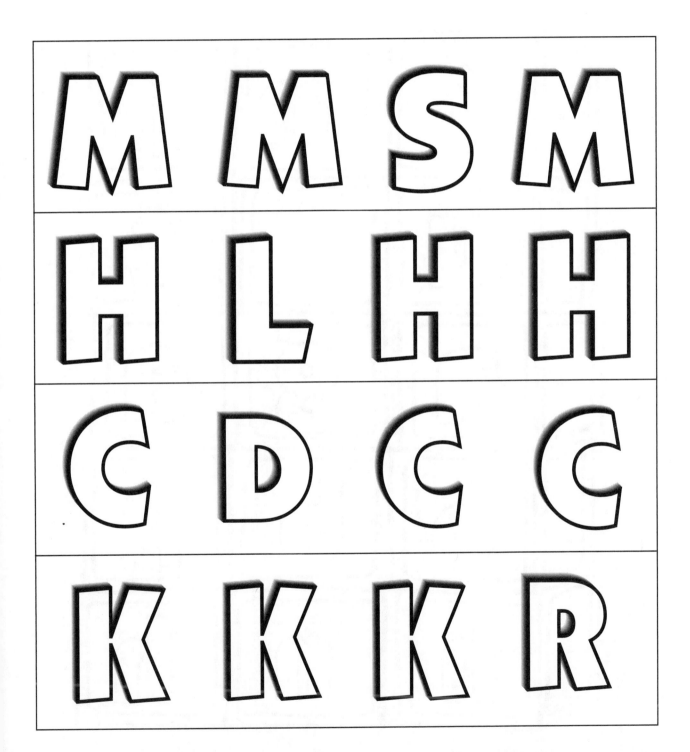

M	M	S	M
H	L	H	H
C	D	C	C
K	K	K	R

Circle the two letters in each row of blocks that are the **same**.
The first row shows you what to do.

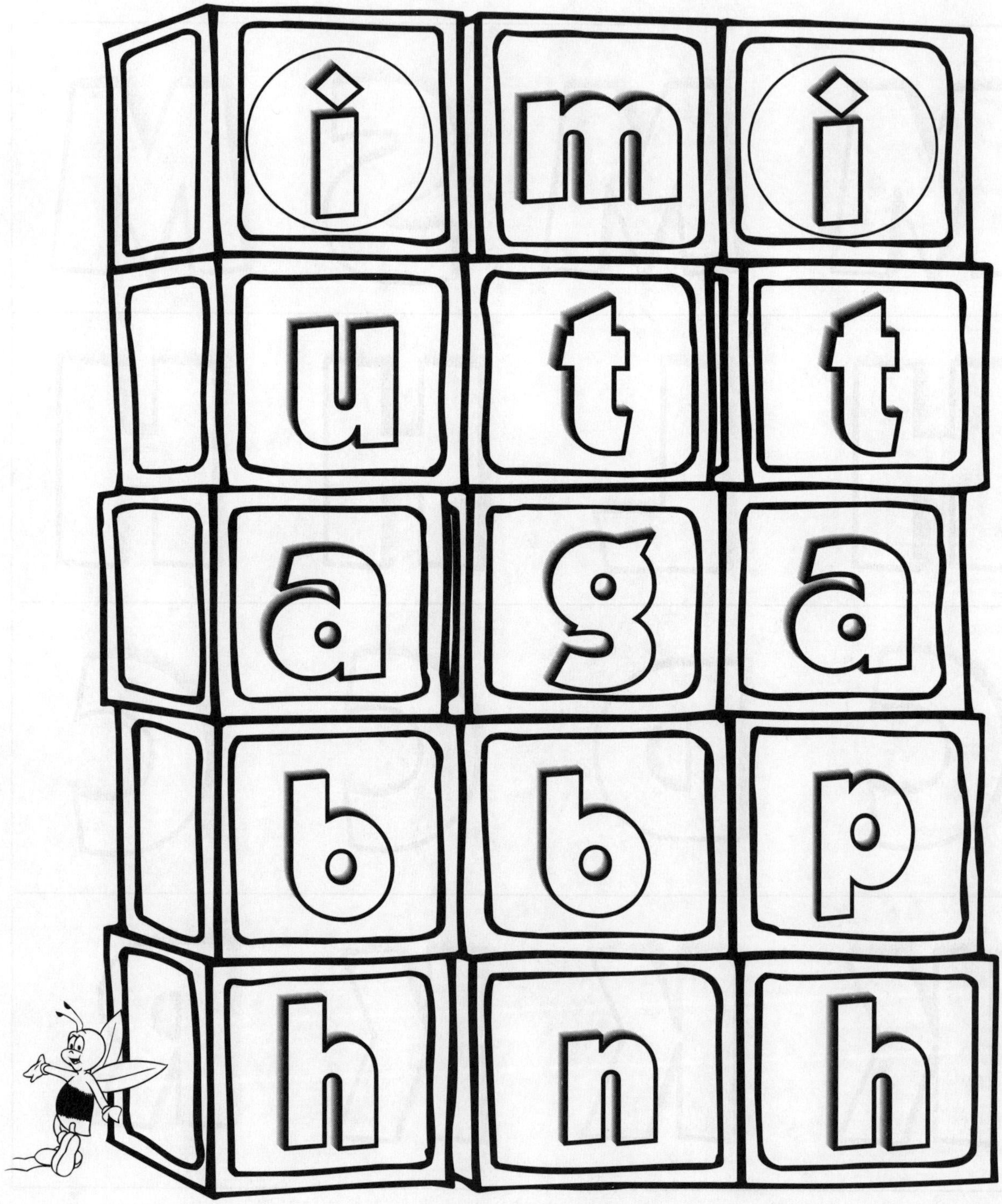

Look at the words below. **Circle** the two words in each row that are the **same**. The first one shows you what to do.

be to be

in do in

at at go

is am am

Look at the words below. **Circle** the word that is the **same** as the first word in the row. The first one shows you what to do.

bug	bug	mug
bat	bat	mat
pin	tin	pin
jam	ham	jam

Look at the picture of the **cat**. **Draw** a **line** from the **cat** to each picture that **rhymes** with the word **cat**. One is done for you. **Color** the pictures.

RHYMES

Look at the picture of the **bug**. **Draw** a **line** from the **bug** to each picture that **rhymes** with the word **bug**. **Color** the pictures.

RHYMES

Look at the picture of the **pail**. **Draw** a **line** from the **pail** to each picture that **rhymes** with the word **pail**. **Color** the pictures.

RHYMES

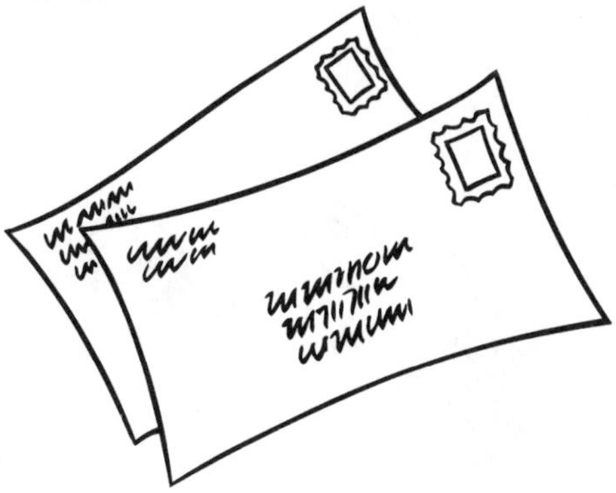

Look at the **first picture** in each row. **Circle** the picture that **rhymes** with it. **Color** the pictures.

RHYMES

Look at the **first picture** in each row. **Circle** the picture that **rhymes** with it. **Color** the pictures.

RHYMES

Look at the **first picture** in each row. **Circle** the picture that **rhymes** with it. **Color** the pictures.

RHYMES

Look at the **first picture** in each row. **Circle** the picture that **rhymes** with it. **Color** the pictures.

RHYMES

Draw a **line** to match each **rhyming** picture. **Color** the pictures.

RHYMES

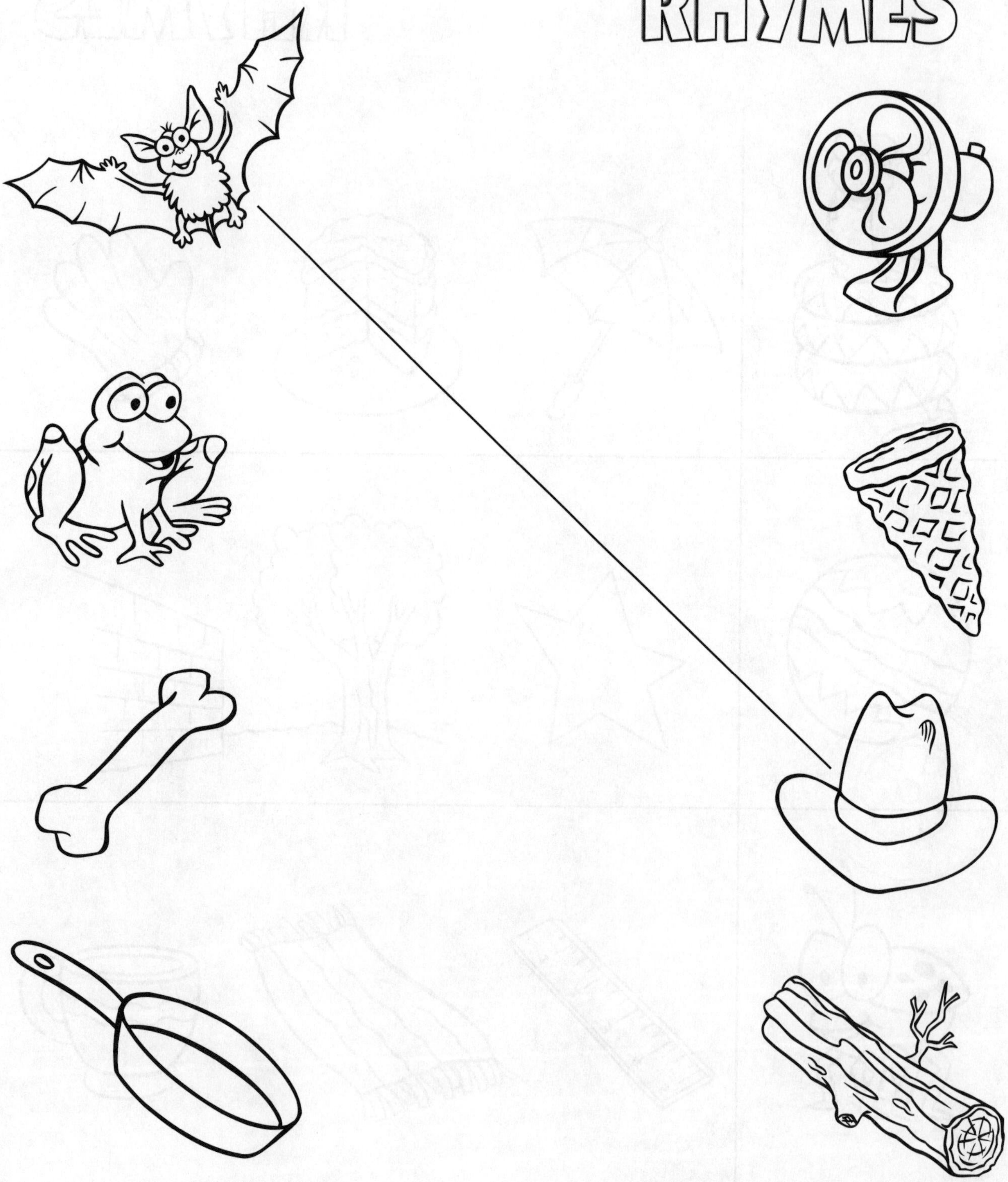

Draw a **line** to match each **rhyming** picture. **Color** the pictures.

RHYMES

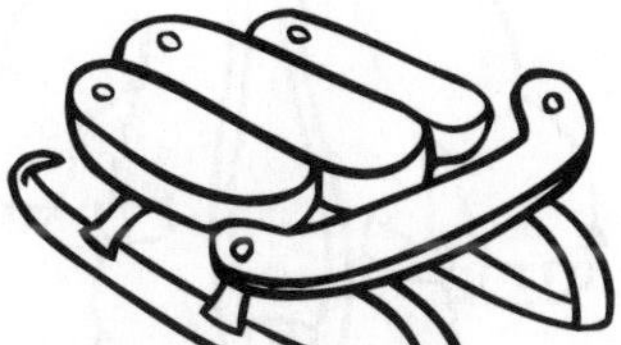

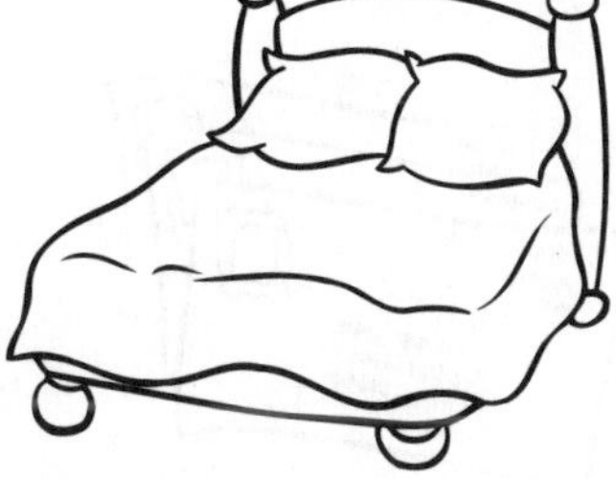

Draw a **line** to match each **rhyming** picture. **Color** the pictures.

RHYMES

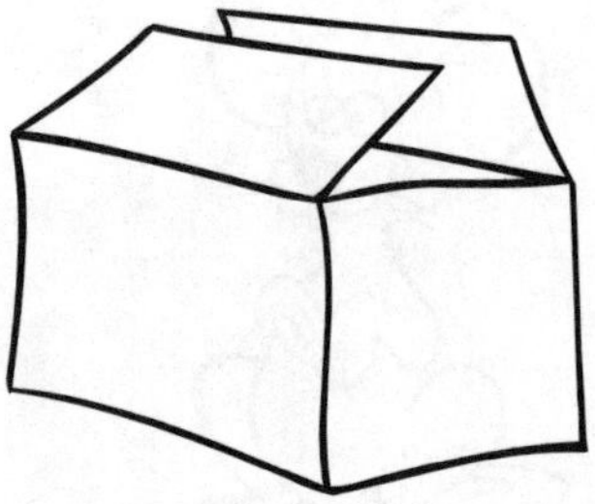

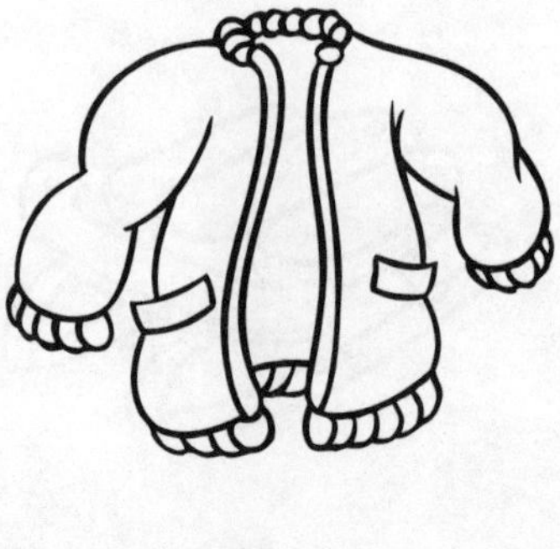

Draw a **line** to match each **rhyming** picture. **Color** the pictures.

RHYMES

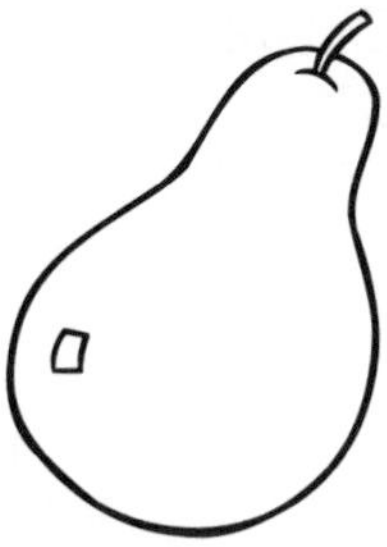

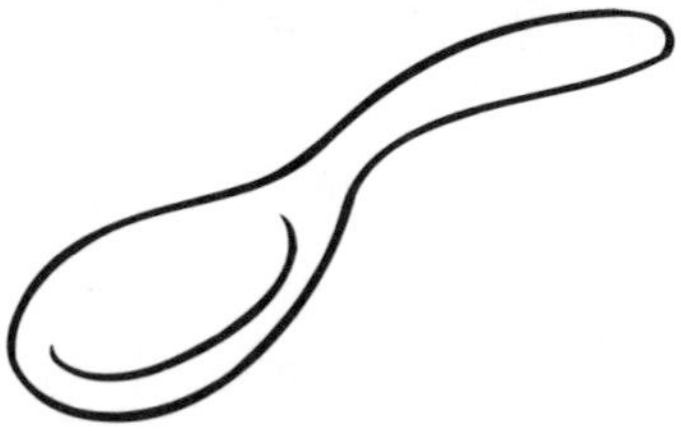

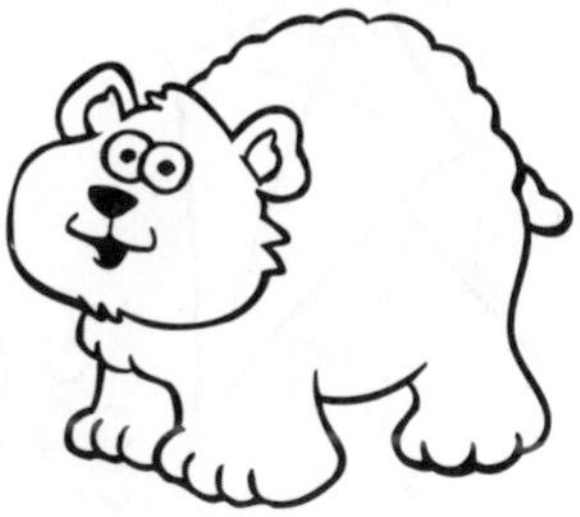

Trace the paths from the pictures on the **left** to some places to play on the **right**. The first one is done for you.

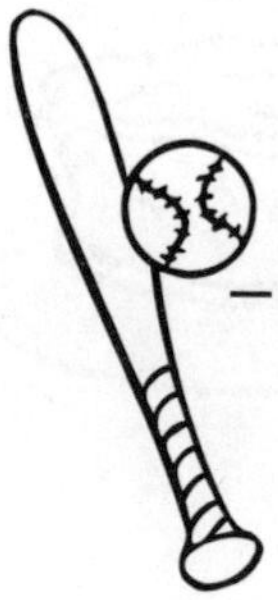

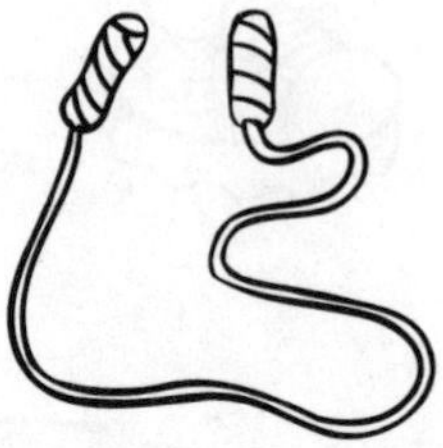

Help the **ants** get back to the **picnic baskets**!

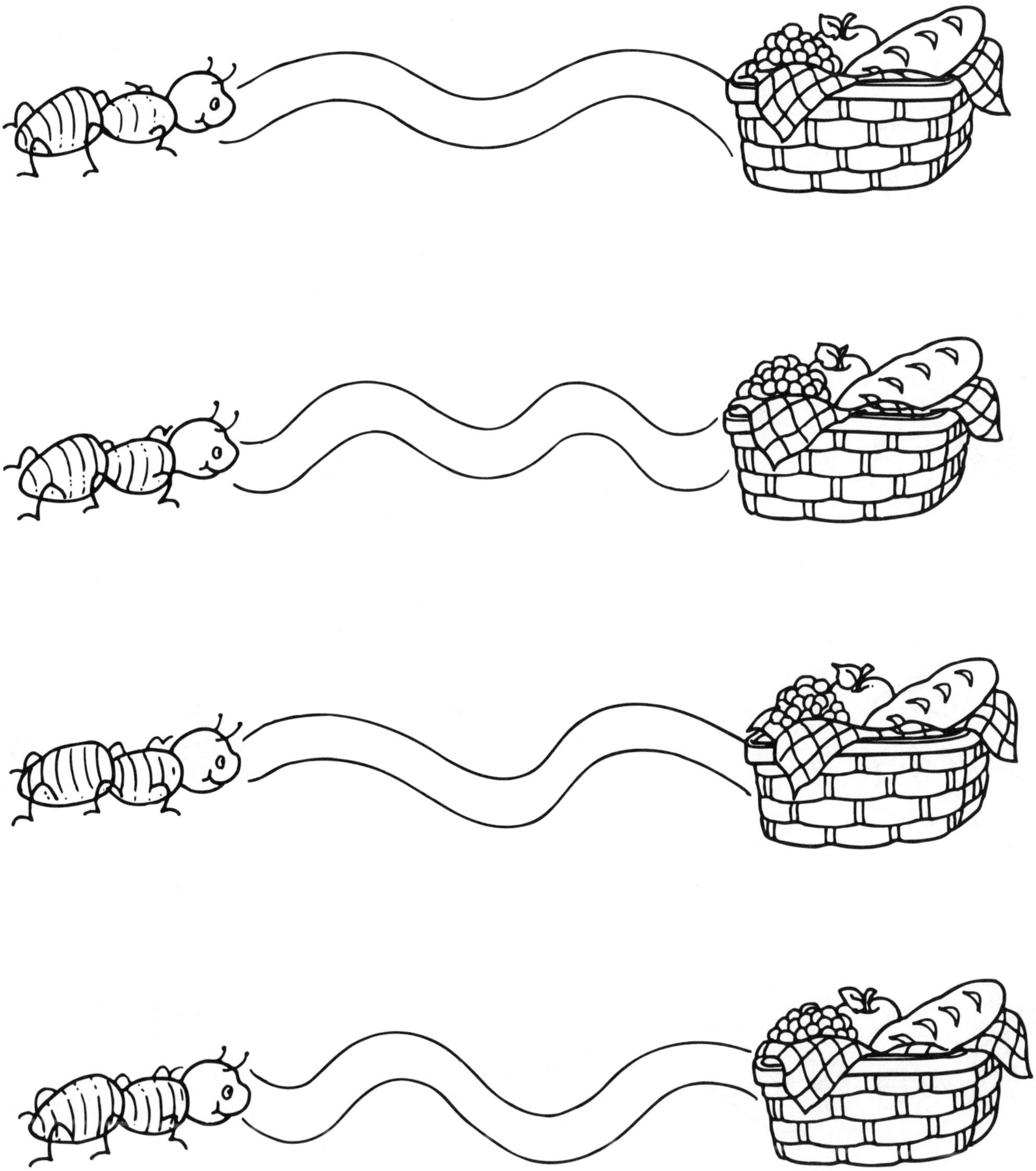

Help the **fish** get back into the **water**!

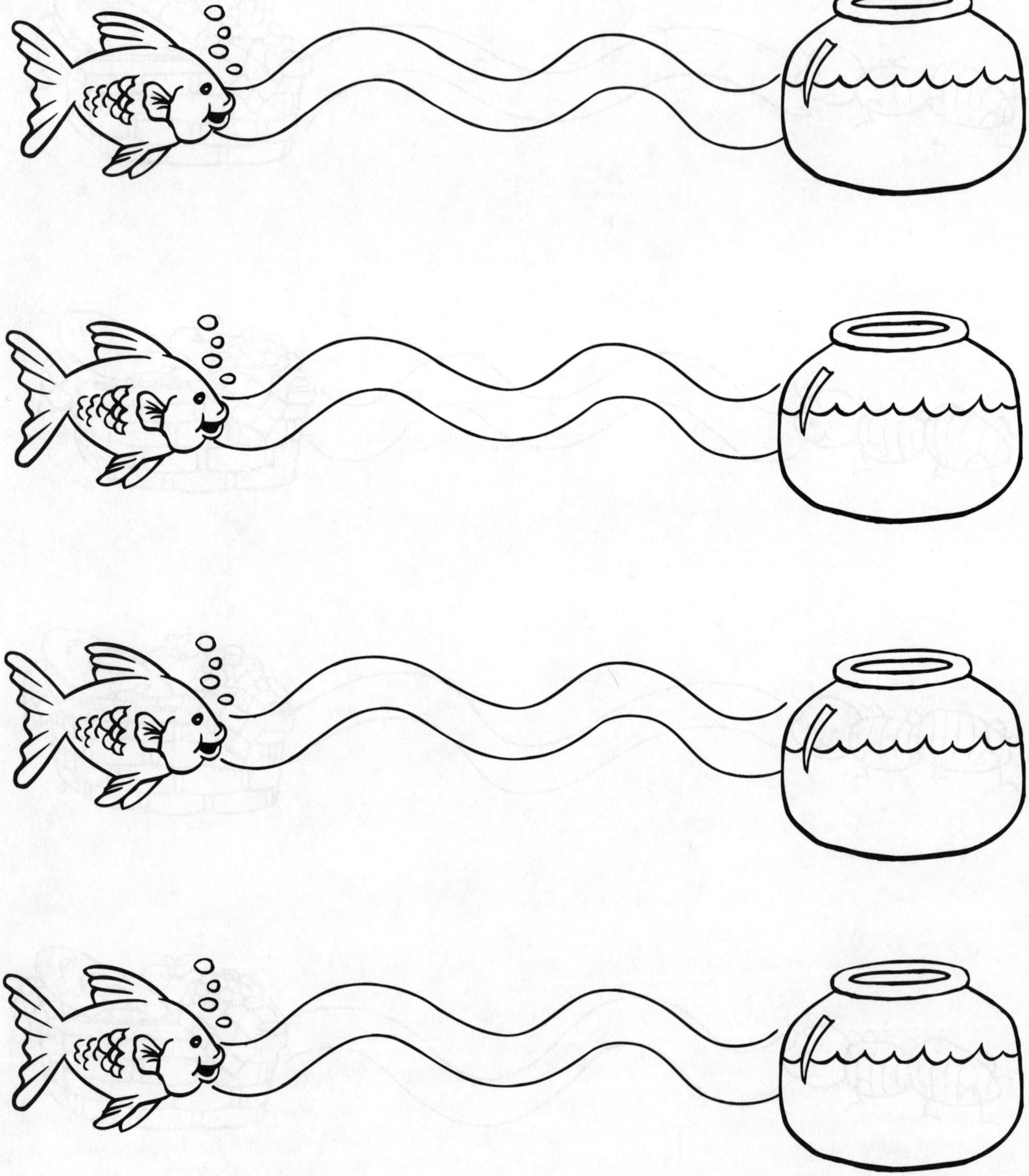

Help the **bunnies** get their **carrots**!

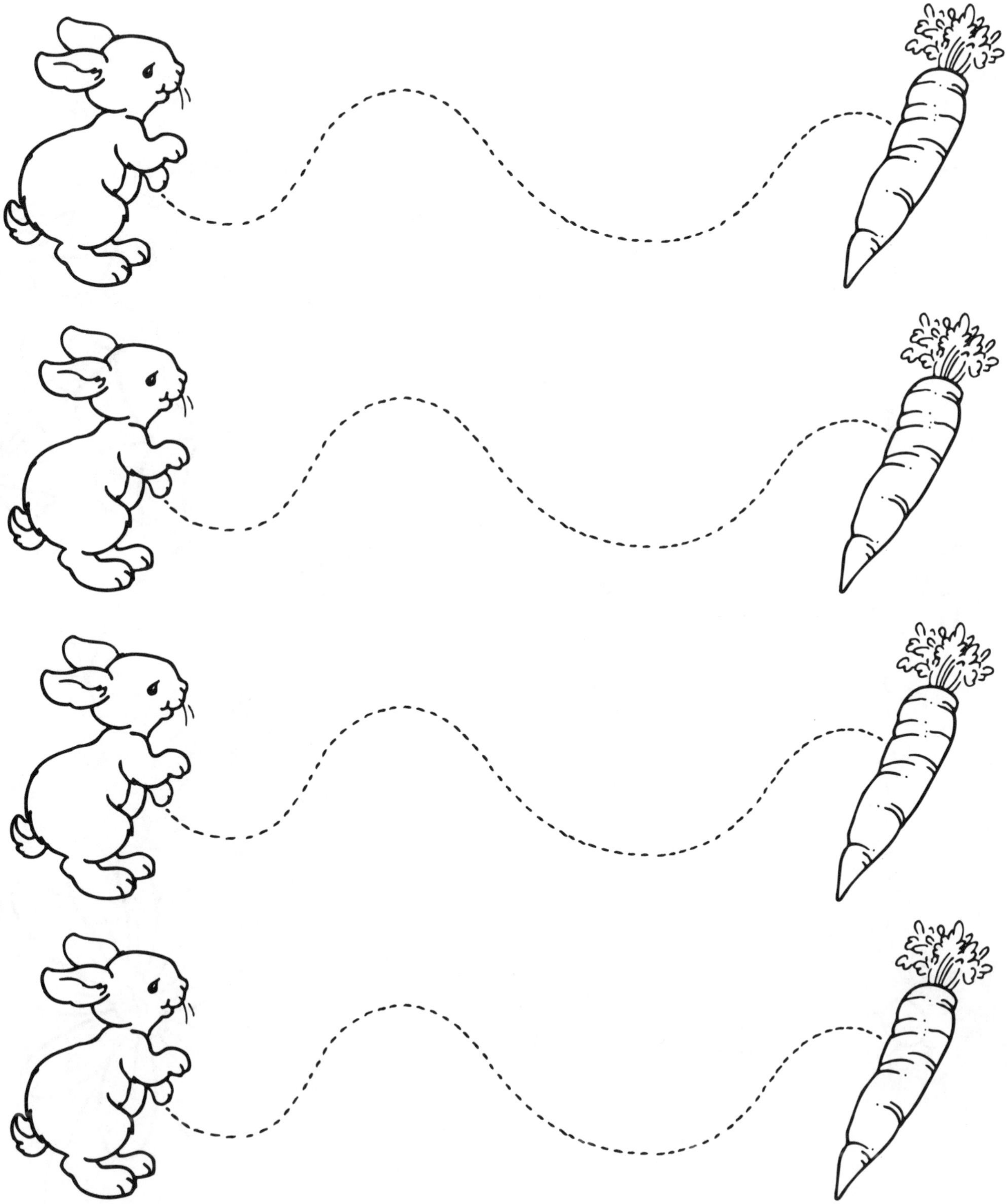

Trace the dotted line. **Start** at the **left** and go to the **right**.

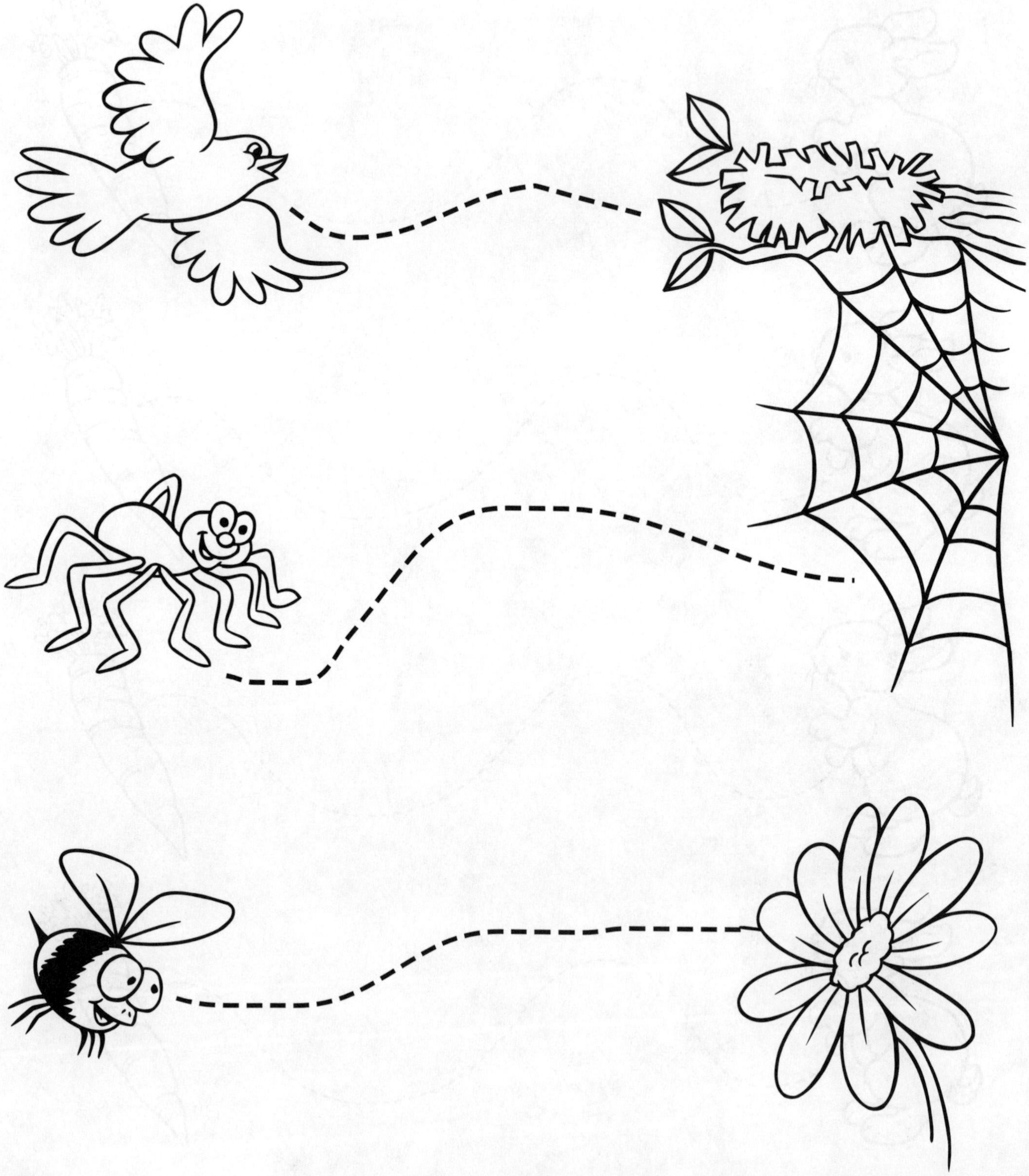

Left-to-Right

Help the **birds** fly to the **clouds**!

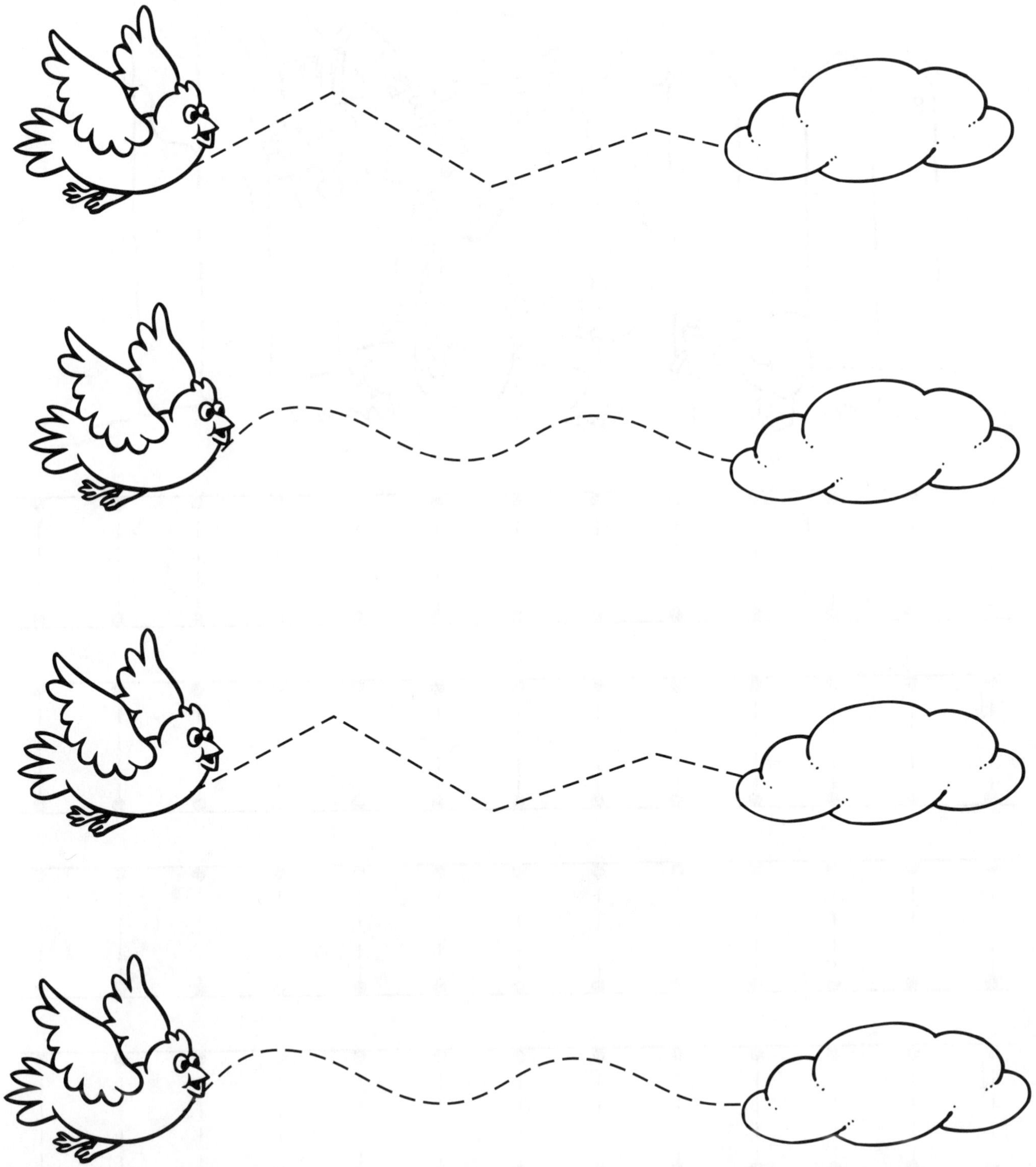

Start at the **dots**. **Trace** the **dotted** lines.

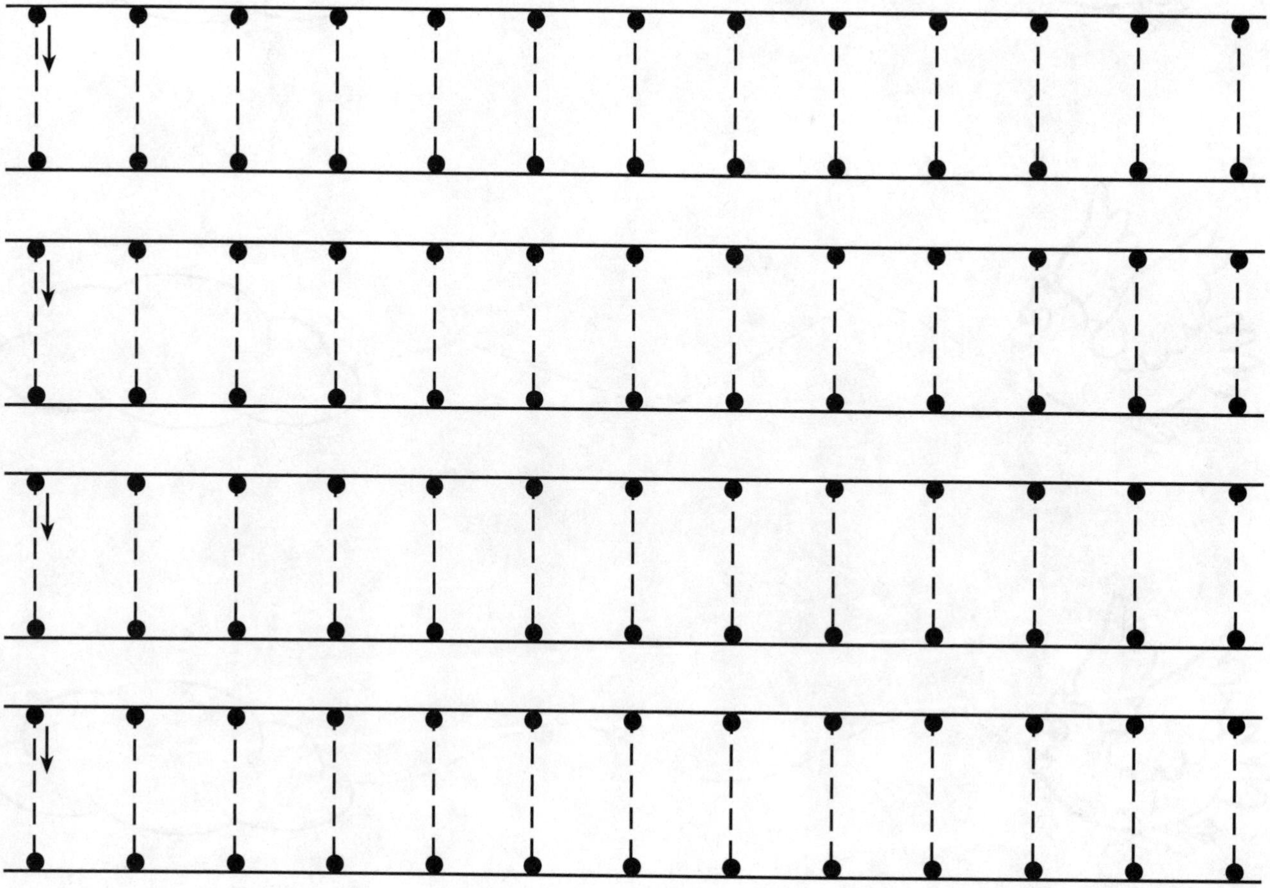

Start at the **dots**. **Trace** the **dotted** lines.

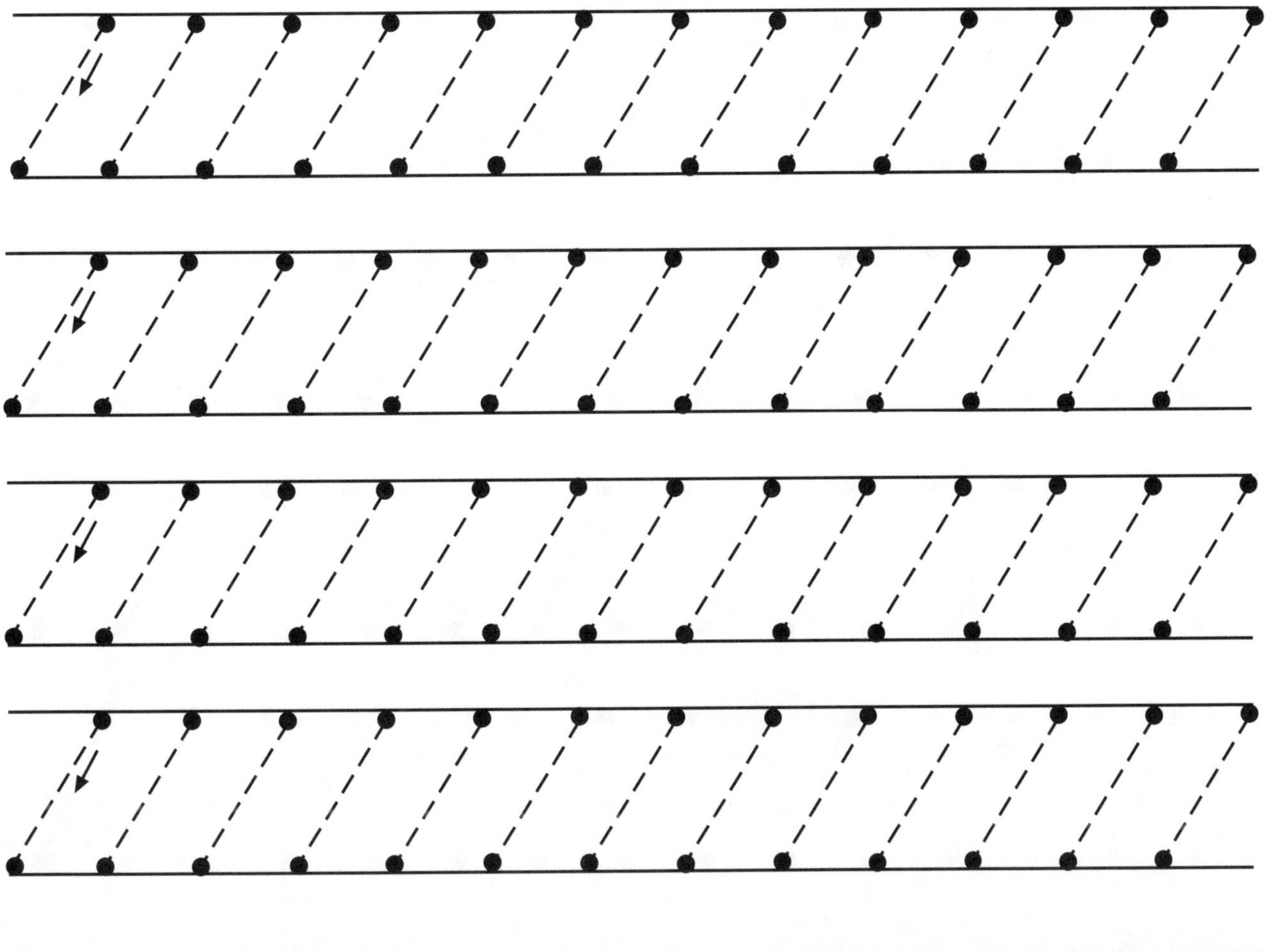

Start at the **dots**. **Trace** the **dotted** lines.

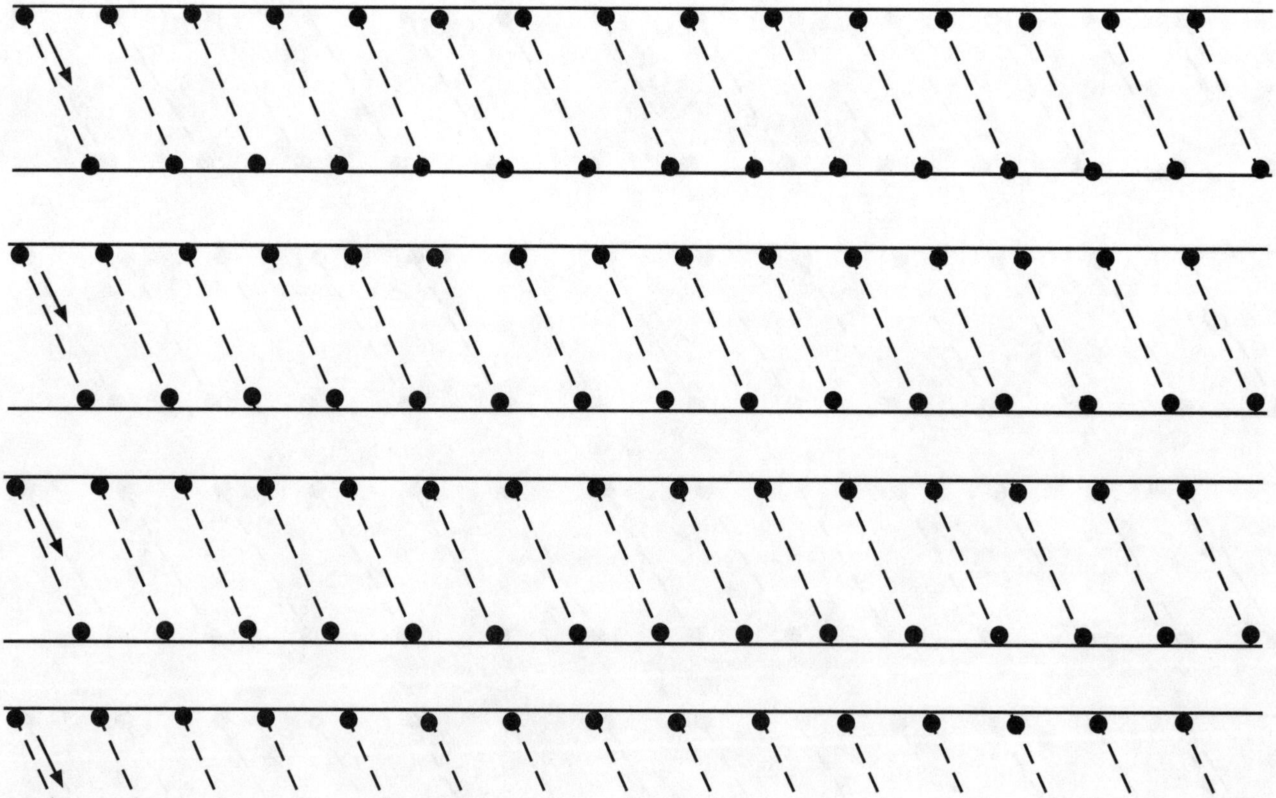

Start at the **dots**. **Trace** the **dotted** lines.

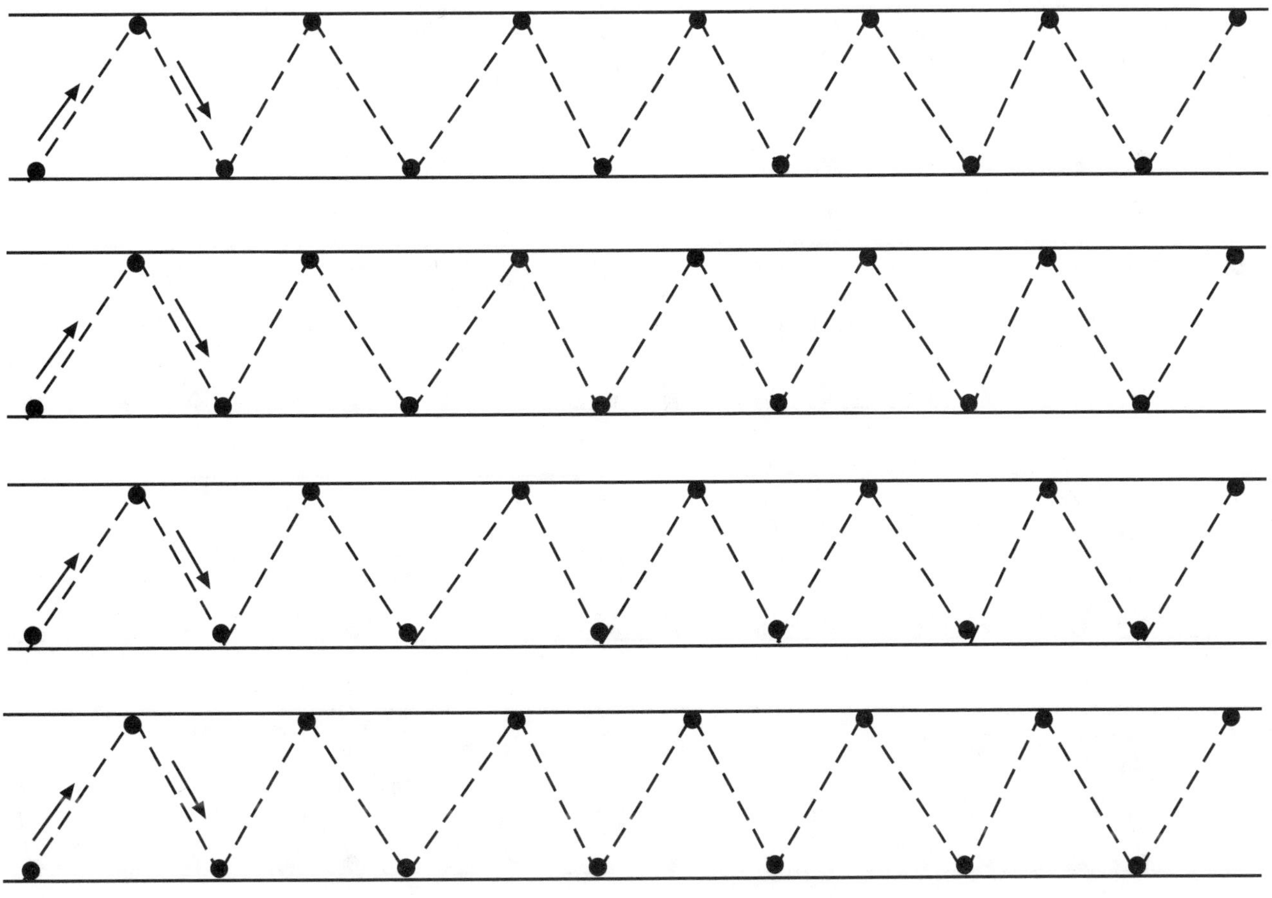

Start at the **dots**. **Trace** the **dotted** lines.

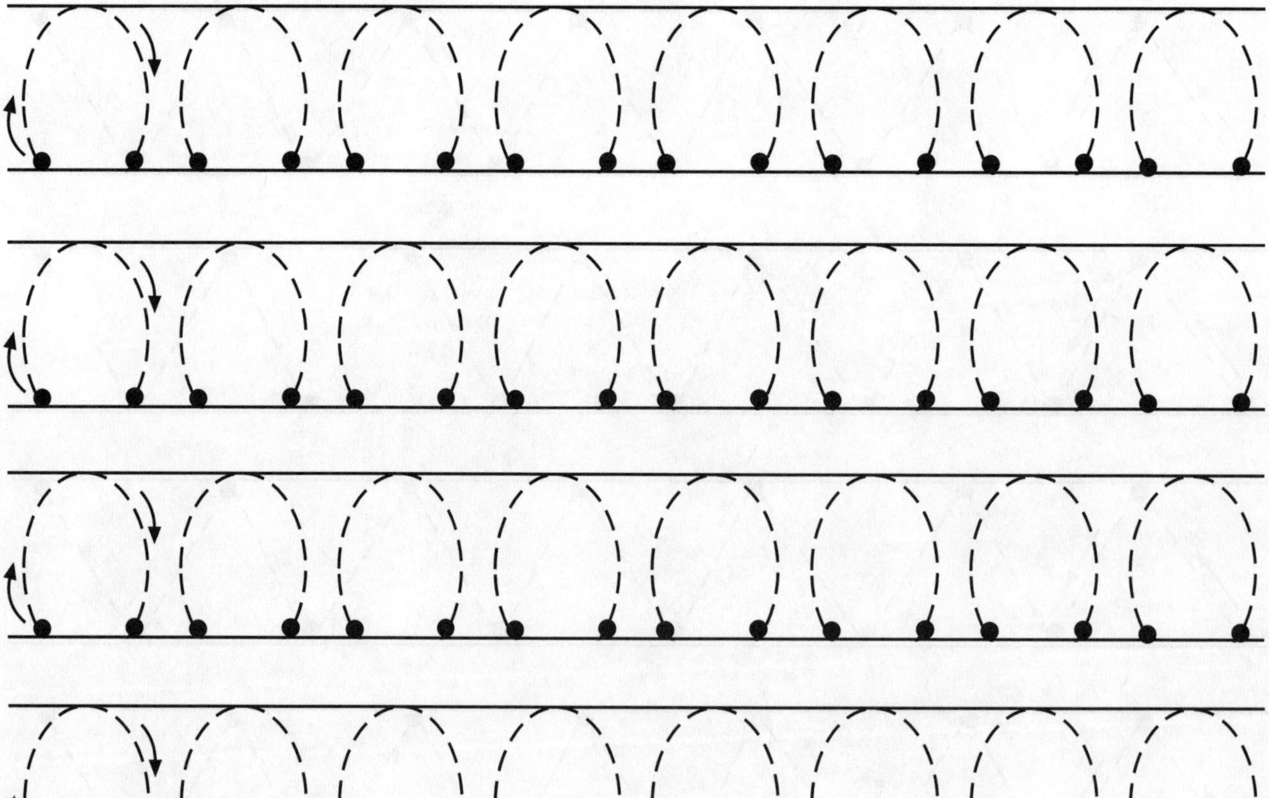

Start at the **dots**. **Trace** the **dotted** lines.

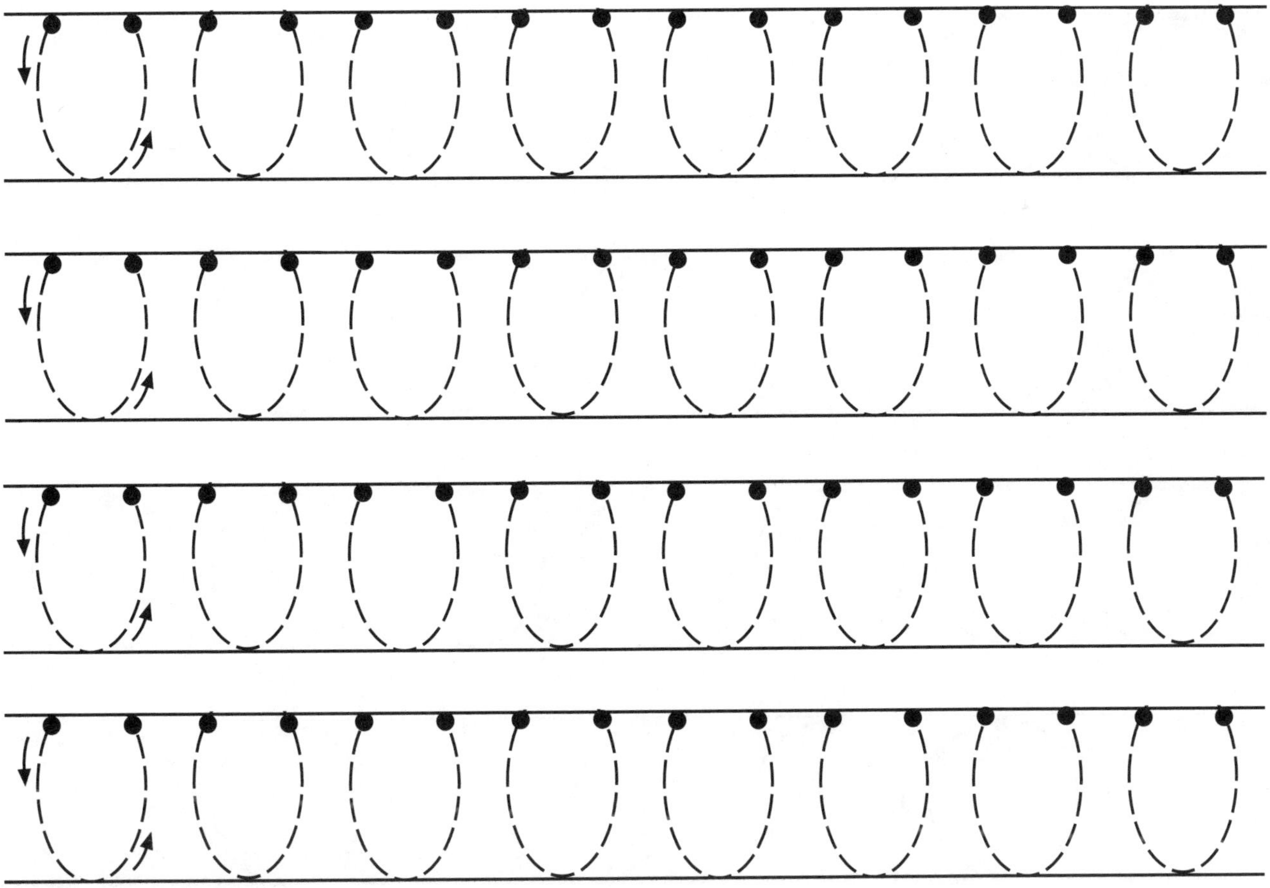

Start at the **dots**. **Trace** the **dotted** lines.

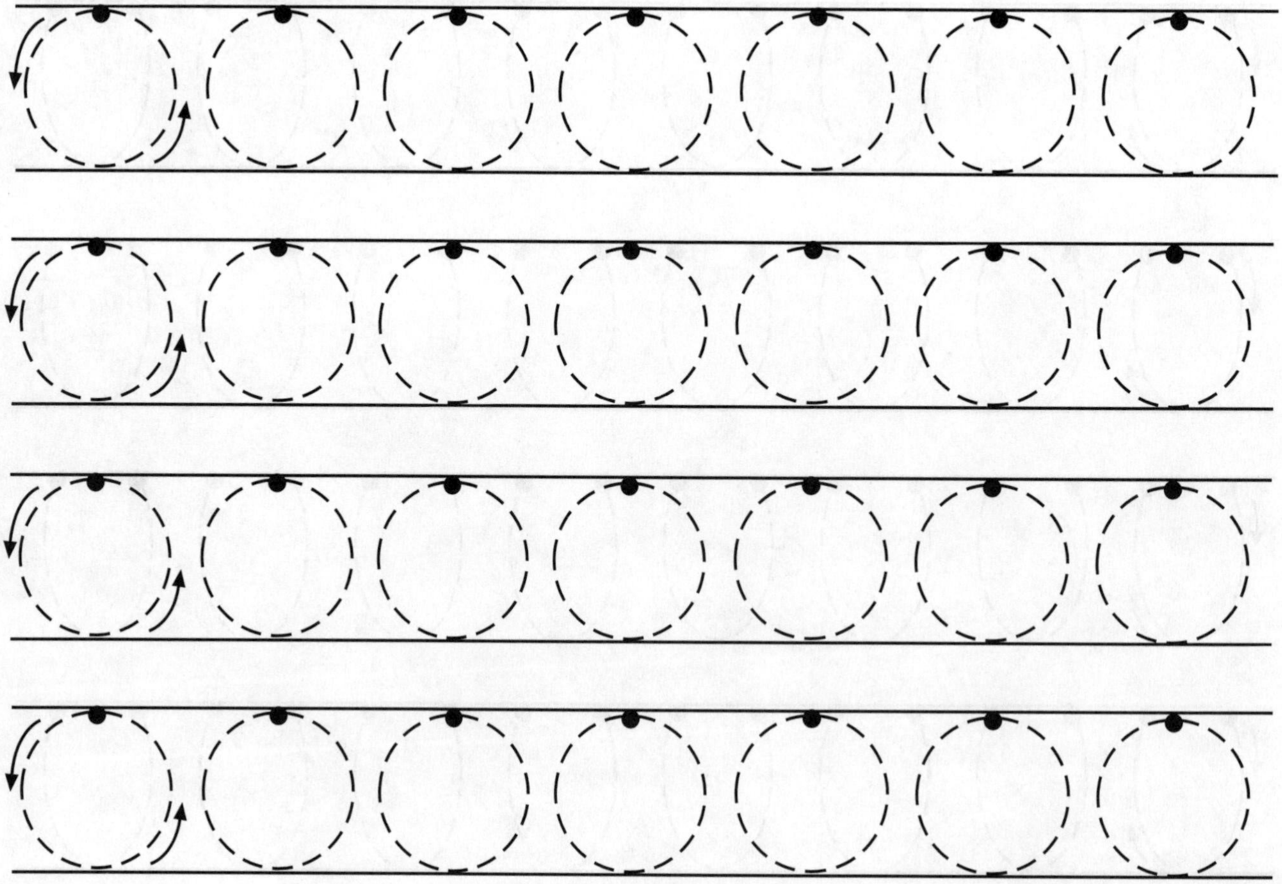

Start at the **dots**. **Trace** the **dotted** lines.

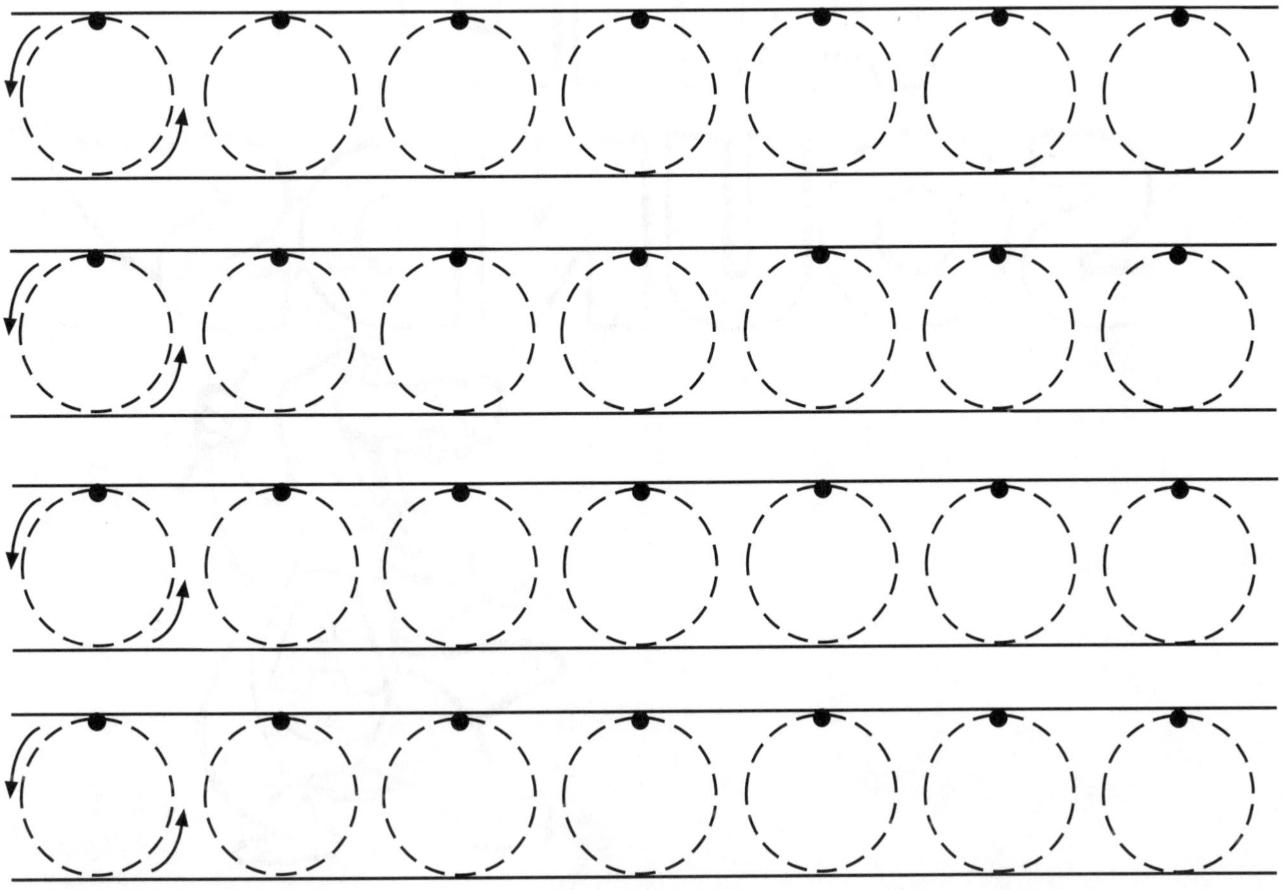

LETTERS AND SOUNDS

Letter A

Upper-case

Trace the letters.

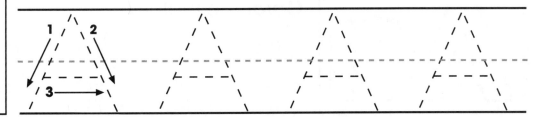

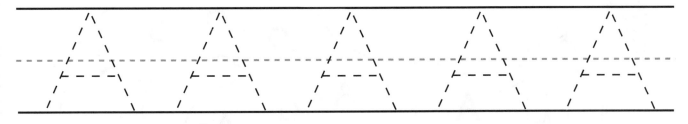

Letter a

Lower-case

Trace the letters.

Letter Aa

Draw a line to follow the letters **A** and **a**.

Color the picture.

Letter Aa

Circle the pictures that start with the sound of **Aa**.

Color the pictures.

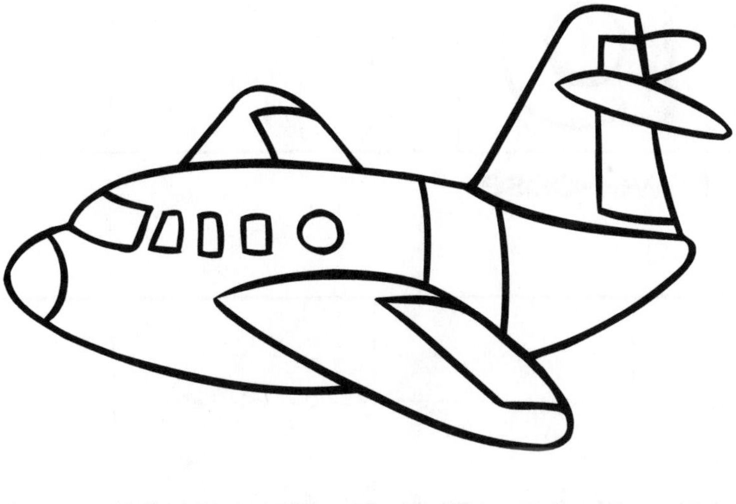

Letter B

Upper-case

Trace the letters.

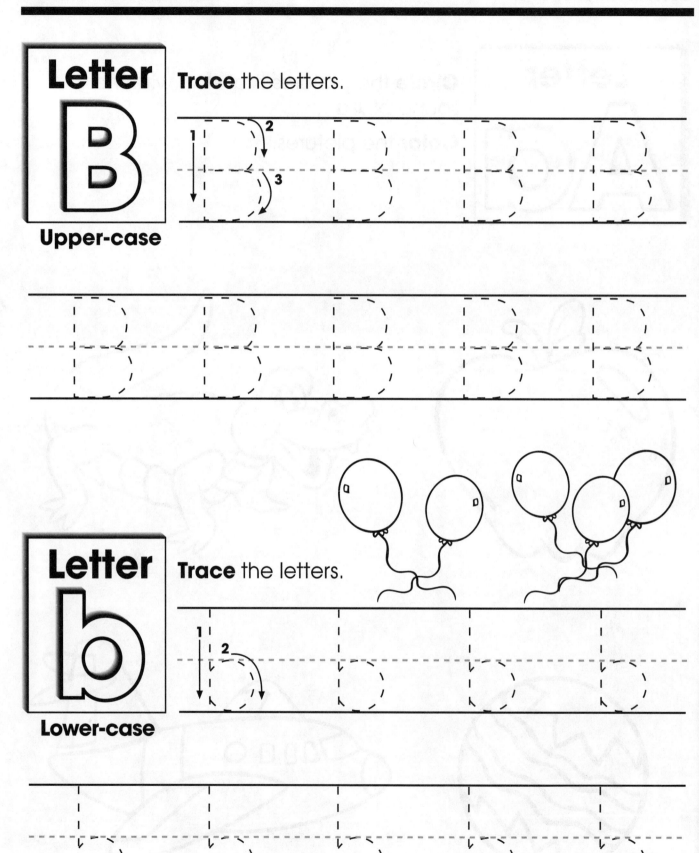

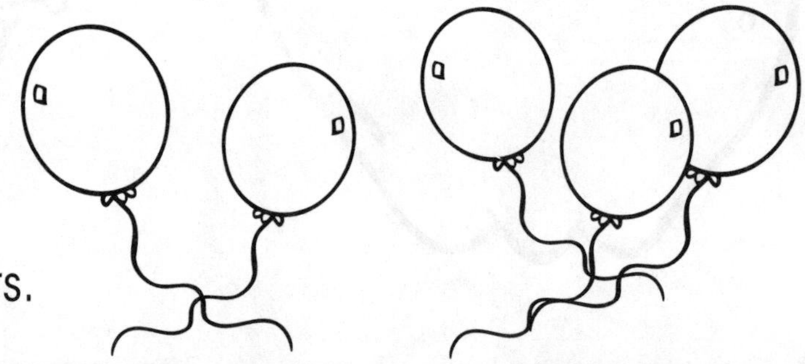

Letter b

Lower-case

Trace the letters.

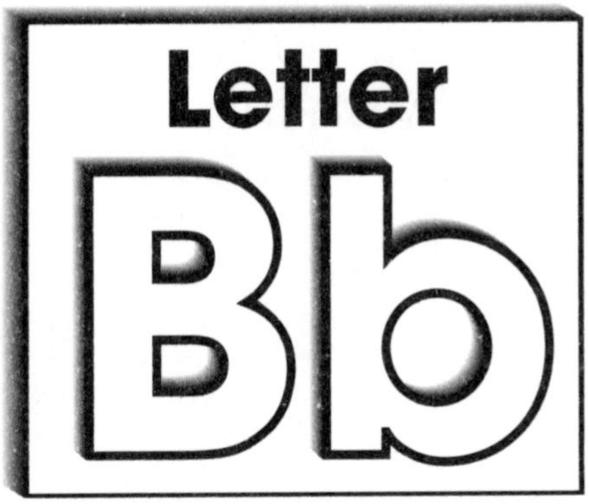

Find each hidden **B** and **b**.

Draw a **blue circle** around each **B**.
Draw an **orange circle** around each **b**.

Letter Bb

Circle the pictures that start with the sound of **Bb**.

Color the pictures.

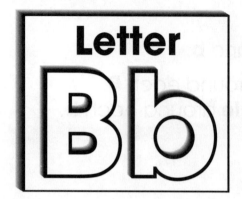

Letter

C

Upper-case

Trace the letters.

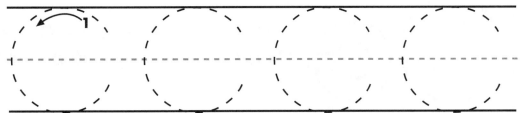

Letter

c

Lower-case

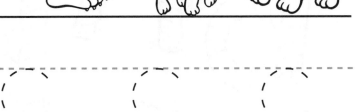

Trace the letters.

Letter Cc

Find each **C** and **c** that the cat has made with the yarn.

Color the **UPPER-case C**'s **red**.
Color the **lower-case c**'s **yellow**.

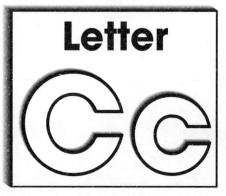

Letter Cc

Circle the pictures that start with the sound of **Cc**.

Color the pictures.

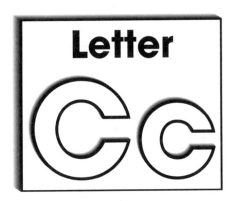

Letter D

Upper-case

Trace the letters.

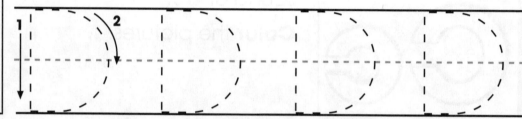

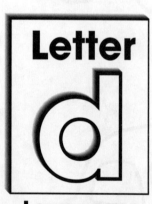

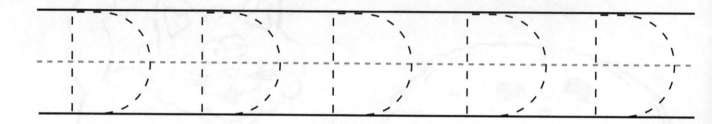

Letter d

Lower-case

Trace the letters.

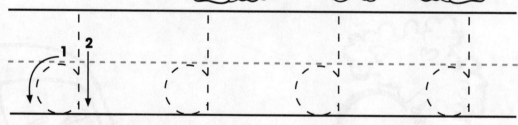

Letter Dd

Color the spaces with the letters **D** or **d** **purple**.

Color spaces with the other letters **orange**.

What did you find?

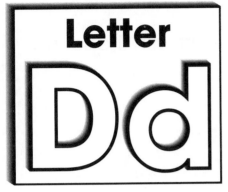

Color the doll, too!

Letter Dd

Circle the pictures that start with the sound of **Dd**.

Color the pictures.

Letter

E

Upper-case

Trace the letters.

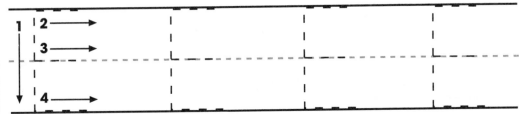

1 2 3 4

Letter

e

Lower-case

Trace the letters.

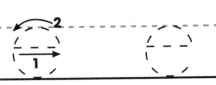

2 1

Letter Ee

Help the elephant find his way to the circus tent.

Color the peanut's with **E** or **e brown**.
Color the other peanut's **green**.
Color the picture!

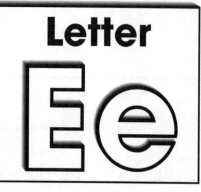

Letter Ee

Circle the pictures that start with the sound of **Ee**.

Color the pictures.

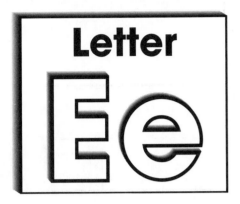

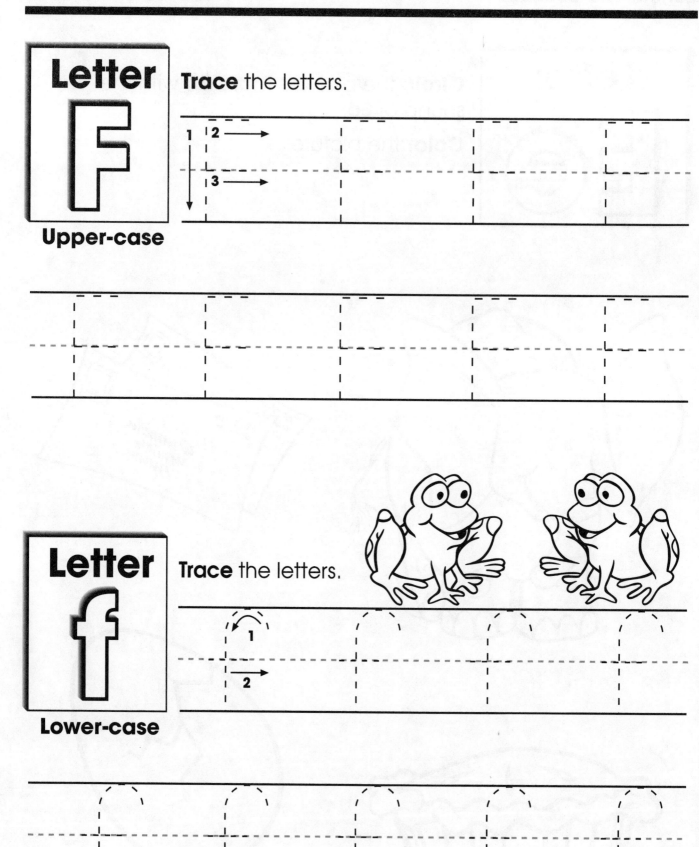

Letter F

Upper-case

Trace the letters.

1 2 3

Letter f

Lower-case

Trace the letters.

1 2

Letter Ff

Color and **cut out** each picture that starts with the sound of **Ff**.
Glue them on the fence.

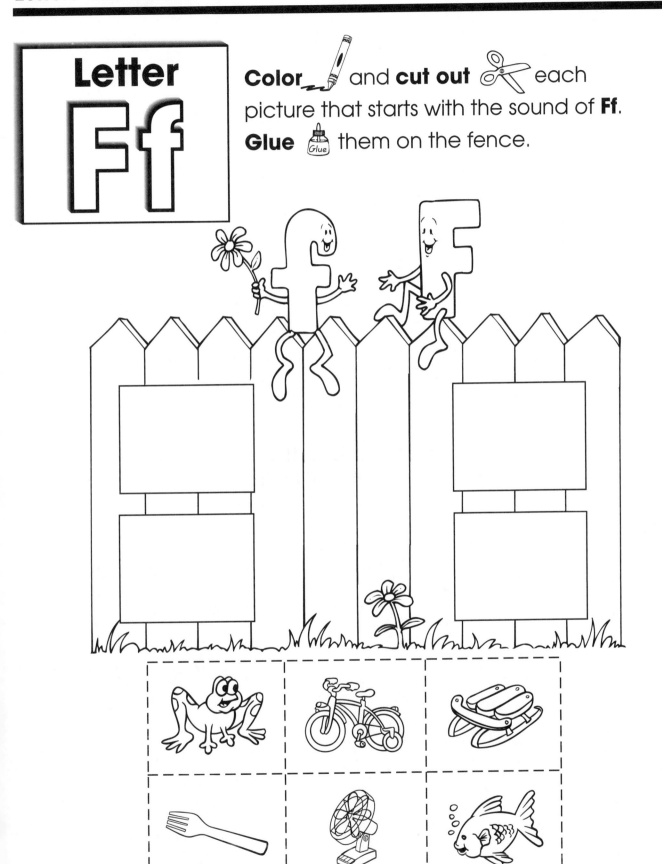

Page is blank for cutting
exercise on previous page.

Letter Ff

Circle the pictures that start with the sound of **Ff**.

Color the pictures.

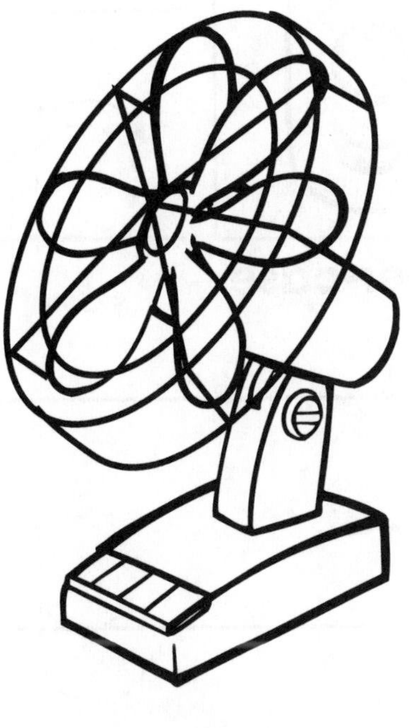

Letter G

Upper-case

Trace the letters.

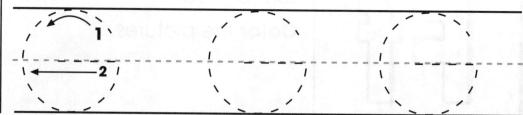

1

2

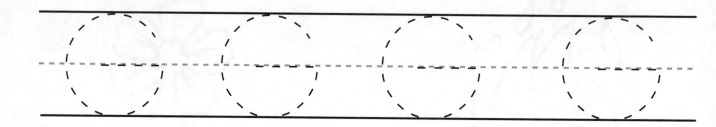

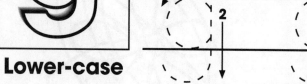

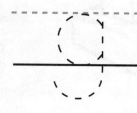

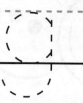

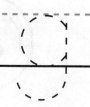

Letter g

Lower-case

Trace the letters.

1

2

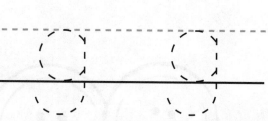

Letter Gg

Look at each sign in the garden.

Trace each **G** and **g**.

Color each sign with **G red**.
Color each sign with **g blue**.

Letter Gg

Circle the pictures that start with the sound of **Gg**.

Color the pictures.

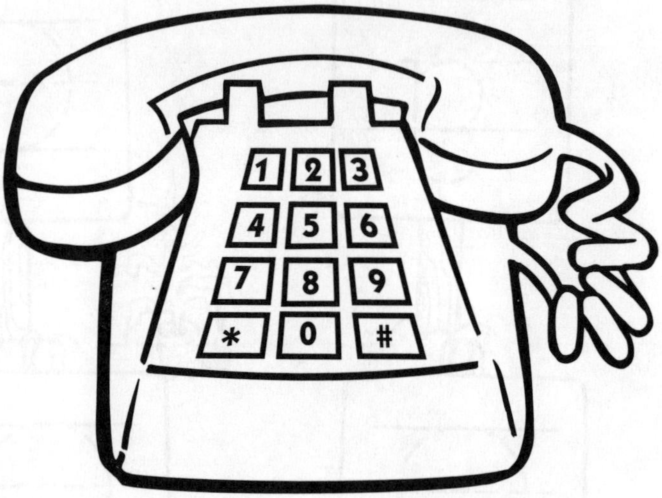

Letter H

Upper-case

Trace the letters.

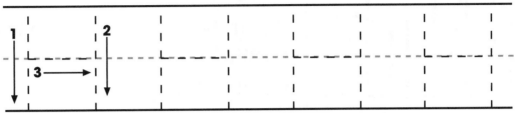

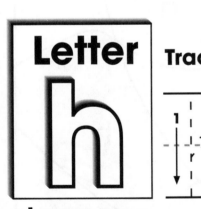

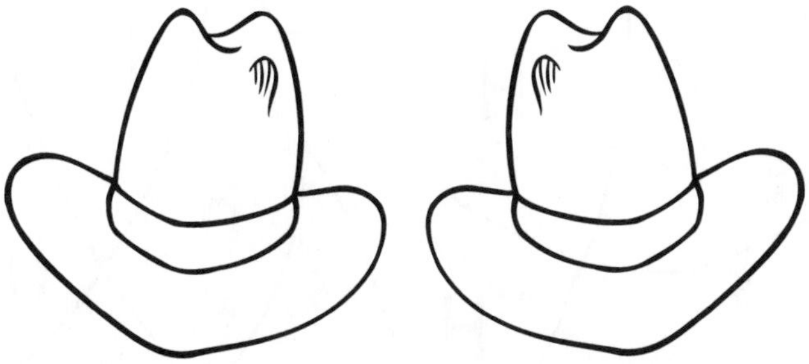

Letter h

Lower-case

Trace the letters.

Letter Hh

Color the spaces with the **UPPER-case H red**.

Color the spaces with the **lower-case h purple**.

What did you find?

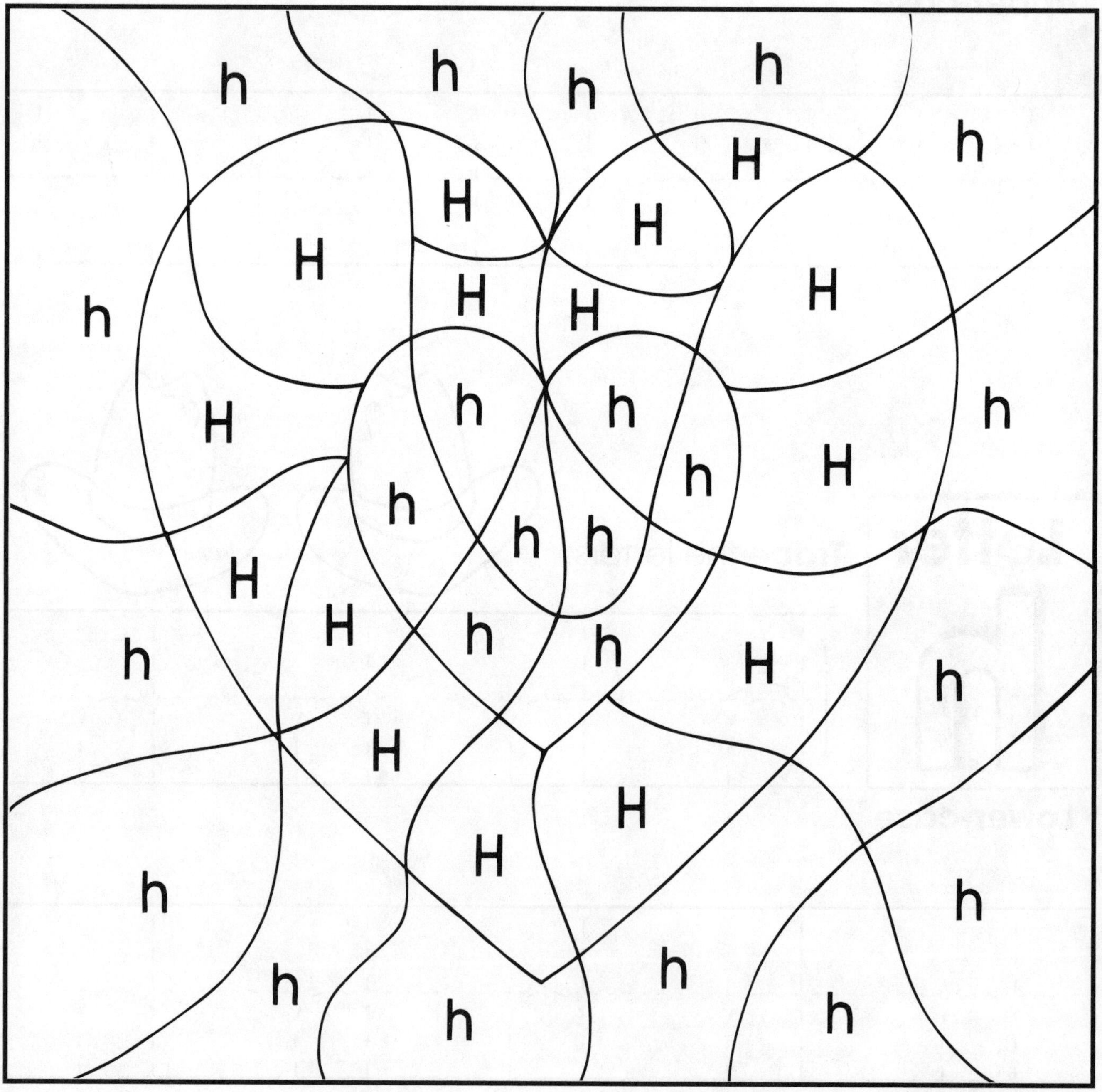

Letter Hh

Circle the pictures that start with the sound of **Hh.**

Color the pictures.

Letter I

Upper-case

Trace the letters.

2 →
1 ↓
3 →

Letter i

Lower-case

Trace the letters.

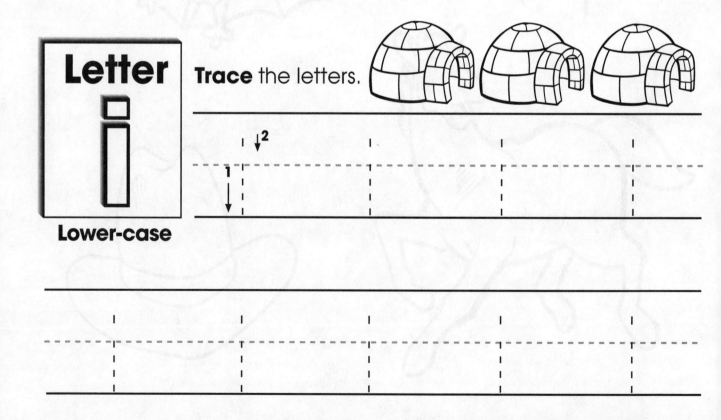

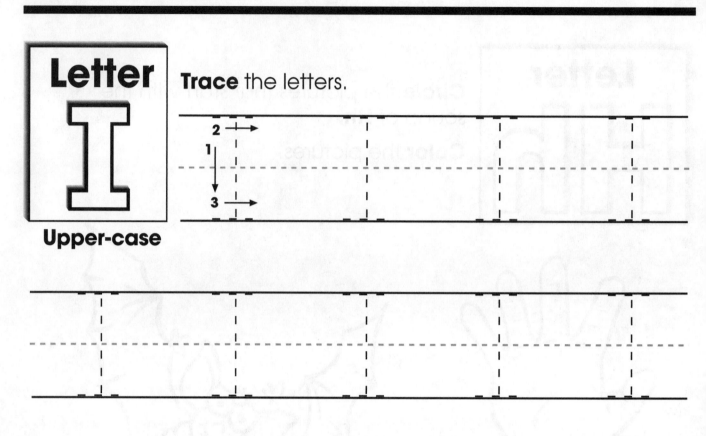

↓2
1 ↓

Letter Ii

Help read the  's smoke signals.

Color each I **red**. **Color** each i **orange**.

Color the picture!

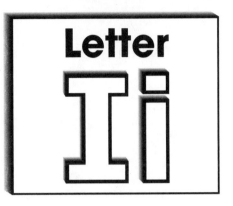

Letter Ii

Circle the pictures that start with the sound of **Ii**.

Color the pictures.

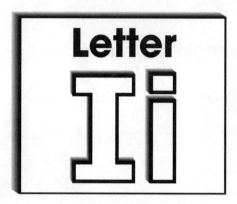

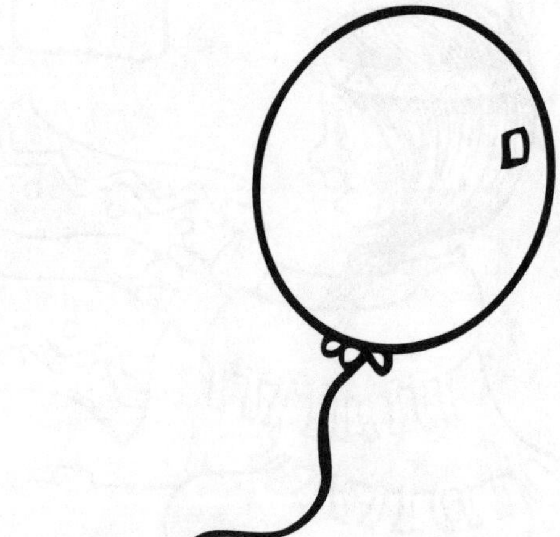

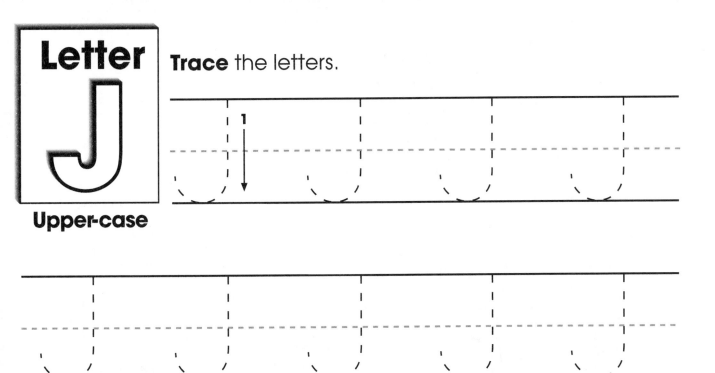

Letter J

Upper-case

Trace the letters.

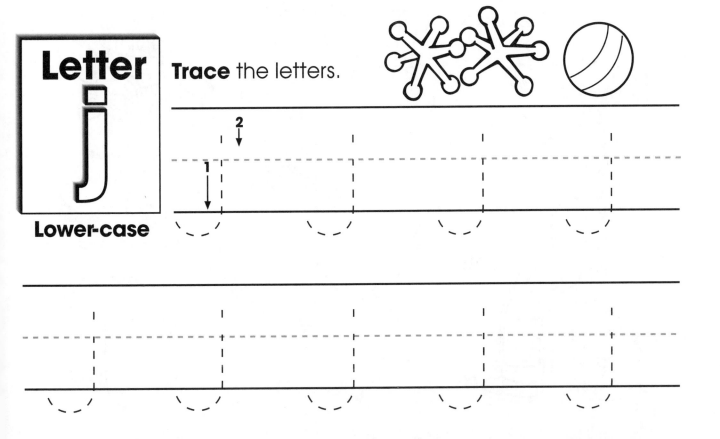

Letter j

Lower-case

Trace the letters.

Letter Jj

Can you **find** each hidden **J** and **j** in the picture?

Color each **J red**.
Color each **j green**.
Then, **color** the rest of the picture!

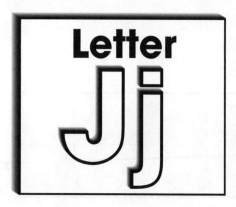

Letter Jj

Circle the pictures that start with the sound of **Jj**.

Color the pictures.

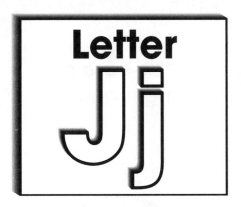

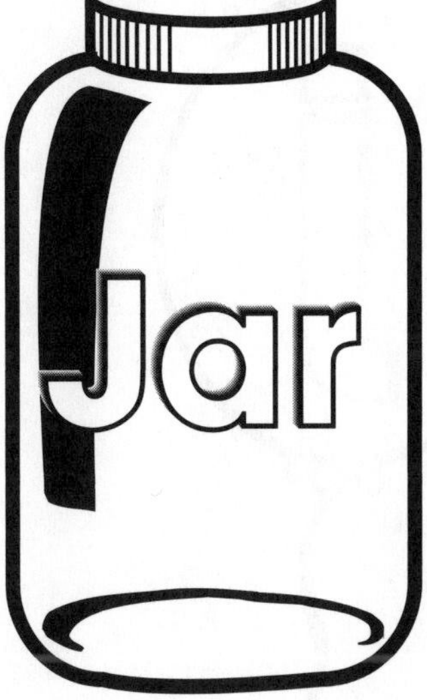

Review Letters A-J

Draw a line to match the **UPPER-case** and **lower-case** letters that belong together.

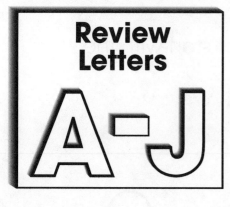

Review Letters A-J

Draw a line to match the **UPPER-case** and **lower-case** letters that belong together.

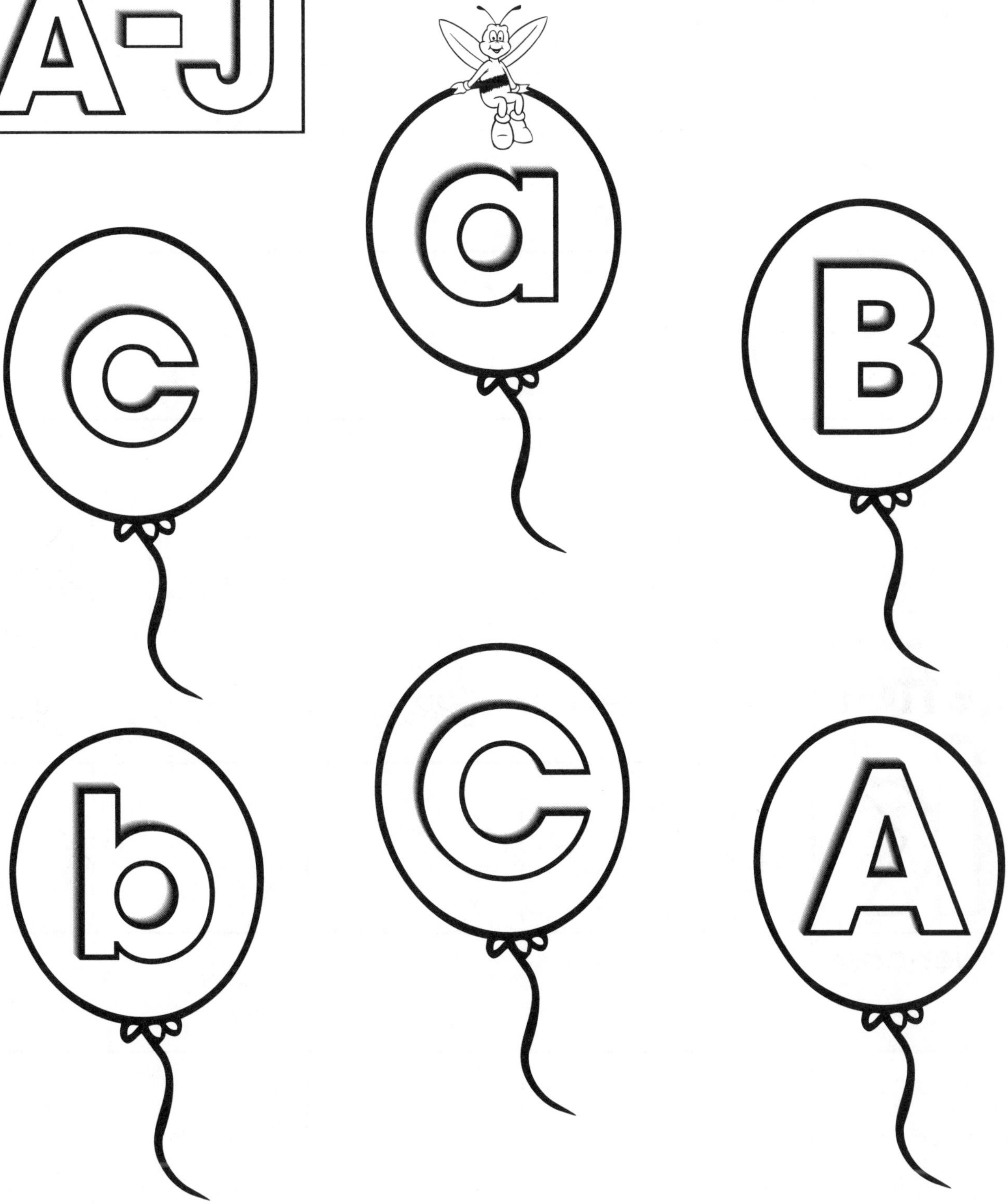

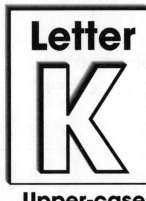

Letter K

Upper-case

Trace the letters.

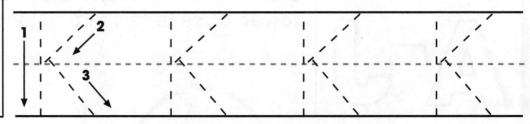

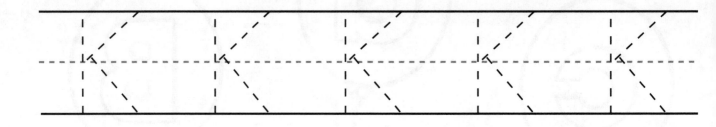

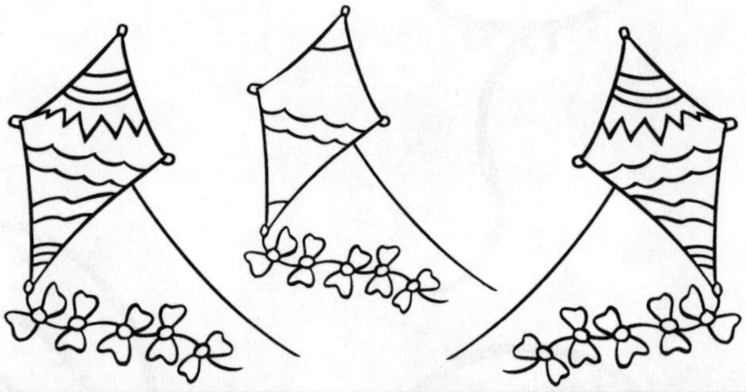

Letter k

Lower-case

Trace the letters.

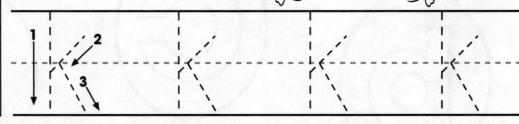

Letter Kk

Look at each letter on the kites.

Match the letters on the kites and **color** them the correct colors.

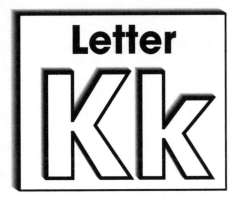

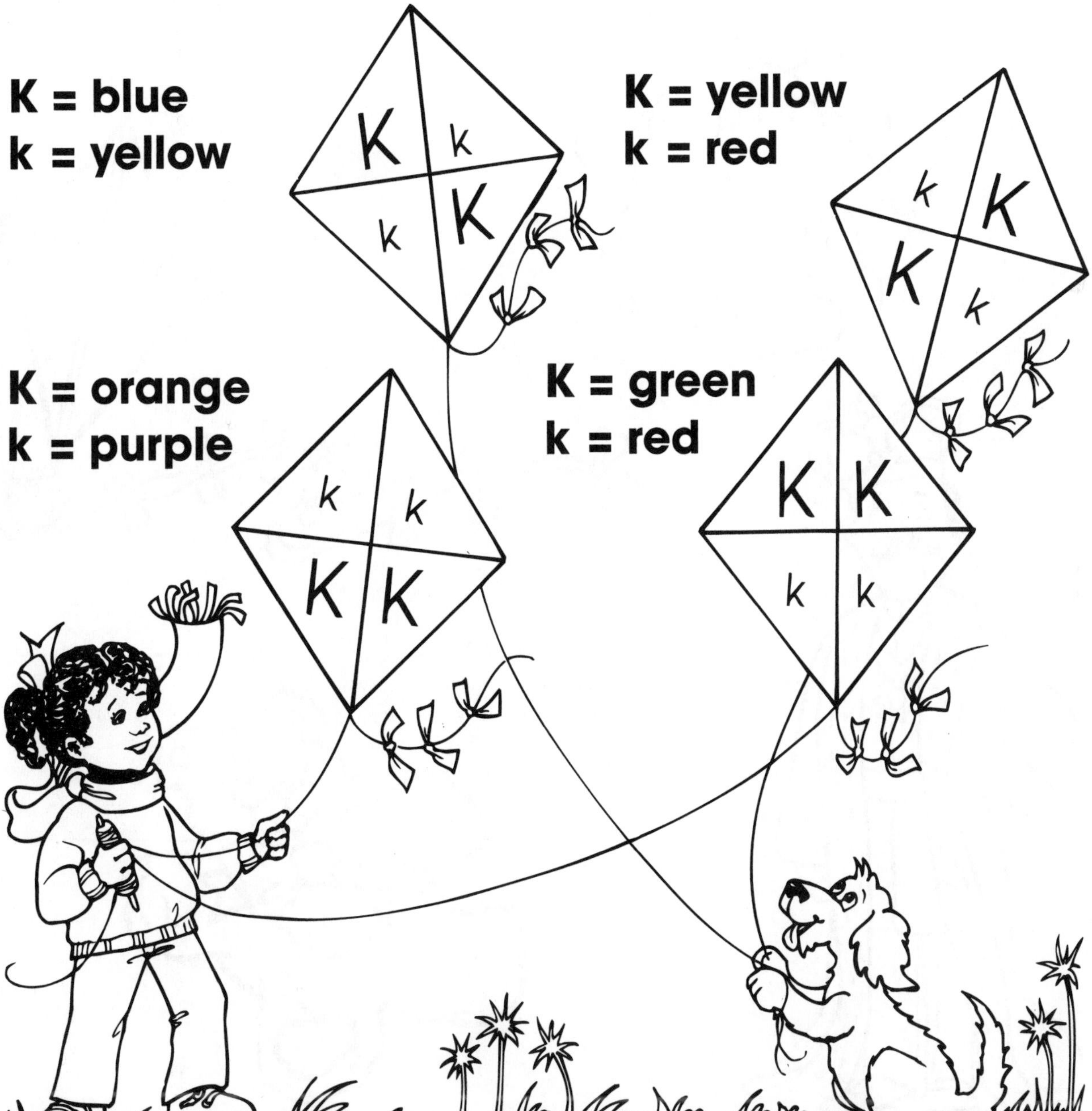

Letter Kk

Circle the pictures that start with the sound of **Kk**.

Color the pictures.

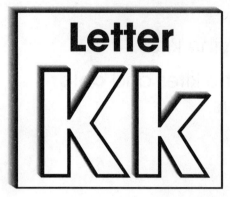

Letter L

Upper-case

Trace the letters.

1 2

Letter l

Lower-case

Trace the letters.

1

Letter Ll

It is fun to rake the fall leaves!

Color the leaves with **L orange**.
Color the leaves with **l red**.

Letter Ll

Circle the pictures that start with the sound of **Ll**.

Color the pictures.

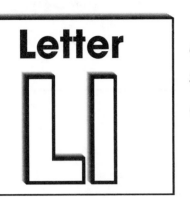

Letter M

Upper-case

Trace the letters.

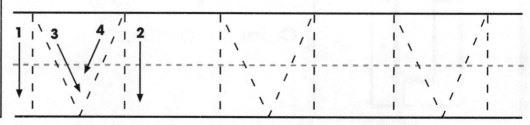

1 3 4 2

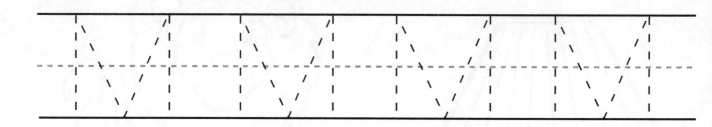

Letter m

Lower-case

Trace the letters.

2 3

1

Letter

Mm

Draw a line from each  to a picture which starts with the sound of **Mm**.

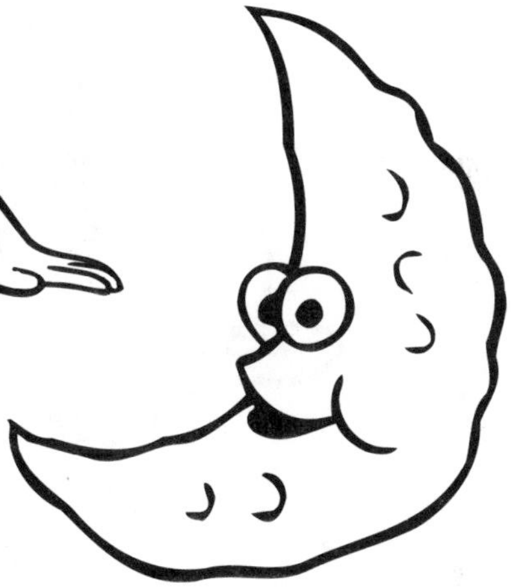

Letter Mm

Circle the pictures that start with the sound of **Mm**.

Color the pictures.

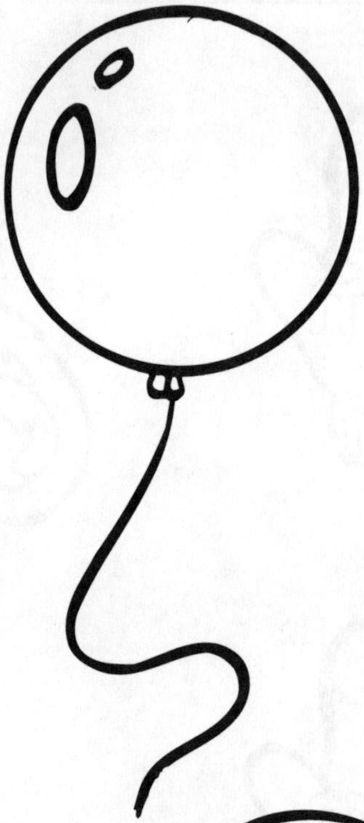

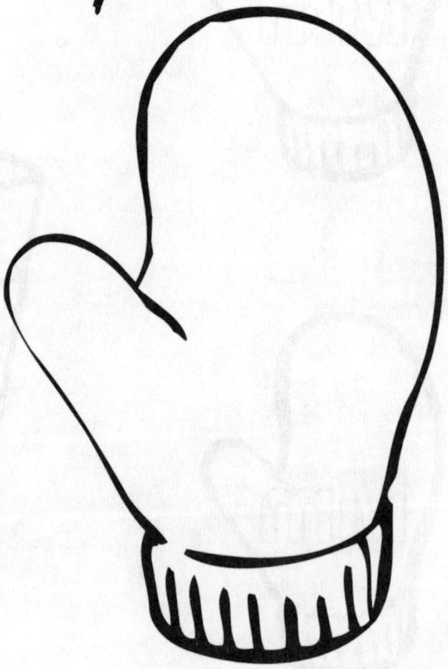

Letter N

Upper-case

Trace the letters.

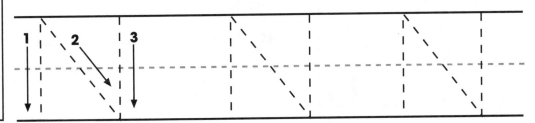

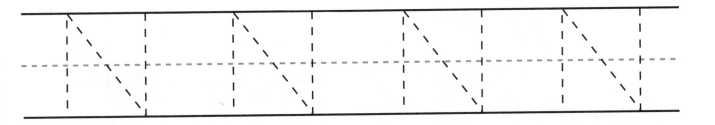

Letter n

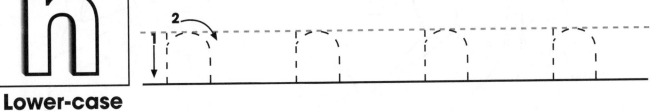

Lower-case

Trace the letters.

Letter Nn

Can you **find** each **N** and **n** that is hidden in the room?

Color each **N purple**. **Color** each **n orange**.

Then, **color** the rest of the picture!

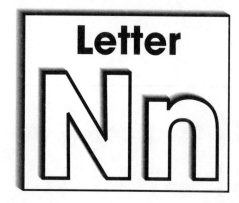

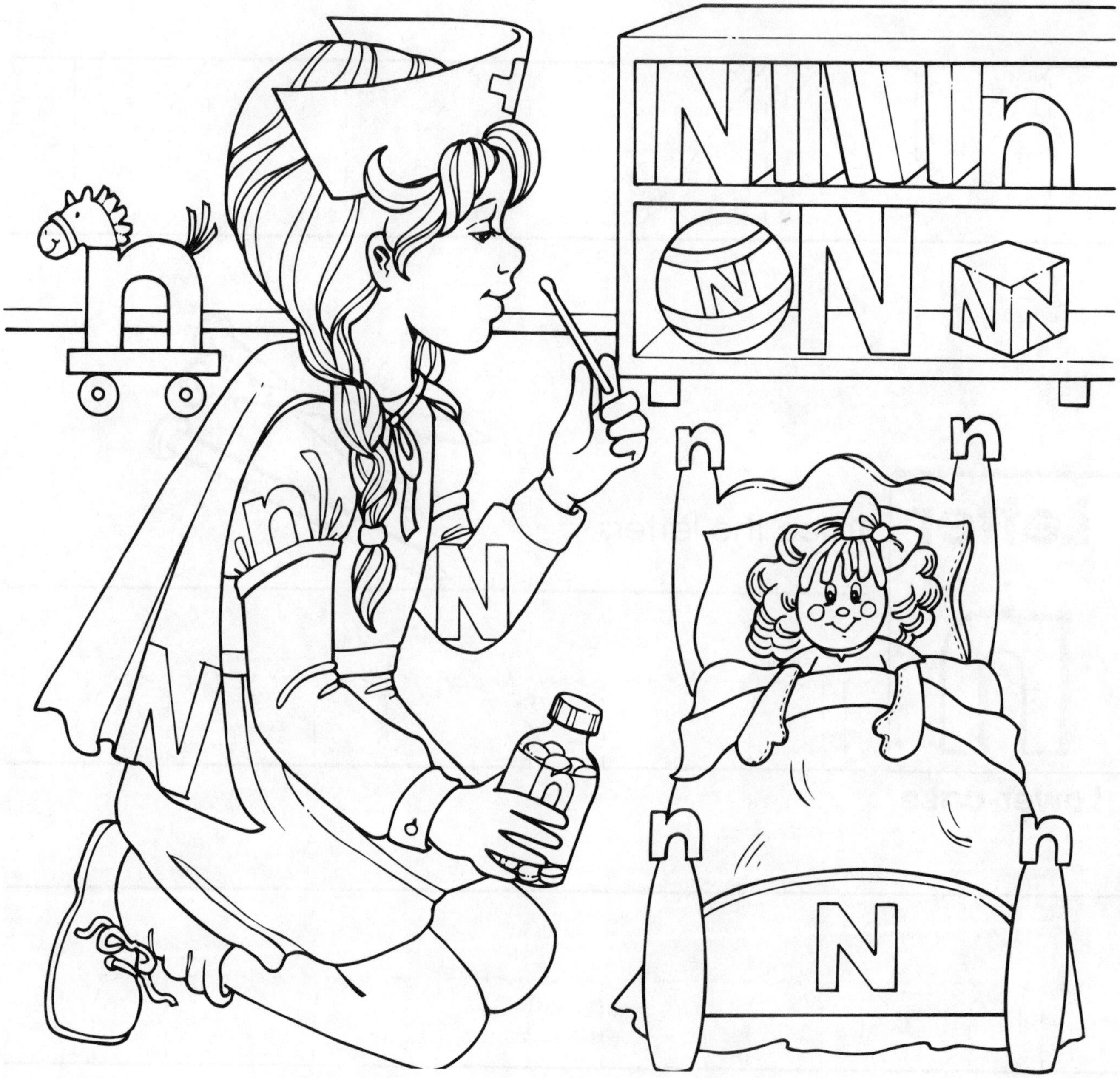

Letter Nn

Circle the pictures that start with the sound of **Nn**.

Color the pictures.

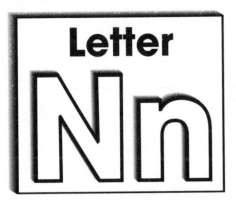

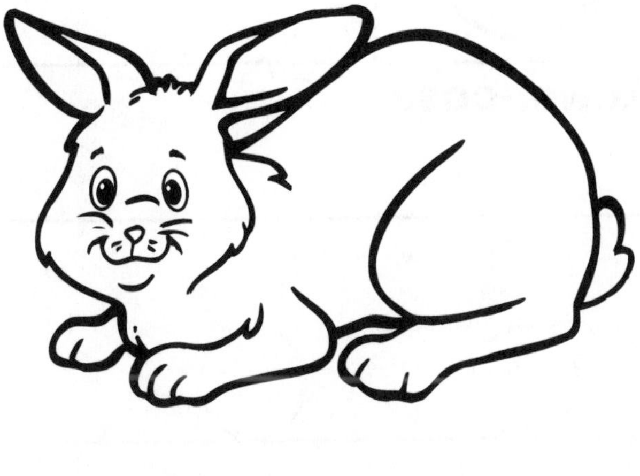

Letter

O

Upper-case

Trace the letters.

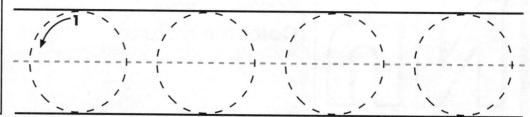

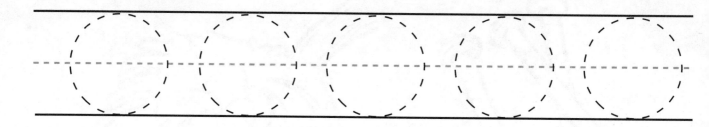

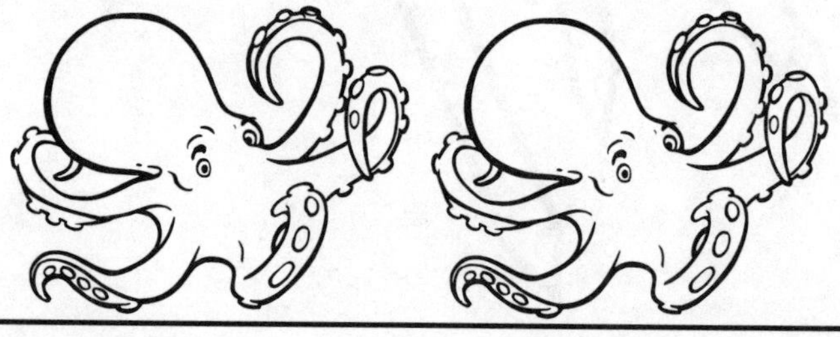

Letter

o

Lower-case

Trace the letters.

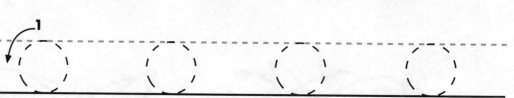

Letter Oo

See who has 8 legs and lives in the ocean.

Color the spaces with **O** or **o brown**.
Color the other spaces **blue**.

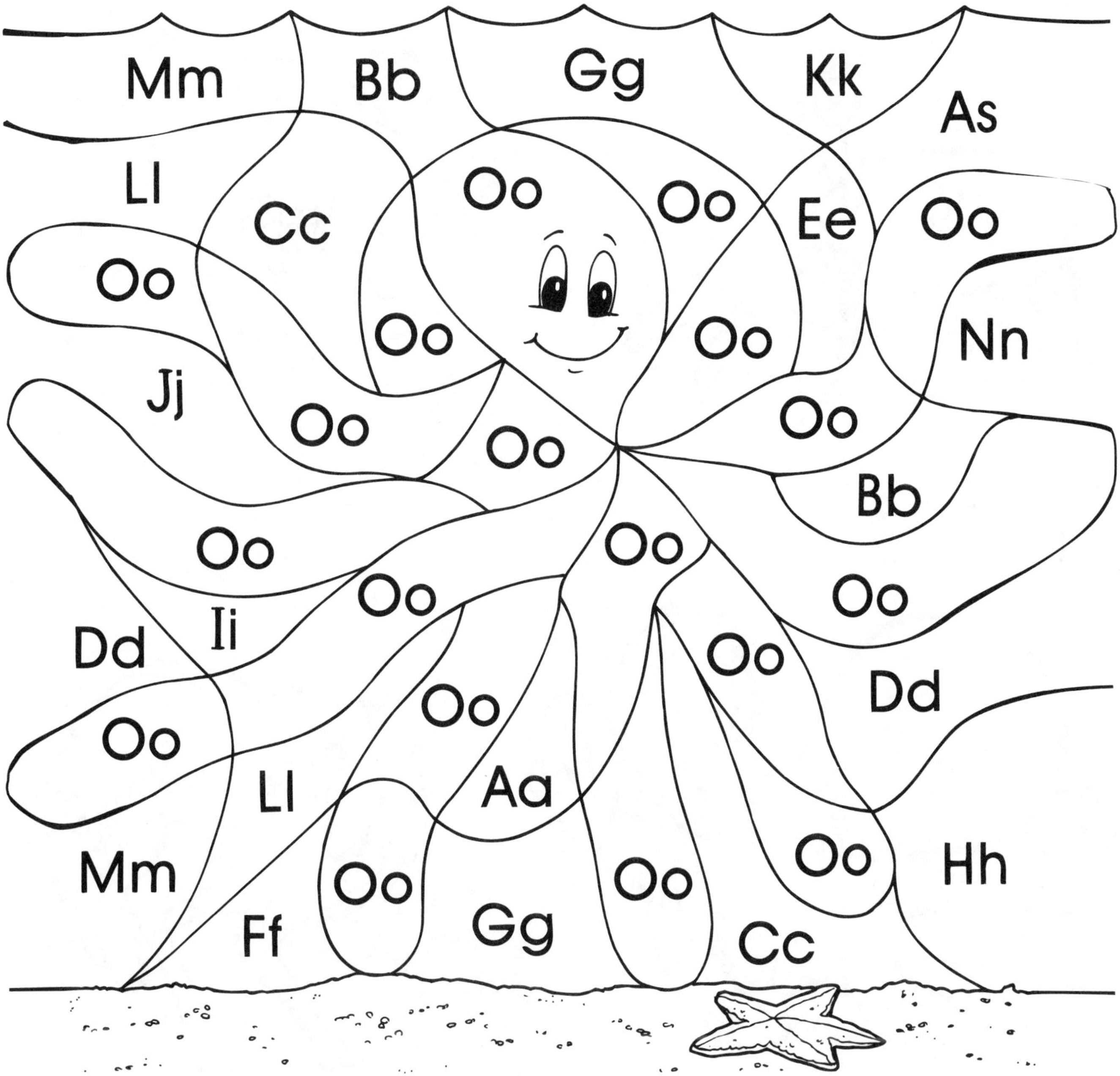

Letter Oo

Circle the pictures that start with the sound of **Oo**.

Color the pictures.

Review Letters

A-O

The Mouse on the Moon

Connect the dots from **A-O**.

Color the picture.

What do you see?

Review Letters A-O

Connect the dots from **a-o** as you **say the alphabet**.

Color the picture.

Start with the letter **a**.

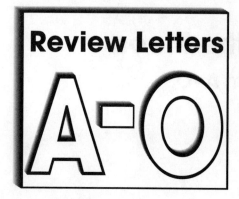

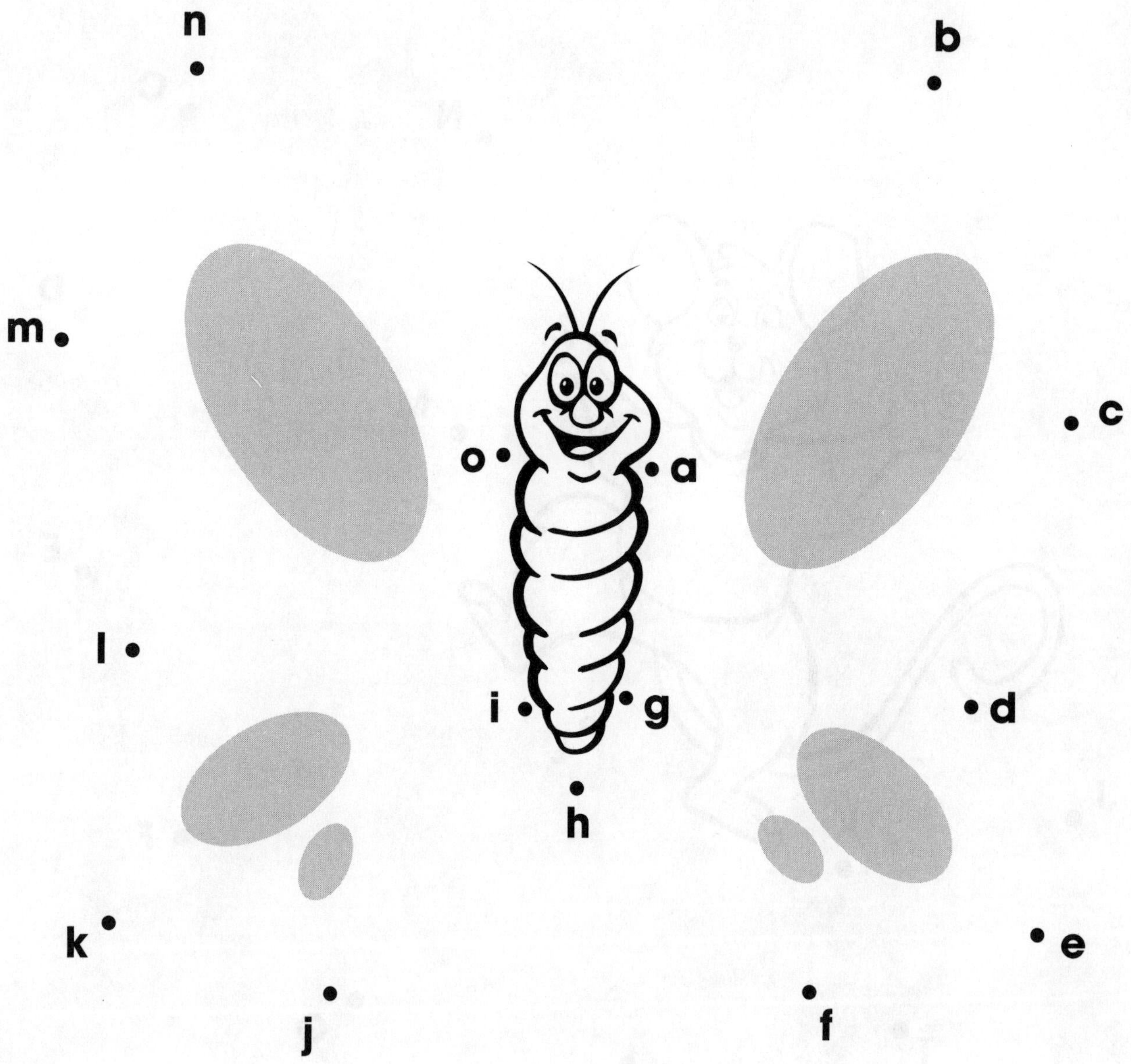

Review Letters A-O

Alphabet Camping

Trace the letters on the tent.

Color the picture!

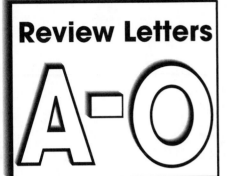

Letter P

Upper-case

Trace the letters.

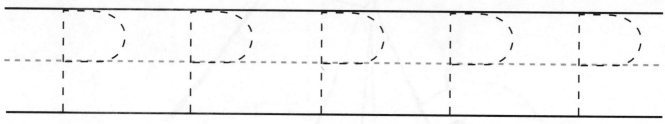

Letter p

Lower-case

Trace the letters.

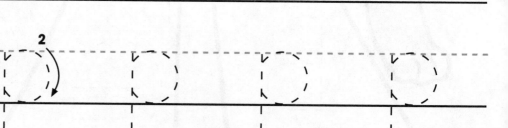

Letter Pp

Trace each **Pp**. Then, **color** each pepperoni **red**.

Cut out each pepperoni and **glue** it on the pizza.

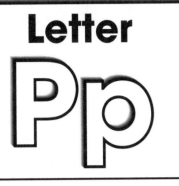

Page is blank for cutting exercise on previous page.

Letter Pp

Circle the pictures that start with the sound of **Pp**.

Color the pictures.

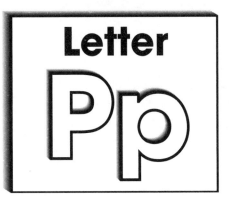

Letter Q

Upper-case

Trace the letters.

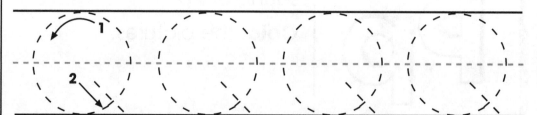

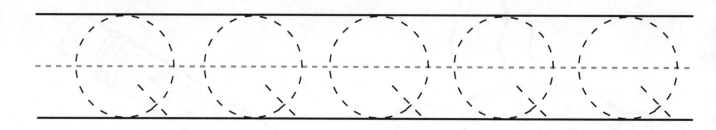

Letter q

Lower-case

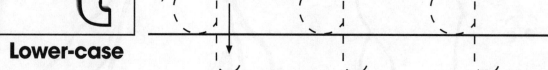

Trace the letters.

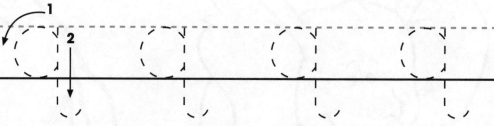

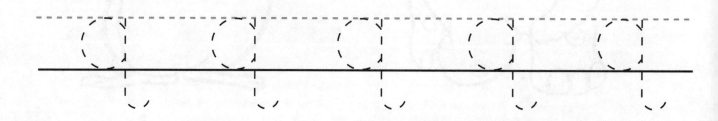

Letter Qq

Look how quiet everything is in the library!

Can you **find** each **Q** and **q**?

Color each **Q blue**.
Color each **q yellow**.

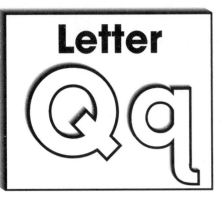

Letter Qq

Circle the pictures that start with the sound of **Qq**.

Color the pictures.

Letter R

Upper-case

Trace the letters.

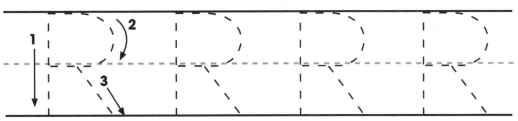

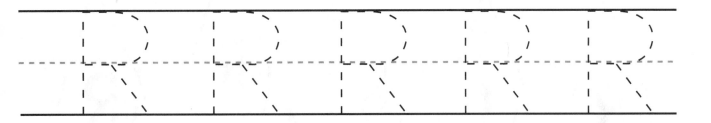

Letter r

Lower-case

Trace the letters.

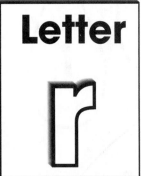

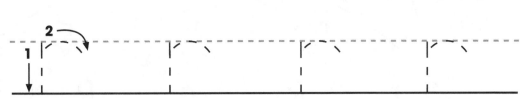

Letter Rr

Trace each **R** and **r**.

Color each raindrop with **R green**.
Color each raindrop with **r blue**.
Color the umbrella, too!

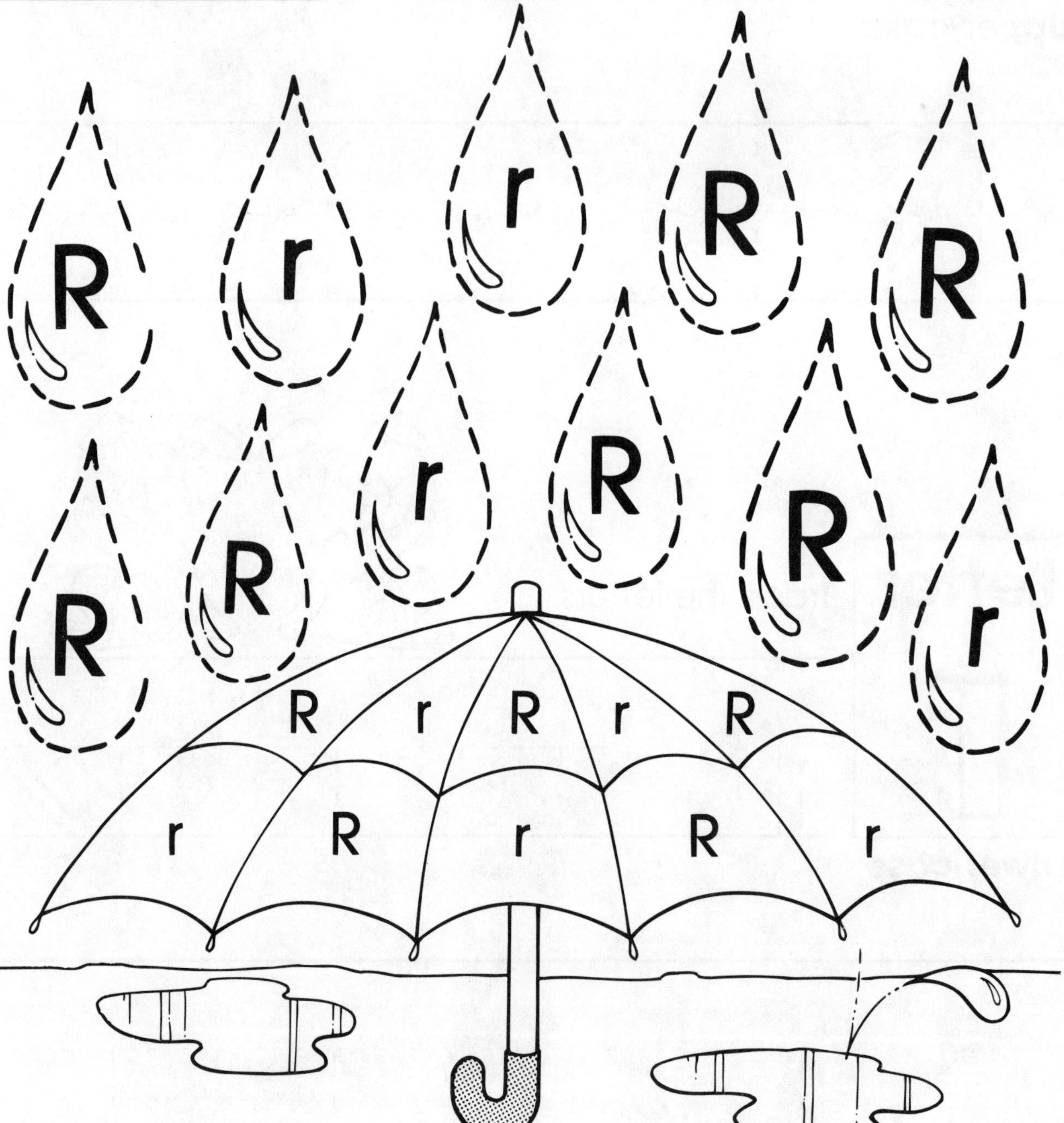

Letter Rr

Circle the pictures that start with the sound of **Rr**.

Color the pictures.

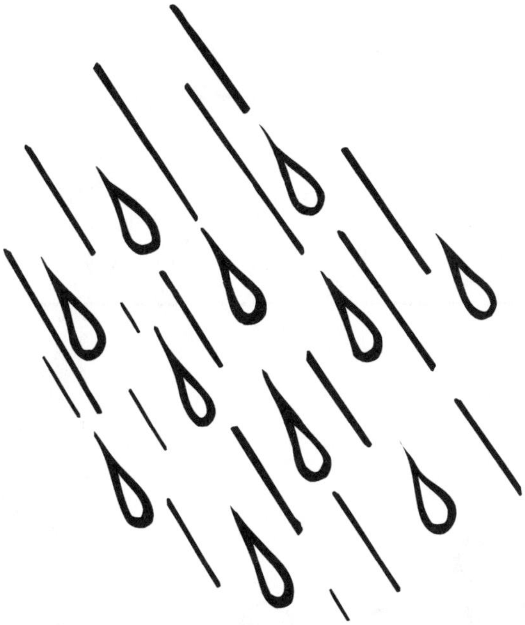

Letter S

Upper-case

Trace the letters.

S S S S

S S S S S

Letter s

Lower-case

Trace the letters.

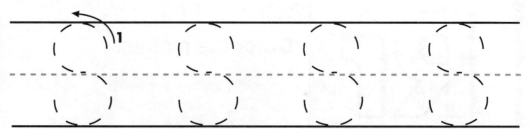

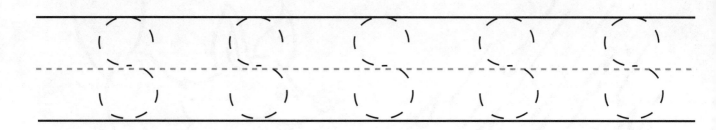

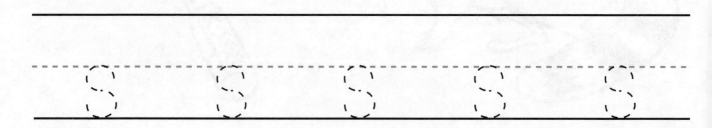

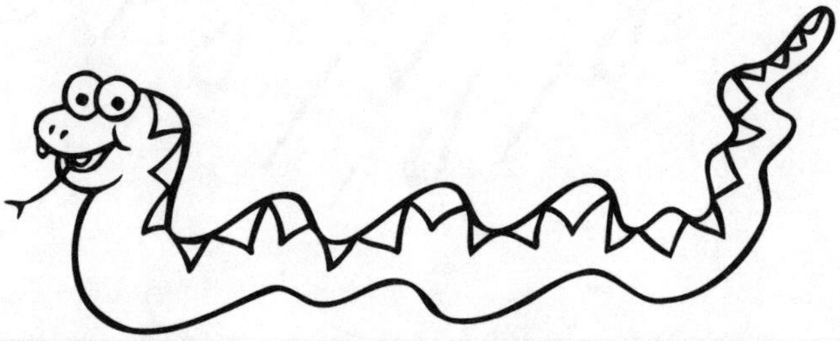

s s s s

s s s s s

Letter Ss

Trace each **S** and **s**.

Color each bubble with **S yellow**.
Color each bubble with **s purple**.

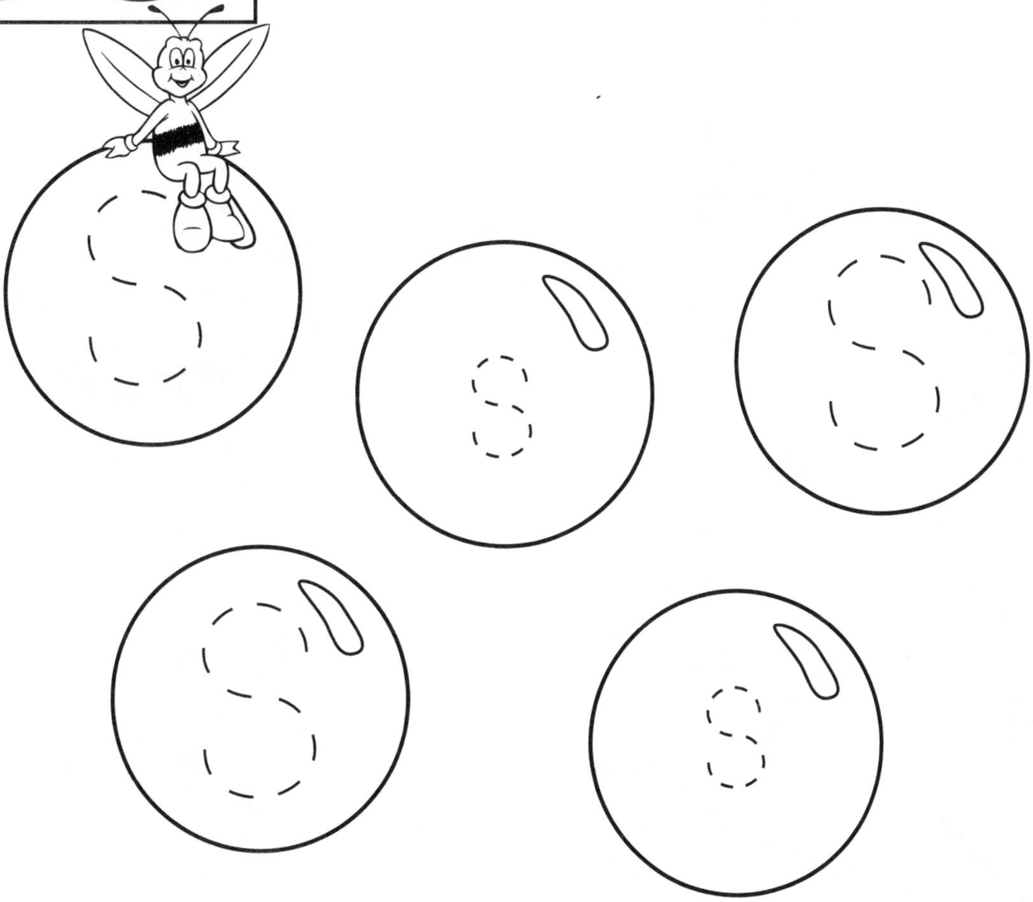

Letter Ss

Circle the pictures that start with the sound of **Ss**.

Color the pictures.

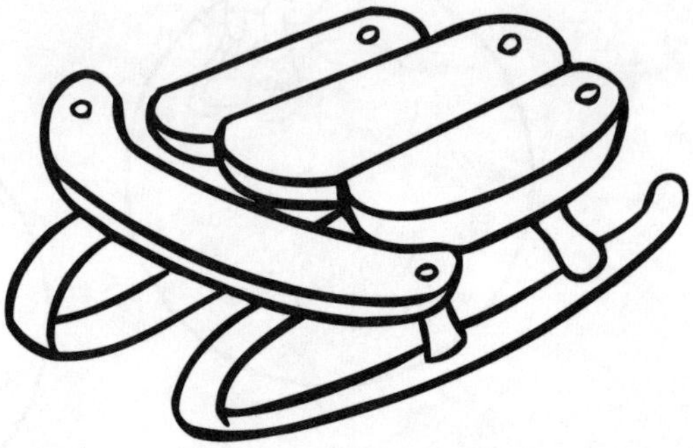

Letter T

Upper-case

Trace the letters.

Letter t

Lower-case

Trace the letters.

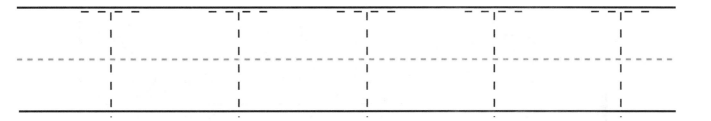

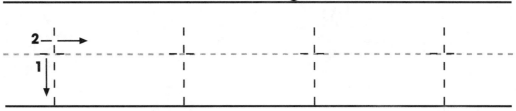

Letter Tt

Color the pictures that start with the sound of **Tt**.

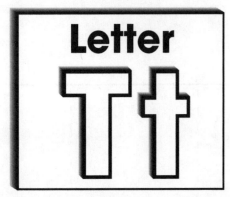

Letter

Tt

Circle the pictures that start with the sound of **Tt**.

Color the pictures.

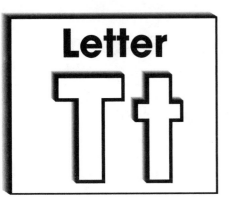

Review Letters A-T

What is the Rabbit Queen jumping out of?

Connect the dots and you will see!

Color the picture.

Review Letters A-T

Follow the maze and **say** each letter. Start with **A** for ant and end with **T** for turtle.

Color the picture!

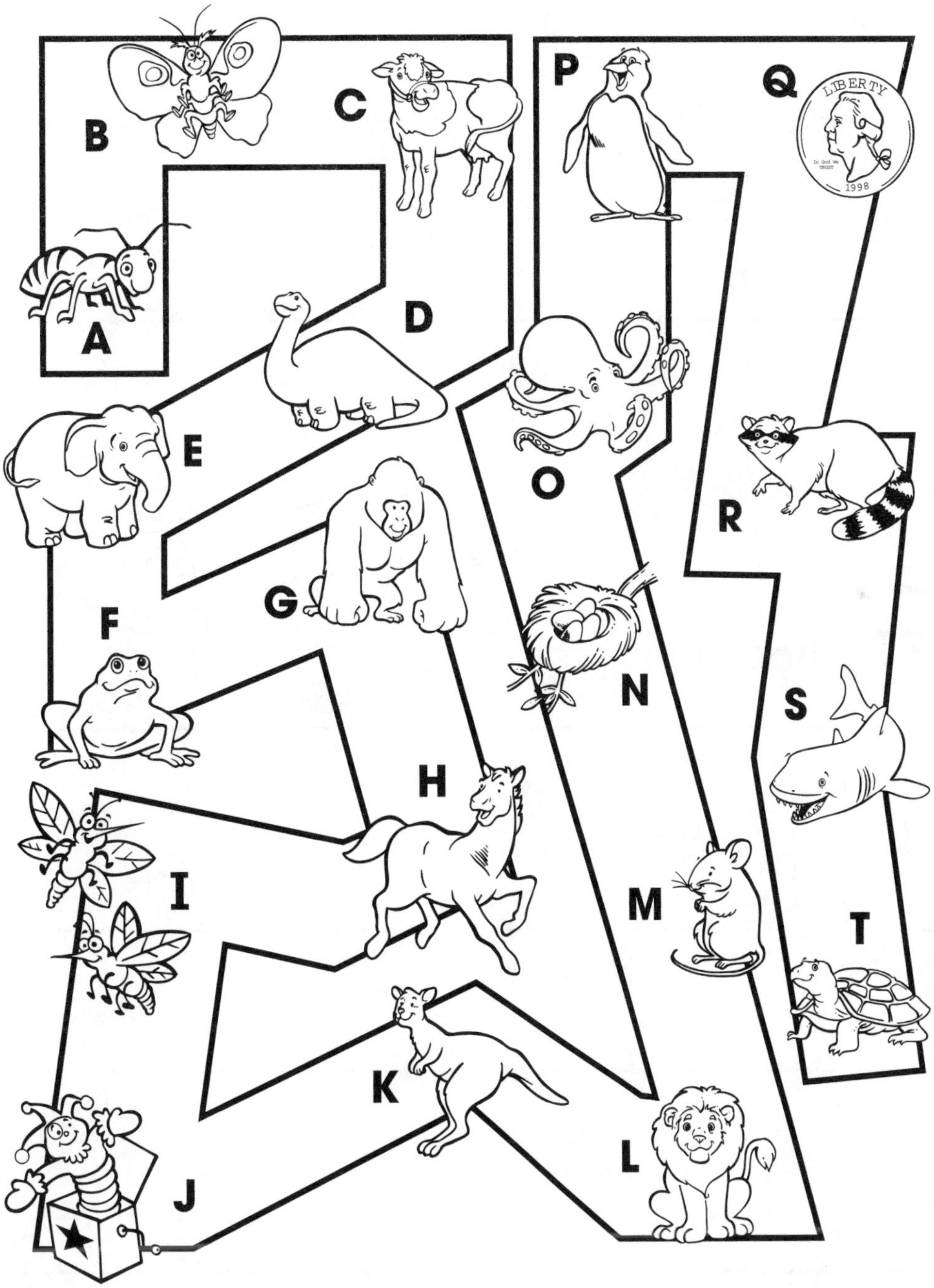

Letter U

Upper-case

Trace the letters.

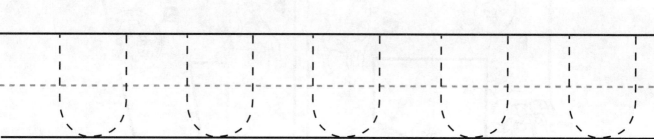

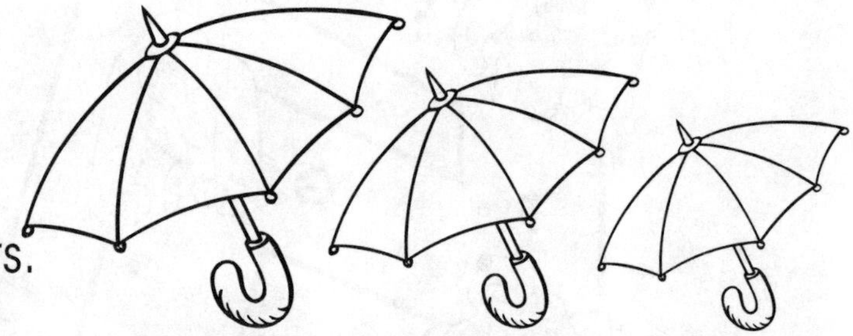

Letter u

Lower-case

Trace the letters.

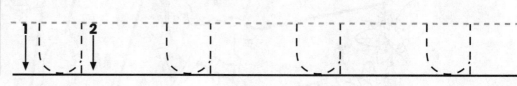

Letter Uu

Find each hidden **U** and **u**.

Color each **U purple**.
Color each **u orange**.
Color the picture.

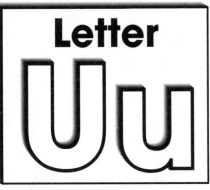

Letter Uu

Circle the pictures that start with the sound of **Uu**.

Color the pictures.

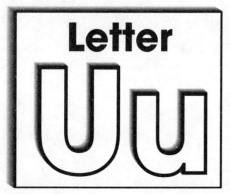

Letter

V

Upper-case

Trace the letters.

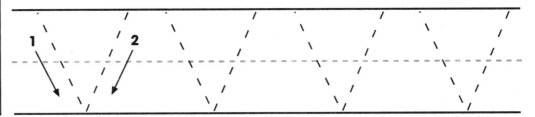

1 2

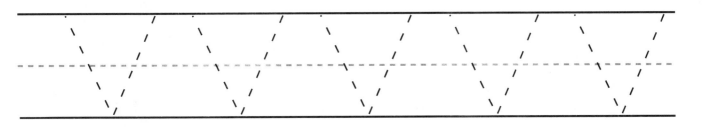

Letter

v

Lower-case

Trace the letters.

1 2

Letter Vv

Circle the pictures that start with the sound of **Vv**.

Color the pictures.

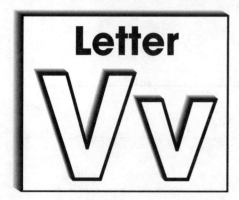

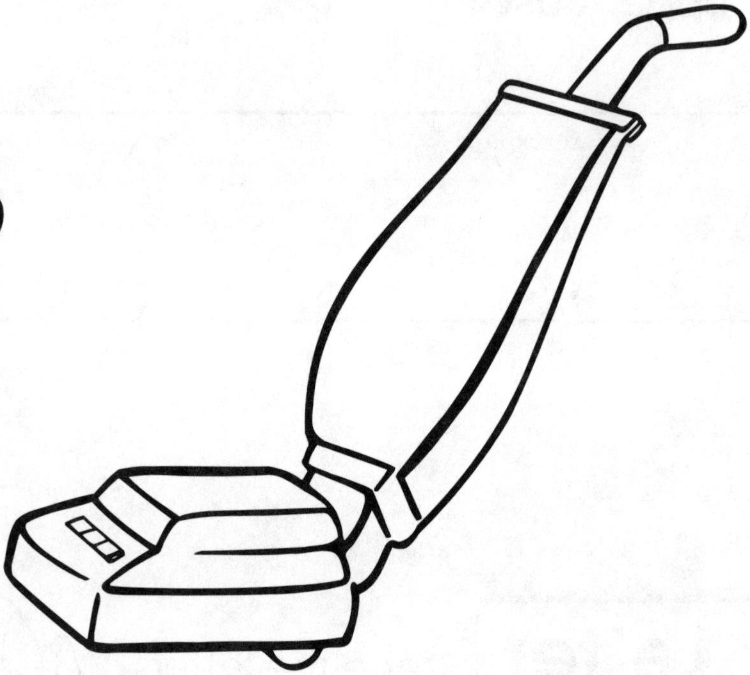

Letter Vv

Trace each **V** and **v**.

Color each heart with **V** or **v** **red**.

Cut out and **glue** each **V** and **v** on a bigger heart.

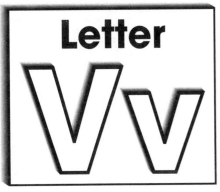

Page is blank for cutting exercise on previous page.

Letter

W

Upper-case

Trace the letters.

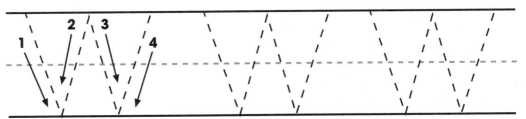

1 2 3 4

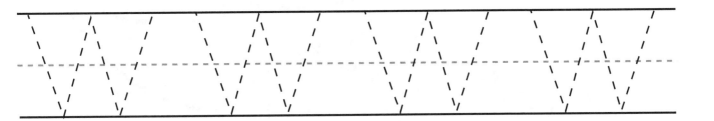

Letter

w

Lower-case

Trace the letters.

1 2 3 4

Letter Ww

Circle the pictures that start with the sound of **Ww**.

Color the pictures.

Letter Ww

Color each watch.
Color and **cut out** each picture that starts with **Ww**.
Then, **glue** them on the watches.

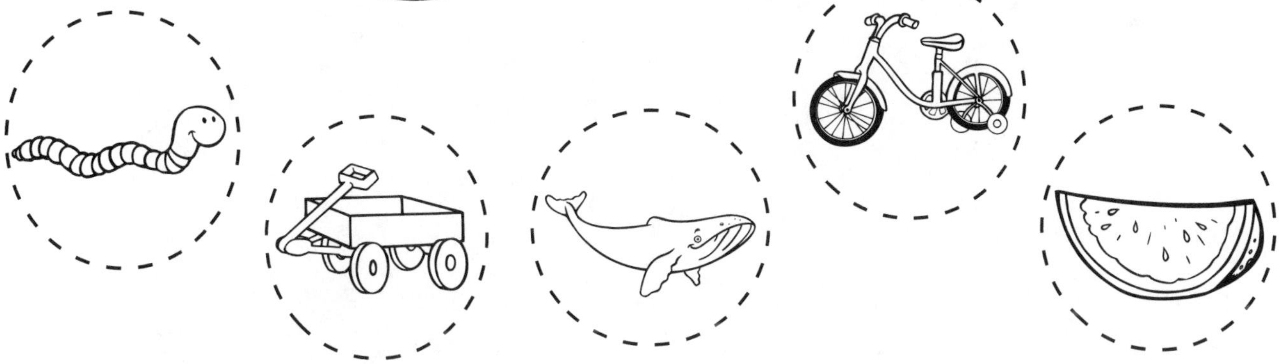

Page is blank for cutting
exercise on previous page.

Letter

X

Upper-case

Trace the letters.

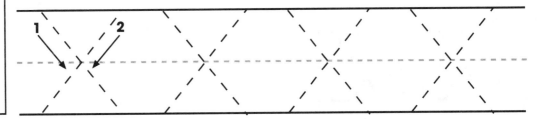

1 2

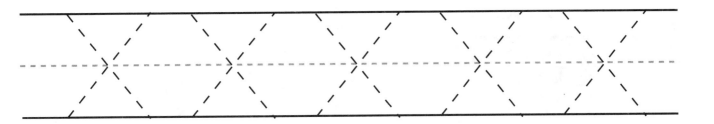

Letter

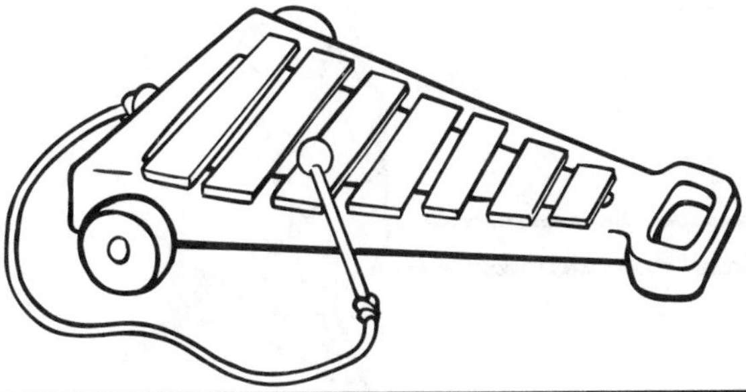

X

Lower-case

Trace the letters.

1 2

Letter Xx

Circle the pictures that start with the letter **Xx**.

Color the pictures.

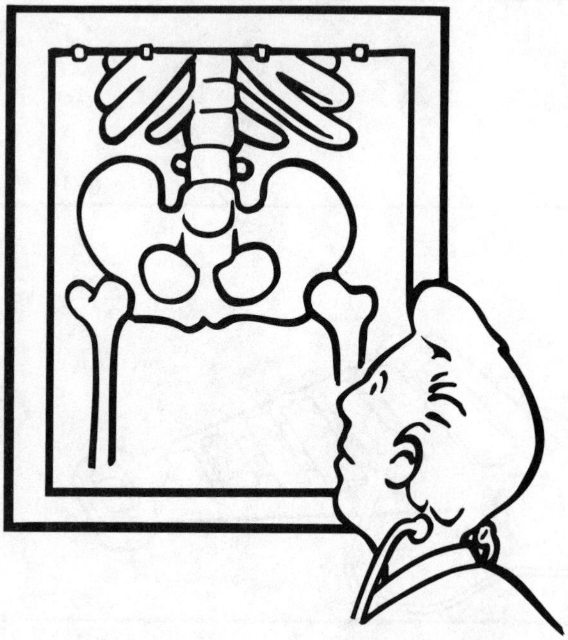

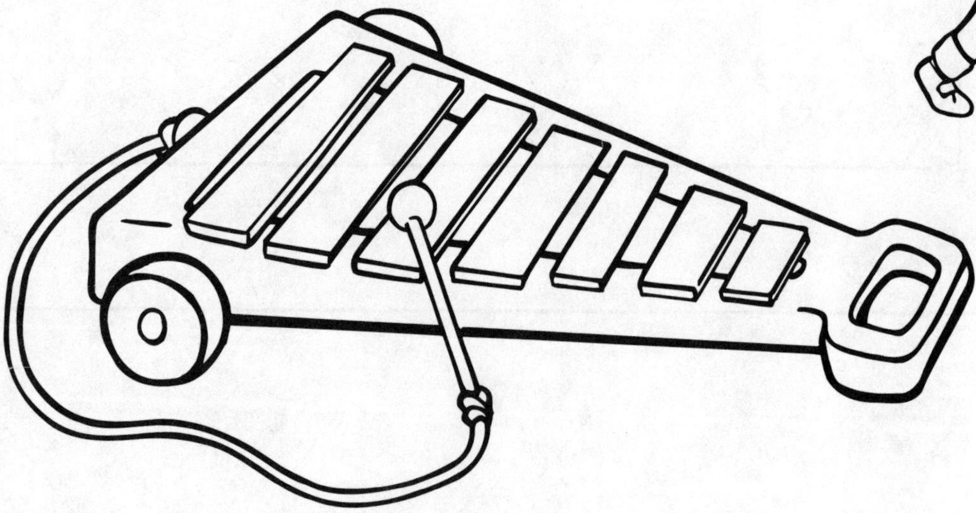

Letter Xx

Color the **UPPER-case X**'s **red**.
Color the **lower-case x**'s **blue**.
Cut out and **glue** each **X** and **x**. Put an **UPPER-case X** and a **lower-case x** in each set.

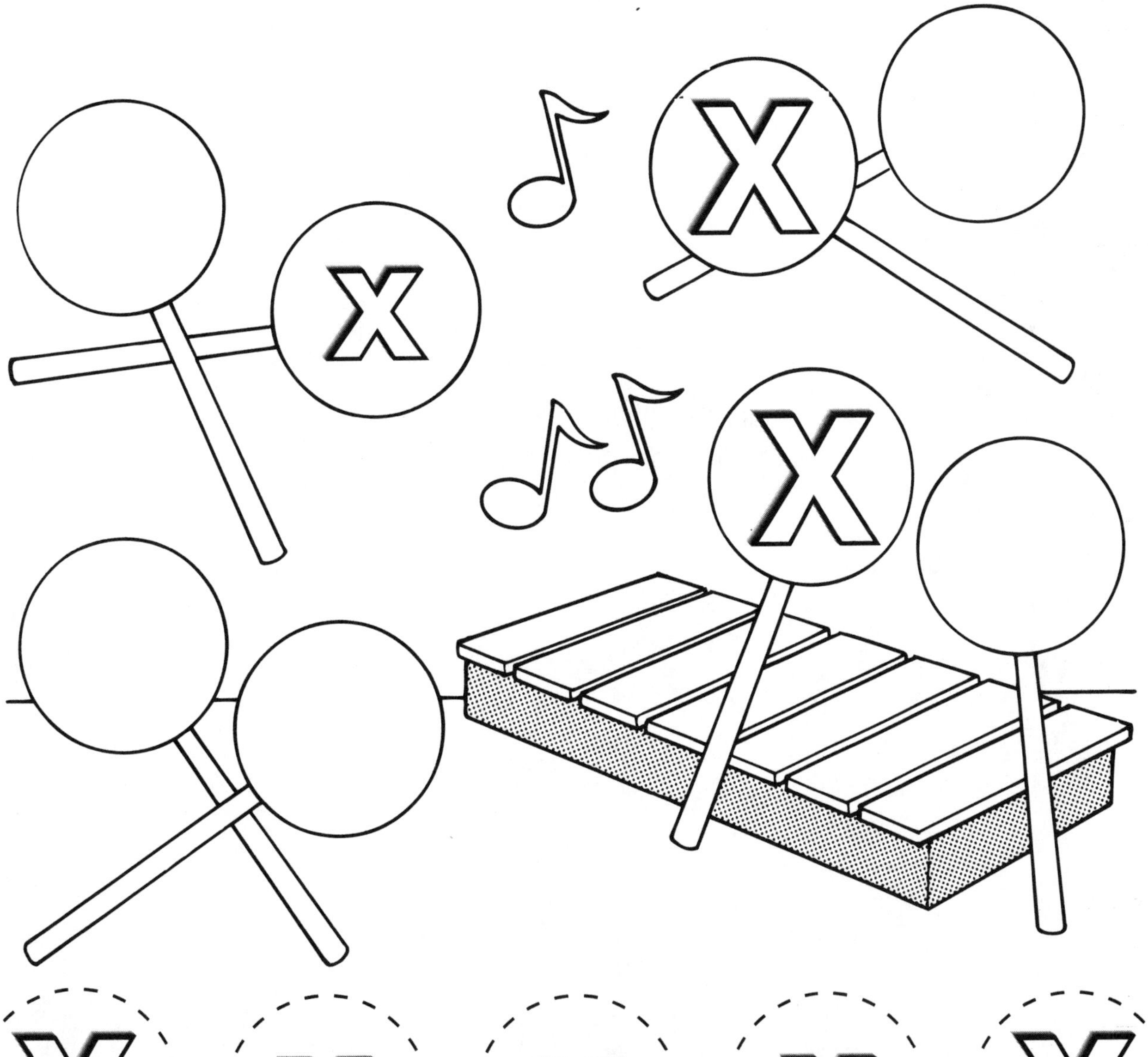

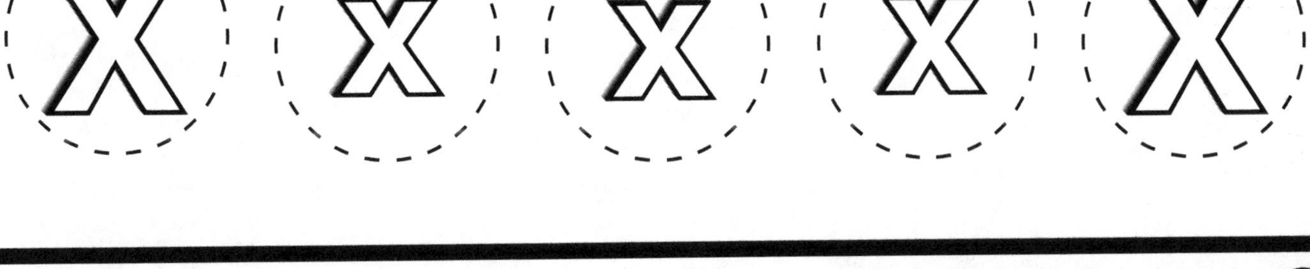

Page is blank for cutting exercise on previous page.

Letter

Y

Upper-case

Trace the letters.

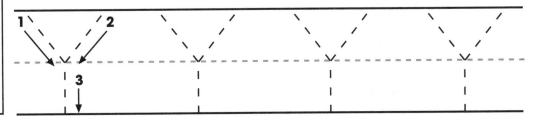

1 2 3

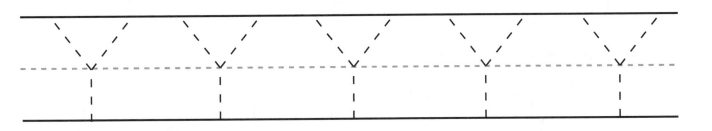

Letter

y

Lower-case

Trace the letters.

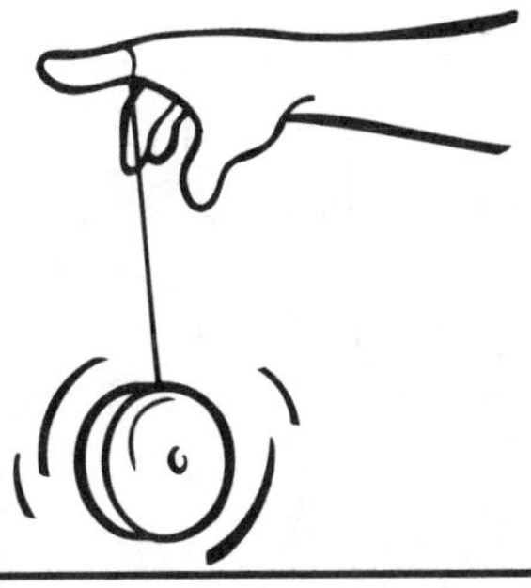

1 2

Letter Yy

Find each **Y** and **y** hidden in the yard.

Color each **Y red**.
Color each **y yellow**.

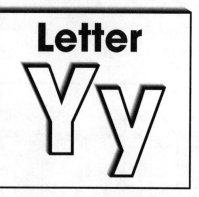

Letter Yy

Circle the pictures that start with the sound of **Yy**.

Color the pictures.

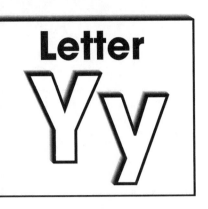

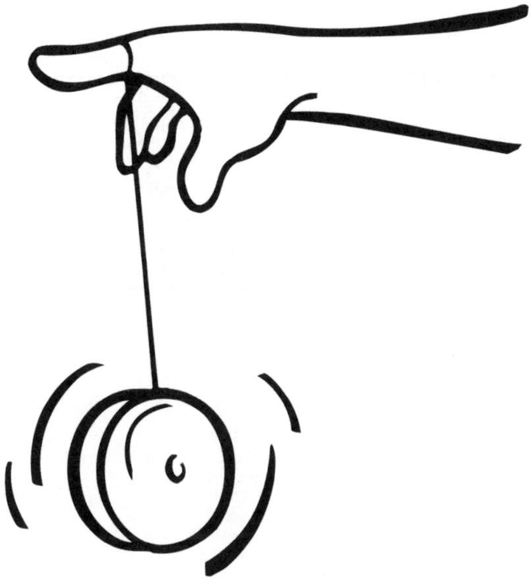

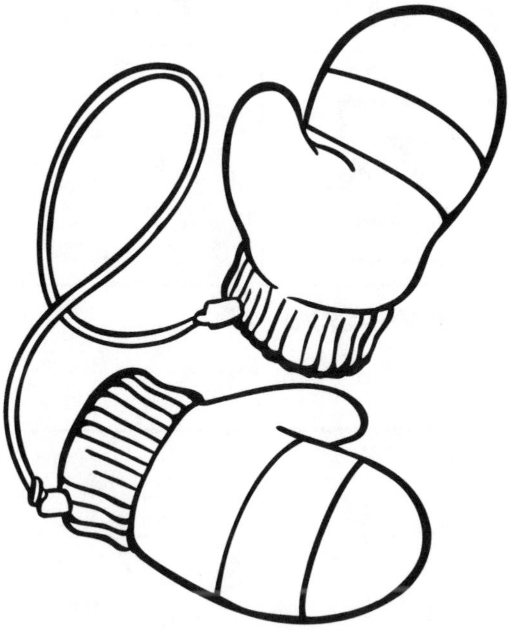

Letter

Z

Upper-case

Trace the letters.

1 2 3

Letter

z

Lower-case

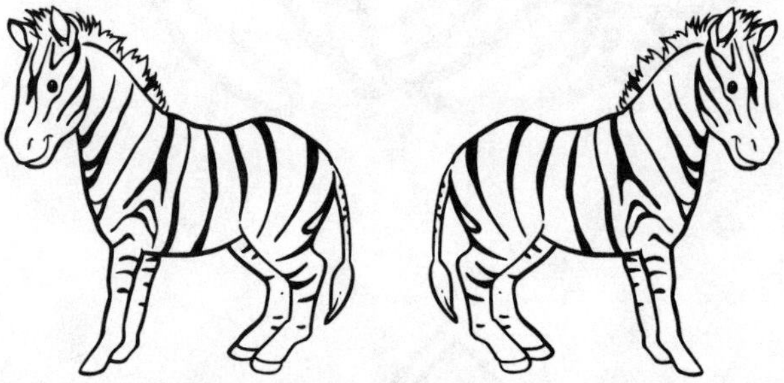

Trace the letters.

1 2 3

Letter Zz

Take a trip through the zoo.

Color only the pictures that start with the sound of **Zz**.

Letter Zz

Circle the pictures that start with the sound of **Zz**.

Color the pictures.

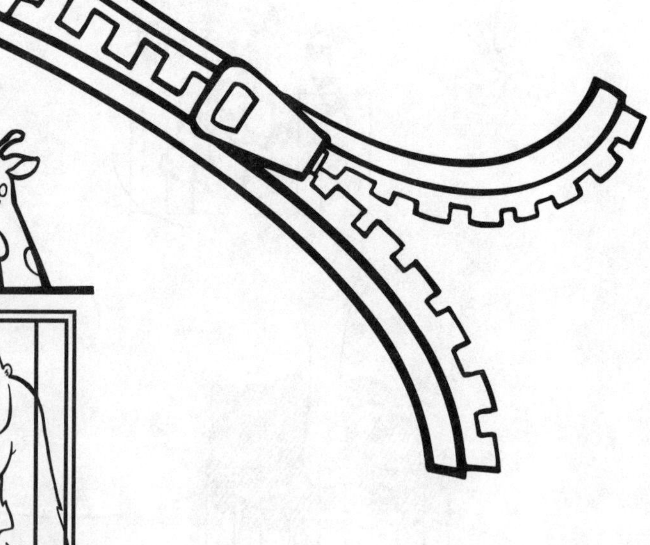

Review Letters A-Z

Connect the dots as you **say the alphabet**.

Color the picture!

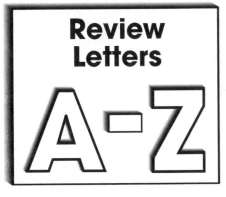

Review Letters A-Z

Connect the dots from **A** to **Z**.

Color the gumballs your favorite colors!

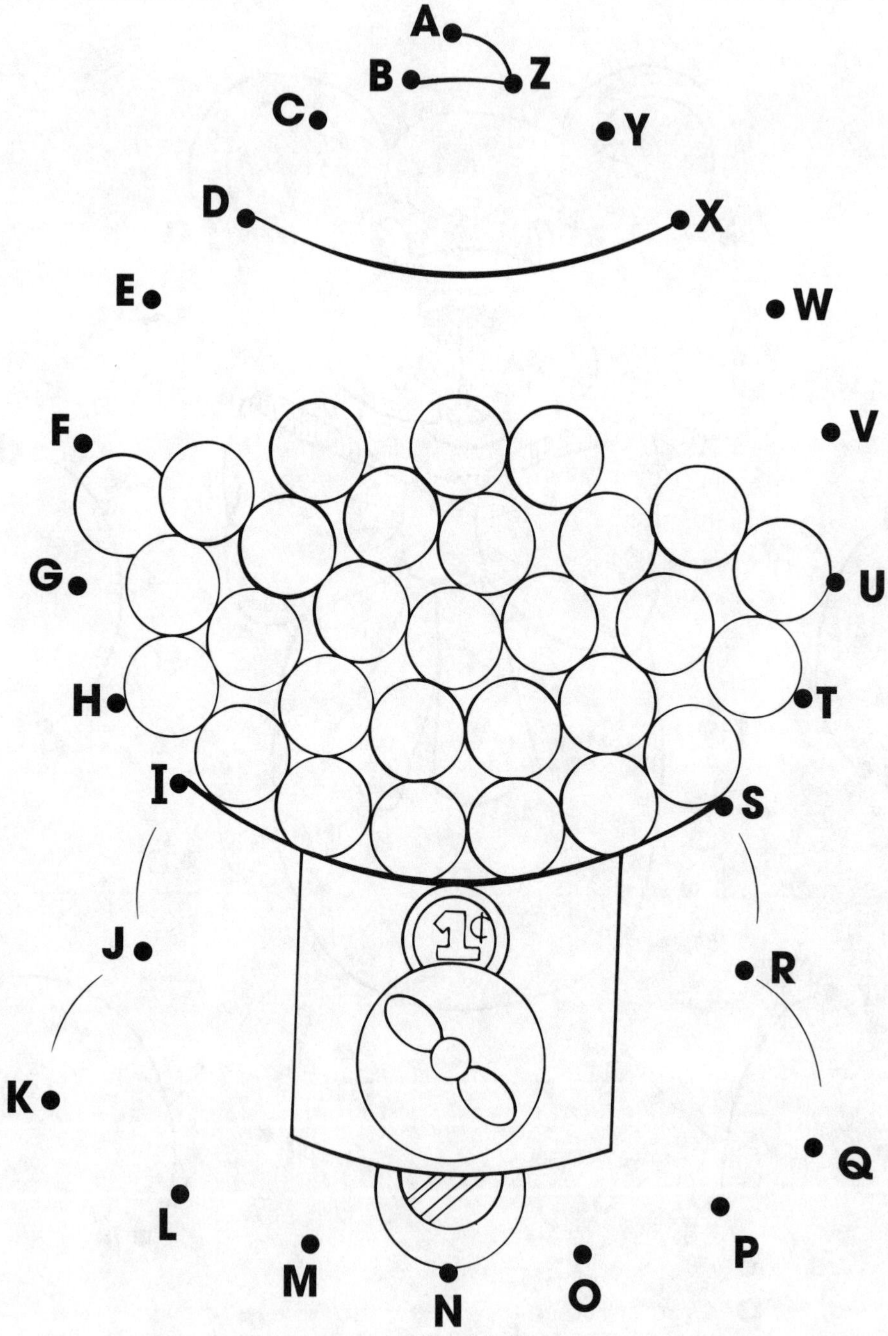

Color and **cut out** the alphabet cards. Use them as flash cards or practice putting your **ABC**'s in order.

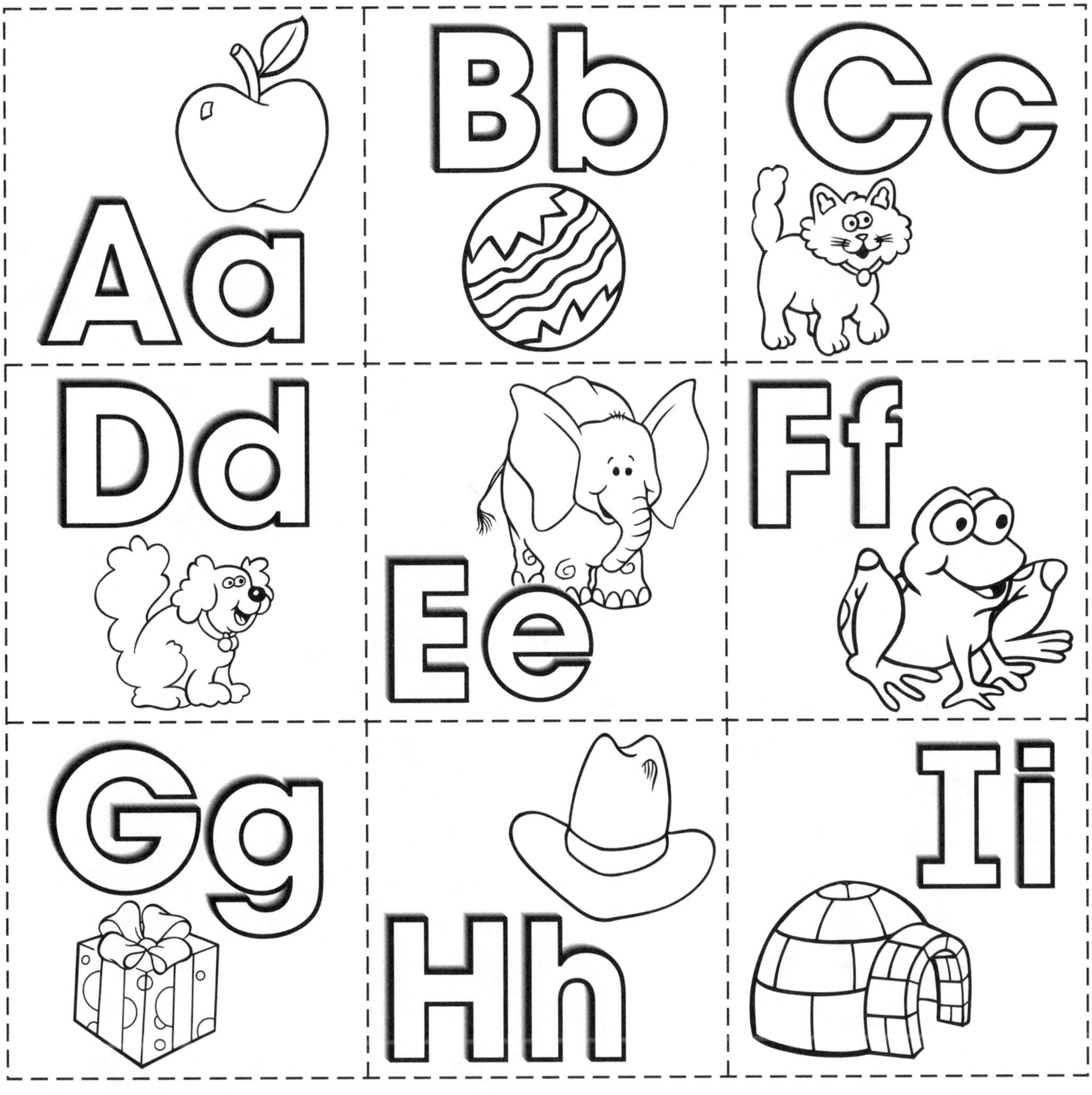

Page is blank for cutting exercise on previous page.

Review Letters A-Z

Color and **cut out** the alphabet cards. Use them as flash cards or practice putting your **ABC**'s in order.

Jj

Kk

Ll

Mm

Nn

Oo

Pp

Qq

Rr

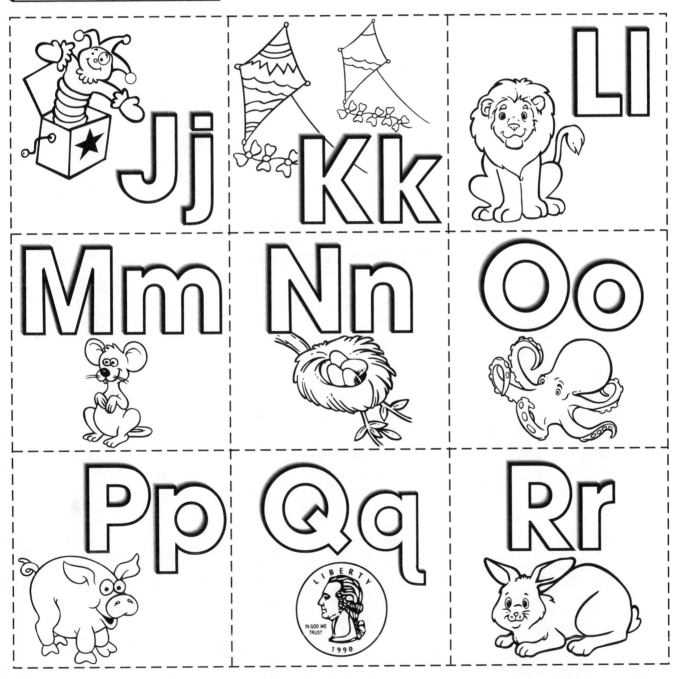

Page is blank for cutting exercise on previous page.

Review Letters A-Z

Color and **cut out** the alphabet cards. Use them as flash cards or practice putting your **ABC**'s in order.

Ss

Tt

Uu

Vv

Ww

Xx

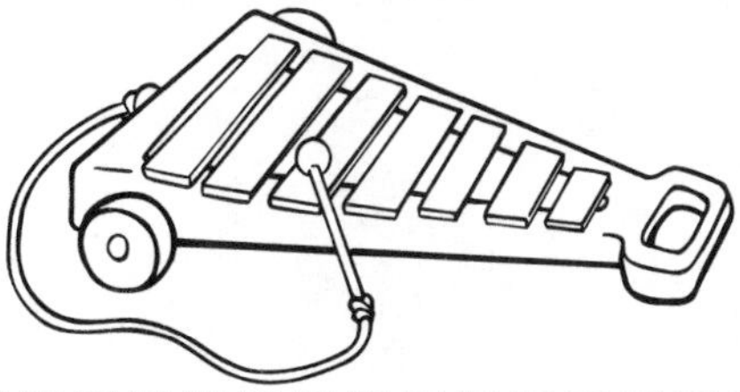

Yy

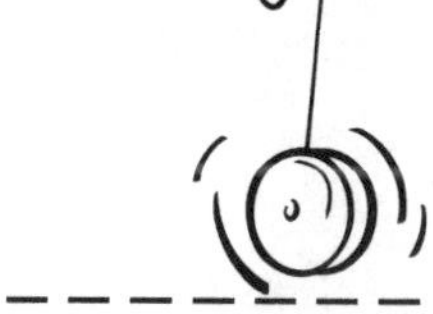

Zz

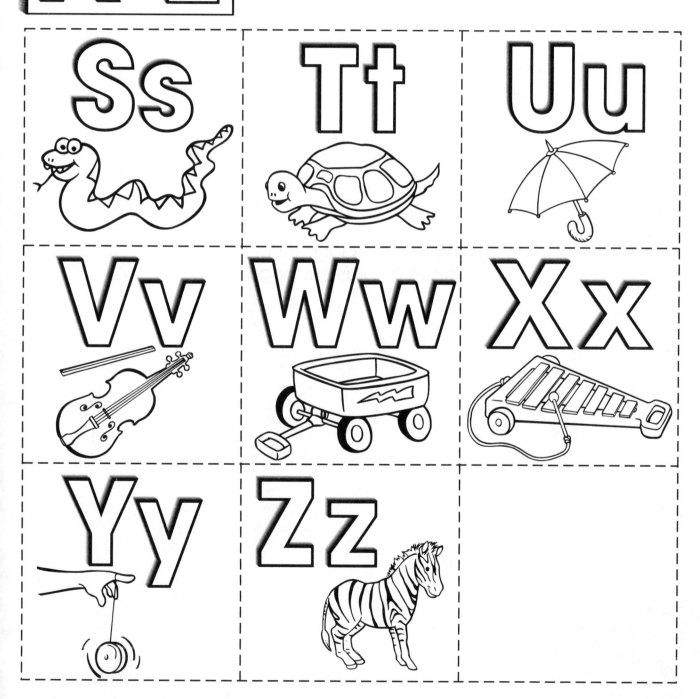

Page is blank for cutting exercise on previous page.